EZRA POUND

Ezra Pound by Wyndham Lewis

EZRA POUND

A collection of essays edited by Peter Russell to be presented to Ezra Pound on his sixty-fifth birthday

HASKELL HOUSE PUBLISHERS Ltd.
Publishers of Scarce Scholarly Books
NEW YORK, N. Y. 10012
1968

First Published 1950

HASKELL HOUSE PUBLISHERS Ltd.
Publishers of Scarce Scholarly Books
280 LAFAYETTE STREET
NEW YORK. N. Y. 10012

Library of Congress Catalog Card Number: 67-31288

Haskell House Catalogue Item # 791

Printed in the United States of America

CONTENTS

ACKNOWLEDGMENTS

Grateful acknowledgments are due to the following for permitting previously published matter to be reprinted: T. S. Eliot, O.M.; Dr. Edith Sitwell and Messrs. Gerald Duckworth & Co. Ltd., the publishers of *Aspects of Modern Poetry*; Wyndham Lewis; Ernest Hemingway; Allen Tate and Messrs. William Morrow & Co. Inc., the publishers of *The Limits of Poetry*; George Seferis; and to Ezra Pound for permission to quote freely from his many works.

The frontispiece, which is in the possession of Mr. T. S. Eliot, is included by his kind permission, and that of the artist, Mr. Wyndham Lewis.

PREFACE

The essays in this book have been collected as a tribute to
Ezra Pound. They are, as is fitting, concerned with Ezra
Pound's works rather than with Mr. Pound himself. Some
are exegetical rather than critical, the intention being, as in
Mr. Drummond's essay for instance, scholarship not criticism.
Both the scholar's and the critic's approach to a work of
art are necessary ones, but it is well to remember—to quote
an early letter of Mr. Pound's—that scholarship and criticism
are only " handmaids to the arts ". One of the best tributes
to a great poet is good criticism of his work, and if these
essays bring to a wider audience the actual poetry of Ezra
Pound, the true intention of both scholarship and criticism
will have been served.

I have to thank many people for their invaluable help to
my own researches into the achievement of Ezra Pound which
originally led me to edit this book—especially Mr. T. S.
Eliot, Mr. Wyndham Lewis, Mr. Ernest Hemingway, Miss
Olga Rudge, Mr. John Drummond, Mr. Ronald Duncan,
Mr. Hugh Gordon Porteus, Mr. A. V. Moore, and Mrs.
Dorothy Pound, whose constant goodwill and accurate
memory have saved me a great deal of labour.

PETER RUSSELL

London,
February, 1950.

INTRODUCTION

by Peter Russell

Ezra Pound was born in Idaho in the wilds of the far Mid-West in 1885, and was already the "country boy" when he went to college at Pennsylvania and Hamilton. After gaining his Master's degree in Romance languages, his career as a University lecturer was short and stormy, for he was thrown out of Wabash College, Crawfordsville, "for being too much the Latin Quarter type". In January 1908 he made his way on a cattle ship to Gibraltar, walked to Venice, and had his first book of poems published there under the title *A Lume Spento*. Arriving in London early in 1909, he was immediately noticeable for his red beard, his huge mop of blonde hair, and his unorthodox opinions on literature. Three books of his poems appeared in London that year. In 1910 another book of poems, and his first prose book, *The Spirit of Romance*, an authoritative, or perhaps one should say, authoritarian, comparative survey of literature in the Romance languages from the Silver Latin poets to Lope de Vega, appeared. By this time he was a member of the circle of the philosopher-poet T. E. Hulme. His literary association with Hulme, F. S. Flint and others of that circle led first to his interest in the concision of Japanese verse forms like the *tanka* and the *hokku*, and later to the Imagist Movement, of which he himself was the leading light (with H.D. and Richard Aldington as close associates). The anthology *Des Imagistes* is the most obvious landmark of the movement. It was compiled (anonymously) by Pound and appeared in 1914. By this time, however, he was much absorbed by other wider problems, notably painting and sculpture. His work with Percy Wyndham Lewis, and his friendship with Henri Gaudier Brzeska, led to a new and more inclusive movement, the Vorticist Movement. If the taste of Roger Fry had seemed outrageous when he had championed the Post-Impressionists in 1910, these young men with their paper, *Blast*, and their twofold attack on Fry and the futurist Marinetti as Impressionist "reactionaries", must have seemed ludicrous. Time

9

has shown who were the more lasting artists and critics.
Pound's own views on Vorticism and on Gaudier are collected
in his life of Gaudier (1916), and there is no better view-
from-the-inside of the movement.

W. B. Yeats met Ezra Pound early on, and throughout the
older poet's life the friendship was a deep one. Mr. Joseph
Hone tells how " It was through Ezra Pound that Yeats first
gained an insight into the tendencies of the generation next
to his own in England and America, afterwards to be led
by T. S. Eliot ". . . . " Yeats appears to have been at once
attracted by the intrepidity of Ezra Pound. . . ." " A rugged
and headstrong nature, and he is always hurting people's
feelings," Yeats wrote of his new friend to Sir William
Rothenstein, " but he has I think some genius and great
goodwill." Later, over the winter 1912-13, Pound was teaching Yeats to fence, and reading to him in the evenings, in
the attempt to win him back to health. The two poets spent
the winter together at Stone Cottage, Holman's Hatch. Yeats
wrote to Lady Gregory " Ezra never shrinks from work . . .
a learned companion and a pleasant one . . . he is full of the
Middle Ages and helps me to get back to the definite and
concrete, away from modern abstractions. . . ." Ezra
Pound's astounding energy and natural intelligence were his
most obvious characteristics. This energy was directed to the
translation of a number of Chinese poems under the title
Cathay, and to the rendering of some of the Japanese *Noh*
plays, which had a considerable influence on Yeats, and in
fact were responsible for the new phase in his career as a
dramatist characterised by *Four Plays for Dancers*. In 1917
Ezra Pound was best man at Yeats' wedding, and in the same
year he edited a selection of letters from J. B. Yeats to his son.

Pound's mind seems never to have been at rest. In 1912
his *Sonnets and Ballate of Guido Cavalcanti* had appeared. He
became European correspondent for the newly-formed Poetry
(Chicago), he " discovered " T. S. Eliot (in 1915), compiled
Catholic Anthology, as he said, with the one object of " getting
sixteen pages of Eliot into print at once ". At the same time,

Introduction

it was through his influence that Joyce's *Portrait of the Artist*
was published by the Egoist Press, that instalments of *Ulysses*
appeared in the *Little Review* in America, and indeed that
Joyce was enabled to live without financial worry, for Pound
was able to persuade Miss Harriet Shaw Weaver to give Joyce
the financial security he needed for the composition of his
masterpiece. This double activity of Pound's—that of poet
and impresario—bears witness to a remarkable energy and
devotion to literature and the arts.

During the same period his study of recent French poetry
did much to sharpen his language into a sardonic colloquialism
which has much in common with the Greek epigrammatists.
His *Ripostes* (1912) and *Lustra* (1915) demonstrate these new
departures. During the war years, apart from his Japanese and
Chinese studies, his careful examination of the work of Henry
James, Remy de Gourmont, the Provençal Troubadours,
Elizabethan Classicists, Renaissance Translators of Greek (into
Latin and French), and his continuing interest in music (expressed in an essay on Arnold Dolmetsch), were all fitting him
for the great task of writing an epic poem, for this is what he
appears to have set himself early on. Three cantos of this poem
appeared in 1917, but were later revised entirely. Before 1920
he had written his finest poetic studies apart from *The Cantos*,
namely the *Homage to Sextus Propertius* and *Hugh Selwyn
Mauberley*.

After the war Ezra Pound went to live in Paris, where he
worked on the early *Cantos*, tried to learn to be a sculptor
under Constantin Brancusi, helped Ernest Hemingway, and
wrote a book on the Polish-American composer George
Antheil. Far more valuable than Antheil's music were
Pound's observations on it, and his collected criticism (under
the pseudonym William Atheling and from the *New Age*)
offers much that is original and interesting, especially on the
difficult subject of "words and music". Three years later,
finding the demands of a Paris full of intellectual activity and
crowded with young American exiles (mostly of very doubtful
integrity) altogether too much for him, Pound removed to

11

Rapallo, returning less and less to Paris as the years went on. From Rapallo he edited *Exile* and in 1926 directed a performance of his opera *Villon*, which was repeated by the B.B.C. in 1932. In 1928 the first of his translations of the Chinese prose classics appeared, in 1931 his transcription from the original MSS. and early editions of the *Rime* of Guido Cavalcanti with critical notes of great insight into the whole mediæval world of thought. This *Cavalcanti* came in for high praise from Professor Etienne Gilson, but has been much neglected both by British and Continental scholars. The anthology *Profile* (1933) contains poetry from the 'nineties up to the date of compilation, together with Pound's interlocking remarks, and *Active Anthology* (1934) is a collection of new experimental writing, with a preface and postscript by Pound. In the *A.B.C. of Reading* (1934) he made a summary of views on the reading of literature, notes which are remarkable for the clarity of outlines which his critical focus gives. More ambitious than the latter was *Guide to Kulchur* (1938). In a series of short chapters he sums up his critical views on almost every subject he has been interested in. He defines *Culture* as "*a direction of the will together with certain ethics, or agreements on the proportionate relationships between moral, intellectual and material values.*"

Pound's interest in economics is assumed by many to be either a crazy pose or an insane obsession. In fact he was writing on general problems of economy in A. R. Orage's *New Age* as far back as 1912, though it was not until his meeting with C. H. Douglas in 1917 that he seems to have given much serious study to the particulars of the subject. As the years went by, Pound became increasingly absorbed in economics. His *Cantos* treat money as a major historical determinant, and his whole attitude is summed up with

. . . History that omits economics is mere bunk.

Between 1932 and the outbreak of the war he wrote *A.B.C. of Economics, Social Credit: An Impact, What is Money*

Introduction

For? and *Jefferson and/or Mussolini.* During the war, when
Pound remained in Italy, he wrote a further four pamphlets
on economic subjects, and translated two Confucian texts
into Italian, one edition being bi-lingual.

After the outbreak of war between Great Britain and Germany, but before Italy's entry into the war, Ezra Pound
started the series of broadcast talks from Rome Radio which
led to his indictment as a traitor to the United States. The
subject matter of these talks varied from cultural or personal
propaganda to actual political and economic exhortation.
The texts of all these broadcasts has not been made available
yet, though a number of them have appeared under private
imprint in Italy. The salient feature of them is a passionate
protest against everything that contributes to the vileness of
what Pound calls usurocracy. His accusations against Roosevelt are extreme, and his attitude to the war itself and the
very pertinent question of who should win, unrealistic. Out
of the talks, however, comes a coherent body of criticism of
men and books which deserves careful study. When it was
plain that the Allies would over-run Northern Italy, Pound
prepared to give himself up to the Americans, for he had
been indicted as a traitor as far back as 1942. He reported
to advance units of the U.S. Army in April 1945, and was
later interrogated at Genoa. After a period there he was taken
by road to Pisa, where he was imprisoned alone in a barbed
wire " cage " where he was exposed to extremes of weather
and physical violence which combined to cause the mental
breakdown he suffered during the following months. After
six weeks of this barbarous treatment he had to be removed
for medical reasons to a tent. There, as he slowly recovered,
he wrote *The Pisan Cantos,* in which the landscape environing
the camp plays so important a part. There also he translated
the only book he had access to (save the Bible and Prayer
Book supplied by the camp)—namely the two shorter Confucian texts, *Chung Yung* and *Ta Hsüeh,* which were bound
together into one volume. This has now appeared in his
translation in the United States and also in India. The titles

he gave these books were *The Unwobbling Pivot* and *The Great Digest*. In the November of 1945 Ezra Pound was flown to Washington to be tried. On the eve of the trial he was however submitted to an examination, and a month later he was declared to be insane. After a short period in the State Penitentiary in Washington he was removed to St. Elizabeth's Hospital, where he has been ever since. While in Washington he has translated the *Analects* of Confucius. Reports suggest that he is a very sick man and able only to work for an hour or so daily, but it may be he has yet much to offer to the world, quite apart from finishing his *Cantos,* which are plainly his most important single work.

One might consider Ezra Pound's whole work under three headings—critical, economic-historical, and poetic. His own opinion of the critic's true purpose is plain enough.

> My opinion of critics is
> The best are those who actually cause an amelioration in the art they criticise.
> The next best are those who focus attention on the best that is written
> and the pestilential vermin are those who distract attention from the best, either to the second-rate, or to their own critical writings. Mr. Eliot probably ranks very high in the first of these three groups. . . .

Mr. Eliot writes of Pound : ' He has enabled a few other persons, including myself, to improve their verse sense ; so that he has improved poetry through other men as well as through himself. I cannot think of anyone writing verse of our generation and the next, whose verse (if any good) has not been improved by the study of Pound's." According to Dr. René Taupin : " Pound n'est pas un critique, si l'on demande à une critique des articles ou des idées neuves et justes dans ' le marbre de la logique ' mais il a le don de voir juste et surtout de dire ce qu'il convient de dire à un moment donné et sur le ton qu'il faut." The fact is that, invaluable as so many of Pound's views are, they are often compensatory exaggerations rather than attempts at absolute evaluations. He shows greater interest in Gautier than in Baudelaire, for instance, and cries down Milton time and again. Both judgments are salutary as warnings, but would be ridiculous if taken as final estimates. Taken all in all, his work marks the first serious " revolt against the crepuscular spirit " in English literature (to quote one of his early titles), and this tendency becomes, through the Imagist demand for exactitude, the *Ching Ming* or "precise definition" of his *Cantos*.

As a prose writer on economics and history he appears to have known his limitations. " It may be that my weekly writings are no more articulate than the trumpetings of a terrified elephant. I have no specific will to preserve them as written. The elephant's noise serves a purpose : to warn its contingent herd." He recognises his purpose, however, in the same essay (written before 1937). " Even as I sit here an editor accuses me of writing Italian propaganda. I am no more writing Italian propaganda than is the calm McNair Wilson. I am writing for humanity in a world eaten by usury. I write for a cultural heritage that includes centuries of anti-usurious doctrine and results thereof in cathedral building. *Usura* was a moral issue, it was a religious issue. It is still an ethical issue, and religious wherever religion merits a name." This is from an essay entitled *We have had no battles but we have all joined in and made roads*. The paragraph is typical of Ezra Pound's forthright moral fervour, his self-opinionated attitude and his obsession with the concept of *usura*. There appears to have been more truth than he could have known in the simile of the trumpeting of the terrified elephant, for the radio talks given from Rome during the war did sound very much like this from all accounts. It is difficult to explain the apparent adherence to the Axis of this obviously " sincere " man. Naturally, " sincerity " is not the only criterion, though Phyllis Bottome, well known as an anti-Fascist, has emphasised in her memoir of Mr. Pound that

" Ezra was never venal ". Mr. Pound has not been tried yet, and it is quite inaccurate, as well as libellous, to describe him as a traitor. The one thing which becomes plain on a perusal of his work is that he was driven to his desperate folly by an almost hysterical fear of what American society was allowing itself to become. The conception of *usura* in Pound's mind is a blend of Dante and Major Douglas. Mr. Pound wrote : " I . . . see . . . clearly the grading of Dante's values, and especially how the whole hell reeks with money. The usurers are there against nature, against the natural increase of agriculture or of any productive work."

" Deep hell is reached via Geryon (Fraud) . . . and for ten Cantos thereafter the damned are all of them damned for money." If the concept of *usura* leaves the reader cold, or if it (as it usually does) sets him against Mr. Pound as an anti-Semite, it would be as well to remember that Shakespeare's view was not dissimilar.

> Which, like a usurer, abounds't in all
> And usest none.   (*Romeo and Juliet.*)

The core of Pound's views on usury and its effect on culture in general is to be found in the forty-fifth Canto, which, whatever one's opinion of the matter, is one of the most moving passages of poetry written in the century. One might go so far as to say that *The Cantos* should be approached through this canto :

> with usura
> seeth no man Gonzaga his heirs and his concubines
> no picture is made to endure nor to live with
> but it is made to sell and sell quickly
> with usura, sin against nature. . . .

Ezra Pound saw Fascism " as the best possible under the circumstances in Italy ". He was impressed with Mussolini's " liberty is not a right, but a duty ", and he wrote in 1937 :

Introduction

" Mussolini has told his people that poetry is a necessity to the state, and Carlo Delcroix is convinced that poets ought ' to occupy themselves with these matters ', namely credit, the nature of money, monetary issue, etc. These two facts indicate a higher state of civilisation in Rome than in London or Washington." He had been writing in this irritating hard-hitting manner ever since his first sardonic articles in 1912 under the title *Patria Mia*. He had embarrassed bankers and financiers as well as professors, and was hated for it. He was speaking from Rome Radio before the war began. He continued throughout the war, becoming increasingly virulent. Nothing could be less typical of the materialist America which today has coined the word " un-American ".

Whatever the value of Pound's criticism and historical or economic writing, his chief and lasting attainment is as a poet. It is tempting, however, to hold to the popular view that Pound as a poet has been side-tracked by economics. If this were so, his most important work, *The Cantos*, now nearly 600 pages in length, would lose three-quarters of its value. Some of the best poetry in them is poetry actually about money. To try to separate the poetic essence from the didactic substance of the poem would be valueless pedantry, or at best, adolescent romantic æstheticism.

The *Selected Poems* contain the best of his work written between 1906 and 1920, omitting *The Cantos* and *Homage to Sextus Propertius*, together with Mr. Eliot's now famous *Introduction*. If Mr. Pound set out with a desire to eradicate the " crepuscular spirit ", it may well be that it was because he felt it in himself. Much of his testy criticism may well be due to a nervous desire to root out from himself the very vices he attributes to others. The fact is, however, that Mr. Pound has steadily rooted out these " vilenesses " and that very early on the dreamy affectations of the early Yeats and the poetical language of the 'nineties, have disappeared. The *Selected Poems* are Mr. Pound's *studies in comparative literature*, the work he might have done in quite other forms had he not abandoned an academic career. The poems seem at

the same time to be the sketches for his life work—*The Cantos*.
In the early poem *Scriptor Ignotus* (*Ferrara* 1715) he wrote :

> And I see my greater soul-self bending
> Sibyl-wise with that great forty-year epic
> That you know of, yet unwrit
> But as some child's toy 'tween my fingers.   (1906)

If this was so, Mr. Pound was all the time schooling himself for the task. He was learning also all he could from
music, especially the music of the troubadours which he
studied (and even edited) with Walter Rummel, as well as
the poems themselves. He considered that "Any study of
European poetry is unsound if it does not commence with a
study of that art in Provence". His later interest in Confucius
brings him back to music again, for Kung insists on the true
value of music to the mind. Mr. Pound wrote in 1937 : "A
fugue a week for a year would teach even a bull-head something." He himself is known to have written a sonnet a day
for a year, and not kept one of them.

Now, Mr. Pound's approach was radically different from
that of many of his contemporaries in that it was entirely
objective. He was out to write a poem and to remove himself
from it as far as possible. He did this by means of *masks*
or *personæ* in which he developed Browning's method of
dramatic monologue, removing verbiage and putting his
whole self into it in order to create not himself, but an independent character, "Cino", "Arnault de Marvoil", "Bertrans de Born", "Sextus Propertius". Ford Madox Ford
had much the same thing in mind when he wrote : ". . .
Poetry . . . is a matter of rendering and not comment. You
must not say 'I am so happy'; you must behave as if you
were happy."

Mr. Pound's preoccupation at the time was largely with
style. Each style was a step to the next. "Imagism was a
point in my development. Some people remained at that
point. I moved on." The *Selected Poems* are the record of his

steps ; they are the best possible witness to his struggle to find a style. Of them Mr. Eliot wrote : " What is curious is his complete and isolated superiority as a master of verse form. No one living has practised the art of verse with such austerity and devotion : and no one living has practised it with more success." The difference in style between a poem by Pound written in 1907 and one written in 1917 is the easiest thing in the world to spot, but if one compares a Canto written in 1920 with one written in 1945, a gap of 25 years, it is not possible to observe any change in style. Pound had by the end of the first world war found the style he wanted, and he set to work on his poem, but whereas his *style* was formed and ready, his *knowledge* needed continued additions and modifications.

The Cantos have to be considered as an epic, the record or story of a struggle. Louis Zukofsky wrote of them :

> Emphasis if not specifically so placed before, may be on their poetic achievement in three respects—
>
> I.   The writing of history.
> II. The writing of narration.
> III. The functioning by concrete example of literary criticism.
>
> The poetry of *The Cantos* is a history. The writing (technique) proceeds towards a living museum of facts about man and his world which displays the validity of his successive positions as against the unwieldy detail of all his story.

To effect this intention many styles of different periods and places are re-animated and used to form a single continuum, just as Picasso's " style " can be recognised in a blue period piece, an adaptation of a Roman portrait or of an African mask.

In making the main work of his life a single poem, Mr. Pound should have claims to being a bigger poetic figure than either Eliot or Yeats *if* he is as successful in particulars as these two poets. At any rate he is the only poet of the century who has attempted an epic in the highest sense— one in which "all knowledge" and "all tradition" are present, whether in the form of myth or anecdote. What makes this epic new in literary history is the fact that its main theme is the power of money as a historical determinant. Seen in this light it is easier to understand why Pound called it "the tale of the tribe". It is a narrative of what he has called "ideas in action", and one can trace various ideas "going into action". For instance, the ten consecutive Cantos describing the history of China make up a history of China *in terms of the Confucian concept.* This is Ezra Pound's typical approach to history, or perhaps one should call it his particular *vision* of history.

Recently both Ezra Pound and T. S. Eliot have been violently attacked on political and poetical grounds. Now whereas these two poets have much in common in their style and their serious approach to literature, the likeness ends at this point. For Mr. Eliot has become essentially a symbolist poet, which Mr. Pound has never been. Mr. Eliot started his literary career with *Prufrock,* an analysis of personal emotions, a *persona* almost indistinguishable from its poet. Mr. Eliot's career might be divided into three stages, the first being that of personal and ironical analysis, the second that of an objectification of person and style under the influence largely of Ezra Pound (*Gerontion, Waste Land, Journey of the Magi*), and the third that of a return, stylistically strengthened, to poems of contemplatory self-analysis, this time by philosophical and theological, as well as literary, method. The influence of Ezra Pound is present in much of Mr. Eliot's verse after 1915, and he himself has recognised it often enough.

I have in recent years cursed Mr. Pound often enough; for I am never sure that I can call my verse my own; just when I am most pleased with myself, I find that I have caught up some echo from a verse of Mr. Pound's.

One other characteristic common to both Ezra Pound and T. S. Eliot is their sense of humour, robust and uproarious or positively ironic in Pound, subtly ironic and sometimes a little grim in Mr. Eliot.

When the *XXX Cantos* first appeared, Dr. F. R. Leavis compared them unfavourably with *The Waste Land*. "The methods of association and contrast employed in *The Waste Land* subserve an urgency pressing from below; only an austere and deep seriousness could have controlled them into significance. But *The Cantos* seem to be little more than a game—a game serious with the seriousness of pedantry. We may recognise what Mr. Pound's counters stand for, but they remain counters; and his patterns are not very interesting, even as schematic design, since, in the nature of the game, which hasn't much in the way of rules ('without reference to a philosophy or to any system of teleological principles'), they lack definition and salience."

Now this probably seemed quite true in 1933 of *XXX Cantos*. Today, with eighty-two Cantos to judge from, this appears to be less the case. Pound's memories, images and characters (for he does not use counters), do stand up and live a life of their own, each lending due significance to the whole history, though they do not necessarily do this until the whole poem (as far as it is finished) has been read. Like a large canvas of Breughel, the detailed incidents are, though amusing, of little significance until seen *as part of a whole*. Each is a painting without a frame, without limits, and fixes into the continuum of the whole, which is musical (i.e. set in time), as well as narrative and visual (i.e. set in space).

Careful reading of the whole of Pound's work suggests rather that the big poem has a consistency and a coherence which the collections of short poems have not, and that the rapid transitions from thought to thought represent the "Conversations with the dead" of one of the quickest minds of our time. The apparent fragmentariness of parts is more like a palimpsest where the reader is carried over the missing parts by the momentum of the extant pieces.

In February 1949 Ezra Pound was awarded the Bollingen
Prize for the best poetry by an American citizen published
during the year in the United States. It was the first award
of the Prize, and the choice made a world-wide sensation.
The situation was ironic, to say the least. For a man under
indictment for treason to receive a prize judged by Government servants, even a prize for poetry, was unprecedented.
The Bollingen Prize was offered by the generosity of Mr.
Paul Mellon, and it was to have been an annual award. Its
value was a thousand dollars. At first, public reaction, if
sceptical of the value of Pound's poetry, suggested that it
was a liberal and civilised gesture, which might reassure
those who saw totalitarian forms overcoming so many of our
national institutions. Later, however, the *Saturday Review of
Literature*, a weekly literary paper of wide circulation, printed
a series of articles in which Pound's poetry was denied any
but corruptive values, and T. S. Eliot was accused of leading
a Fascist plot in awarding the prize to Pound. It was suggested
that Eliot had proposed Pound's name and coerced the other
judges into awarding it to him. The judges were the Fellows
of the Library of Congress. They have since denied in a
strenuously-worded pamphlet[1] all the accusations of the
Saturday Review. Many of the facts printed by the *Saturday
Review* have been shown to have been false, and American
academic circles have been embarrassed by the critical in-
judiciousness of one of the biggest weeklies in the country. The
controversy has continued in many reviews and magazines,
and has become a straight fight between the old and the New
Critics, rather than an examination of the merits of Pound's
poem. An enquiry was demanded in the House of Representatives by the Democratic Representative Javitts. The enquiry
was refused, but the practice of judging prizes was condemned
and discontinued. The Bollingen Prize has, however, been
re-inaugurated, for it is in future to be awarded under the
auspices of Yale University instead of the Library of Congress.

It would be idle to deny that he has incurred intense

1. The case against the *Saturday Review of Literature* (Poetry, Chicago, 1949).

hostility, but when one considers him, with all his human imperfections, Ezra Pound cannot but command the respect of all liberal-minded people who examine his work fairly. They may not agree with him, yet they cannot but see the remarkable genius which has informed his works, especially *The Cantos*. And if they do not recognise the single-mindedness with which he has pursued his purpose over the years of his life, they are blinding themselves to one of the most remarkable phenomena of the century—a dedicated poet.

EZRA POUND

by T. S. Eliot [*1946*]

Whatever may have been the literary scene in America between the beginning of the century and the year 1914, it remains in my mind a complete blank. I cannot remember the name of a single poet of that period whose work I read: it was only in 1915, after I came to England, that I heard the name of Robert Frost. Undergraduates at Harvard in my time read the English poets of the '90s who were dead: that was as near as we could get to any living tradition. Certainly I cannot remember any English poet then alive who contributed to my own education. Yeats was well-known, of course; but to me, at least Yeats did not appear, until after 1917, to be anything but a minor survivor of the '90s. (After that date, I saw him very differently. I remember clearly my impression of the first performance of *The Hawk's Well*, in a London drawing room, with a celebrated Japanese dancer in the rôle of the hawk, to which Pound took me. And thereafter one saw Yeats rather as a more eminent contemporary than an elder from whom one could learn). There were, in the early years of the century, a few good poets writing in England, but I did not know of their existence until later; and it was often Pound (whose appreciation was much more comprehensive than most people realise) who directed my attention to them. But I do not think it is too sweeping to say, that there was no poet, in either country, who could have been of use to a beginner in 1908. The only recourse was to poetry of another age and to poetry of another language. Browning was more of a hindrance than a help, for he had gone some way, but not far enough, in discovering a contemporary idiom. And at that stage, Poe and Whitman had to be seen through French eyes. The question was still: where do we go from Swinburne? and the answer appeared to be, nowhere.

It is as well, in writing at the present moment about Pound, to acknowledge one's greatest personal debt at once. I had kept my early poems (including *Prufrock* and others eventually published) in my desk from 1911 to 1915—with the exception of a period when Conrad Aiken endeavoured, without success, to peddle them for me in London. In 1915 (and through Aiken) I met Pound. The result was that *Prufrock* appeared in *Poetry* in the summer of that year; and through Pound's efforts, my first volume was published by the Egoist Press in 1917.

Pound was then living in a small, dark flat in Kensington. In the largest room he cooked, by artificial light; in the lightest, but smallest room, which was inconveniently triangular, he did his work and received his visitors. There he lived until he moved, in 1922 I think, to Paris : but he seemed always to be only a temporary squatter. This appearance was due, not only to his restless energy—in which it was difficult to distinguish the energy from the restlessness and the fidgets, so that every room, even a big one, seemed too small for him —but to a kind of resistance to growing into any environment. In America, he would no doubt have always seemed on the point of going abroad ; in London, he always seemed on the point of crossing the Channel. I have never known a man, of any nationality, to live so long out of his native country without settling anywhere else. For a time, London, and then Paris, seemed to him the best centre for his attempts to revitalise poetry. But though young English writers, and young writers of any nationality, could count on his support if they excited his interest, the future of American letters was what concerned him most.

No one could have been kinder to younger men, or to writers who, whether younger or not, seemed to him worthy and unrecognised. No poet, furthermore, was, without self-depreciation, more unassuming about his own achievement in poetry. The arrogance which some people have found in him, is really something else; and whatever it is, it has not expressed itself in an undue emphasis on the value of his own poems. He liked to be the impresario for younger men, as well as the animator of artistic activity in any milieu in which he found himself. In this rôle he would go to any lengths of generosity and kindness; from inviting constantly

to dinner a struggling author whom he suspected of being
under-fed, or giving away clothing (though his shoes and
underwear were almost the only garments which resembled
those of other men sufficiently to be worn by them), to trying
to find jobs, collect subsidies, get work published and then
get it criticised and praised. Indeed, he was ready to lay out
the whole of life for anyone in whose work he was interested—
a degree of direction which not all the beneficiaries deserved,
and which was sometimes embarrassing. Yet, though the
object of his beneficence might come to chafe against it, only a
man of the meanest spirit could have come to resent it. He was
so passionately concerned about the works of art which he
expected his protegés to produce, that he sometimes tended to
regard the latter almost impersonally, as art or literature
machines to be carefully tended and oiled, for the sake of
their potential output.

Pound was, in fact, a dominating director. He has always
had a passion to teach. In some ways, I can think of no one
whom he resembled more than Irving Babbitt—a comparison
which neither man would have relished. Perhaps the back-
grounds were not unlike; perhaps if Pound had stopped at
home, and become, as he might have become, a professor of
comparative literature, the resemblance might have been
closer still. Babbitt had been my teacher; and by "teacher"
I do not mean merely a tutor, or a man whose lectures I
attended, but a man who directed my interests, at a particular
moment, in such a way that the marks of that direction are
still evident. Babbitt's closest friend was Paul More: many
years later, More became my friend also. But, once having
been a pupil of Babbitt, one did not later become his
"friend" in quite that sense; one retained, certainly, not only
admiration but warm affection—the affection of the ex-
disciple. For when one had come to hold a conviction,
religious, social or political, contrary to one of Babbitt's, the
status of ex-disciple was the highest to which one could aspire.
Some men are so devoted to ideas, that they cannot engage in
profitable discussion with those whose ideas differ from their own.

I do not know how good a judge of men Babbitt may
have been : when I was his pupil I was too immature to know.
But I suspect that he was more inclined to judge men by the
ideas they held, than to judge ideas by his understanding of
the men who held them. This difference distinguishes two
types of intelligence. Pound was always a masterly judge of
poetry; a more fallible judge, I think, of men; and he was
not at all interested in those who did not strike him as eligible
for the ideal intellectual and artistic milieu which he was
always trying to find or to found. I think also that sometimes
he not only judged too favourably those who shared his
views, but was deceived, in judging men by the ideas which
they professed to share with him, rather than by appreciation
of their personality and character.

I have been writing mainly in the past tense; for I have
been writing of a particular period, that between 1910 and
1922—or, with reference to myself, between 1915 and 1922.
(It was in 1922 that I placed before him in Paris the manuscript of a sprawling chaotic poem called *The Waste Land*
which left his hands, reduced to about half its size, in the
form in which it appears in print. I should like to think that
the manuscript, with the suppressed passages, had disappeared
irrecoverably : yet, on the other hand, I should wish the blue
pencilling on it to be preserved as irrefutable evidence of
Pound's critical genius). This is the period which ended with
Mauberley and *Propertius* and the first drafts of the early *Cantos*.
It is also the period in which he exercised a vital influence
upon English and American poetry, although his influence
has been largely felt by a younger generation, many of whom
never knew him personally, and some of whom may be
unaware of the extent of the influence upon them. I am not
in this statement taking account of "imagism". Whether the
name and principles of imagism were Pound's invention or
Hulme's, I do not know, and I am not very much interested.
Imagism produced a few good poems—notably those of H.D.
—but it was quickly absorbed into more comprehensive
influences, including Pound's. Then, with *The Catholic*

Anthology, The Egoist, The Little Review, Pound accomplished more than any other man could have done with anthologies and periodicals of such limited circulation. (To Pound, and to Miss Weaver, we owe the publication of Joyce's *Portrait of the Artist* and Lewis's *Tarr*). Pound did not create the poets: but he created a situation in which, for the first time, there was a "modern movement in poetry" in which English and American poets collaborated, knew each other's works, and influenced each other. Who, I wonder, in England (to say nothing of the rest of Europe) has read any American poetry written between Whitman and Robert Frost? If it had not been for the work that Pound did in the years of which I have been talking, the isolation of American poetry, and the isolation of individual American poets might have continued for a long time. I am not forgetting Miss Lowell, but it seems to me that the work she did, in putting over American poetry upon an American public, was on a lower level. She was a kind of demon saleswoman; and unless my memory of her methods is at fault (for it is a great many years since I read her *Six American Poets*) they were more enthusiastic than critical. If today it is a matter of course that London should take an interest in poetry published in New York and that New York should be interested in poetry published in London—not simply in the decorated reputations, but in the new verse—this is largely due to what Pound achieved for poetry in a decade.

I cannot say what Pound's critical writing will mean to those who have not known the man, because to me it is inextricably woven with his conversation. I still consider it to be almost the only contemporary writing on the Art of Poetry, that a young poet can study with profit. It forms a corpus of poetic doctrine: it has thus a particular relation to poetry in a particular age; and it is moreover addressed primarily to the poet. The opinion has been voiced, that Pound's eventual reputation will rest upon his criticism and not upon his poetry. (I have been paid the same compliment myself). I disagree. It is on his total work for literature that

he must be judged: on his poetry, *and* his criticism, *and* his
influence on men and on events at a turning point in literature.
In any case, his criticism takes its significance from the fact
that it is the writing of a poet about poetry; it must be read in
the light of his own poetry, as well as of poetry by other men
whom he championed. Criticism like Pound's is advocacy for
a certain kind of poetry; it is an assertion that poetry written
in the immediate future must, if it is to be good poetry,
observe certain methods and take certain directions. The
important question is, whether the critic is right in his judgment of the situation: if so, his criticism will be permanent, as
Dryden's and Wordsworth's are. Only, it will have to be read,
in the more distant future, with an understanding of the
situation for which the critic wrote. You cannot wholly understand Aristotle's doctrine of tragedy without reference to the
remains of the Attic drama upon which Aristotle's generalisations are founded. To readers in the future who do not trouble
to put Pound's criticism in its proper setting, as to many
contemporary readers to whom "literary criticism" means
something quite different from the notes of a poet on his craft,
Pound will seem irritatingly biassed. Such readers will be
annoyed, as some have already been annoyed, by his irrever-
ence for reputations which they have been educated to regard
as above dispute, and by his affirmation of the importance of
writers whom they have never read. To those, however, who
appreciate the necessity of some abrupt mutation of poetic
form and idiom in the period of which I have been speaking,
and who concede that Pound not only grasped the situation
but saw the direction which poetry ought to take, these
exaggerations and depreciations will appear in their proper
setting, and find their justification.

On the whole, I prefer the collected papers as one finds
them in the two volumes published in New York, to the later
book, *Make It New*, published in London. For me, at least,
the former volumes recall the first appearance of several items,
in periodicals, and so have a savour of their original timeliness
which they cannot have for those who know only the collected

criticism. Of the essays in *Make It New,* the essay (which is also a small anthology) on French Poets of the Symbolists Movement does not wear so well as some of the others. Certainly, a different approach would be appropriate now; some of the poets included may now be ignored; Mallarmé is not discussed; and Valéry's finest work was not known. The essay reads like the report of a tourist in French poetry, rather than like the conclusions of a reader who has digested the matter slowly and over a long period of time. The essay on Henry James remains of value, though the study of the subject has now reached a different phase. On the other hand, Remy de Gourmont does not now appear to have the importance which Pound attributes to him. The observations on the troubadours, on Arnaut Daniel, and on the Elizabethan and other early translators, are as good as they ever were. And the short papers at the beginning and end, *Date Line* and *A Stray Document,* are just as necessary for the beginner in the art of verse as they were when they were written. The most important principle of Pound's criticism is contained in the following paragraphs:

Theoretically (criticism) tries to forerun composition, to serve as gun-sight, though there is, I believe, no recorded instance of this foresight having ever been of the slightest use except to actual composers. I mean the man who formulates any forward reach of co-ordinating principle is the man who produces the demonstration.

The others who use the principle learn usually from the example, and in most cases merely dim and dilute it.

I think it will usually be found that the work outruns the formulated or at any rate the published equation, or at most they proceed as two feet of one biped.

A Stray Document is advice to poets. I had not read it for a long time; and in re-reading it for my present purpose, I found that some of the advice in it is substantially advice that I must have given to many young poets. For instance:

Let the candidate fill his mind with the finest cadences he can discover, preferably in a foreign language so that the meaning of the words may be less likely to divert his attention from the movement; e.g. Saxon charms, Hebridean folk songs, the verse of Dante, and the lyrics of Shakespeare —if he can dissociate the vocabulary from the cadence. Let him dissect the lyrics of Goethe coldly into their component sound values, syllables long and short, stressed and unstressed, into vowels and consonants.

The only qualification this precept needs, is the warning that one is not likely to get a full appreciation of the way poetry in a foreign language should sound, until one knows that language very well indeed—at which stage the danger arises that the meaning of the words will divert attention. But the advice is nevertheless valuable: for instance, I myself have got a good deal of stimulation from Carmichael's *Carmina Gadelica*, a collection of Highland folk poetry.

As for the errors against which Pound warns the beginner, I find them turning up, week after week, in verse submitted for my opinion.

Be influenced by as many great artists as you can, but have the decency either to acknowledge the debt outright, or to try to conceal it.

The weakness of the greater amount of verse I have to read —apart from that class, abundantly represented, in which the authors do not appear to have read *any* poetry—is that the authors have indeed been influenced, but not by enough, or by enough variety, of first-rate poetry. Often they appear to have read the shorter poems of Donne, several pieces by Gerard Hopkins, and some of the work of their own elder contemporaries. Some poems submitted suggest that the author has opened a volume of Whitman and noted how the lines look on the printed page. What most of the "free verse" derives from (except from the rumour that verse has been liberated) I cannot tell.

Half of the work that Pound did as a critic can be known only from the testimony of those who have benefited from his conversion or correspondence. At a certain moment, my debt to him was for his advice to read Gautier's *Emaux et Camées*, to which I had not before paid any close attention. I have already spoken of his operation upon *The Waste Land*. I have sometimes tried to perform the same sort of maieutic task; and I know that one of the temptations against which I have to be on guard, is trying to re-write somebody's poem in the way in which I should have written it myself if I had wanted to write that poem. Pound never did that: he tried first to understand what one was attempting to do, and then tried to help one do it in one's way. There did come a point, of course, at which difference of outlook and belief became too wide; or it may have been distance and different environment; or it may have been both.

I have already said that Pound's criticism would not have the great value it has, without his poetry; and in his poetry there is, for the analytical reader, a great deal of criticism exemplified. I find nothing to alter in my introduction to a volume of Pound's *Selected Poems*, published in London in 1928, except that I should now speak more respectfully of Whitman—a matter irrelevant to my present theme. In that introduction I said nothing about the *Propertius*, which I rate very high indeed. (I am aware of the censure of those who have treated it as a translation; and if it is treated as a translation, they are of course right). If I am doubtful about some of *The Cantos*, it is not that I find any poetic decline in them. I am doubtful on somewhat the same ground as that on which I once complained to him about an article on the monetary theory of Gesell, which he had written at my suggestion for *The Criterion*. I said (as nearly as I can remember): "I asked you to write an article which would explain this subject to people who had never heard of it; yet you write as if your readers knew about it already, but had failed to understand it." In *The Cantos* there is an increasing defect of communication, not apparent when he is concerned with Sigismondo

Malatesta, or with Chinese dynasties, but, for instance: when-
ever he mentions Martin Van Buren. Such passages are very
opaque: they read as if the author was so irritated with his
readers for not knowing all about anybody so important as
Van Buren, that he refused to enlighten them. I am incidentally annoyed, myself, by occasional use of the peculiar
orthography which characterises Pound's correspondence, and
by lines written in what he supposes to be a Yankee dialect.
But the craftsman up to this moment—and I have in mind
certain recent and unpublished *Cantos*—has never failed.
There is nobody living who can write like this: how many
can be named, who can write half so well.

I have before now expressed the opinion, that the "greatness" of a poet is not a question for critics of his own age to
raise: it is only after he has been dead for a couple of generations that the term beings to have meaning. "Greatness",
when the term means anything at all, is an attribute conferred
by time. The question of "genuineness" is the first question
for contemporary criticism to raise. But there is a third aspect,
under which it is proper to consider a poet, a third kind of
judgment which may be passed upon him in his later years,
the material for which is not only his poetry, but the principles
of writing which he has exemplified and defended. I avoid the
word *influence*, for there are dangers in estimating a poet by his
influence. It takes at least two to make an influence: the man
who exerts it and the man who experiences it. The latter may
be a writer whose verse would have been bad, whatever
influences had gone to form it; or he may have been influenced
in the wrong way, or by the wrong things in the work of the
poet under whose influence he has come; or he may be born
into a period less favourable to the creation of art—though
this is a subject we cannot know very much about. So I am not
speaking of influence, but of the things for which a man like
Pound has stood, in his own time. To appreciate these, we
need first, as I suggested at the beginning, some understanding
of the state of poetry when the poet began writing. And that
is soon forgotten, for each generation tends to accept the

situation it finds, as if that situation had always prevailed.
I think that Pound was original in insisting that poetry was an
art, an art which demands the most arduous application and
study; and in seeing that in our time it had to be a highly
conscious art. He also saw that a poet who knows only the
poetry of his own language is as poorly equipped as the
painter or musician who knows only the painting or the music
of his own country. The business of the poet is to be more conscious of his own language than other men, to be more
sensitive to the feeling, more aware of the meaning of every
word he uses, more aware of the history of the language and
of every word he uses, than other men. He needs, however,
to know as much as he can of several other languages:
because one advantage of a knowledge of other languages is
that it makes us understand our own language better. Pound's
"erudition" has been both exaggerated and irrelevantly
under-estimated: for it has been judged chiefly by scholars
who did not understand poetry, and by poets who had
little scholarship. Pound's great contribution to the work of
other poets (if they choose to accept what he offers) is his
insistence upon the immensity of the amount of *conscious*
labour to be performed by the poet; and his invaluable sug-
gestions for the kind of training the poet should give himself—
study of form, metric and vocabulary in the poetry of divers
literatures, and study of good prose. Poets should continue to
study—and if poetry survives they no doubt will—Pound's
poetry, which bridges the gap separating Browning and
Swinburne from the present day, and his writings about
poetry. He also provides an example of devotion to "the art
of poetry" which I can only parallel in our time by the
example of Valéry, and to some extent that of Yeats: and to
mention these names is to give some impression of Pound's
importance as an exponent of the art of poetry in a time when

> The 'age demanded' chiefly a mould in plaster
> Made with no loss of time,
> A prose kinema, not, not assuredly alabaster
> Or the 'sculpture' of rhyme.

POSTSCRIPT, 1950.—To this article there is nothing that I should at present wish to add, unless I were to engage upon a deeper and more analytical examination of Pound's poetry; and that would be a different essay. On one point I should like to qualify my opinion. The foregoing was written shortly after the end of the War, when I had not yet had the opportunity to study *The Pisan Cantos* ; and these *Cantos*—apart from their immense weight and solidity in themselves—do I find go far towards justifying the *longeurs* of earlier passages about mysteries of American history, in the first half of the last century, in which I, like most readers, am not adept. Nor would I now complain, re-reading all of the existing *Cantos* continuously, of obscurities which irritated me in reading sections of the poem, at wide intervals, in the form of a serial. Such a change of view, of course, is merely a question of habitation and gradual adaptation. How very straightforward, lucid and orderly we now find *Ulysses* to be!

T.S.E.

EZRA POUND

by Edith Sitwell [1934]

In the year 1908, amidst the silvery tintinnabulations of tea-spoons left over from the tea-parties of the Victorian Aunts of Poetry, amidst the noise of the shufflings of football boots, amidst the odd and circumscribed movements (penned between wooden wickets) of literary cricketers making their runs, appeared a new poet who, heedless of wickets and careless of tea-parties, walked with natural, free, and beautiful movements according to the law of his nature.

Tea-spoons were clashed, football boots were hurled at the offender, in vain. Mr. Pound continued on his way, "disturbing"—to paraphrase a later criticism of one of the tea-spoon school—"the most mobile placidity."

I confess I am unable to understand why Mr. Pound's poems aroused so much fury, for, as Mr. Eliot has pointed out in his preface to Mr. Pound's *Selected Poems*, his "originality is genuine in that his versification is a logical development of the verse of his English predecessors," and "The earliest of the poems in this volume show that the first strong influence upon Pound, at the moment when his verse was taking direction, were those of Browning and Yeats. In the background are the 'nineties in general, and behind the 'nineties, of course, Swinburne and William Morris."

The intense vitality which inhabited every poem of Mr. Pound's, the sharp and clear visual sense, the apparent easiness of the movement—these qualities, however, frightened readers with debilitated senses and no power of living. They were alarmed at the fact that life was forming itself into new rhythmic lines, which are yet a logical development to those to which they were accustomed.

"They knew that (to quote Mr. Eliot once more) a man who devises new rhythms is a man who extends and refines our sensibility; and that is not merely a question of technique; and of this extension of sensibility they were afraid."

Of this fear, Mr. Pound paid no heed. He developed his technique according to the necessities of his time, and of his

nature. In the Augustan age, the outward structure of poetry
was the result of logic alone, whilst variations of speed, the
feeling of heat or of cold, the variations of different depths
and heights, were produced by means of texture, and was
the result of sensibility and of instinct. Poetry was therefore,
in that age, as far as outward structure was concerned, the
sister of architecture ; with the romantics, and their heightened
vowel-sense, resulting in different melodic lines, she became
the sister of music ; now she appears like the sister of horti-
culture, each poem growing according to the laws of its own
nature, but in a line which is more often the irregular though
entirely natural shape of a tree or of a flowering plant—
bearing leaves, bearing flowers, bearing fruit—than a sharp
melodic line, springing like a fountain.

In the work of a great artist like Mr. Pound, however, the
shape of the line, its outline and colour are perfectly and
miraculously balanced, and may be claimed as being that
"compound of freedom and of order" which, according to
Mr. Pound's essay on Dolmetsch, constitutes a work of art.
"It is perfectly obvious that art hangs between chaos on the
one hand and mechanics on the other ; a pedantic insistence
upon detail tends to drive out major form. A firm hold on
major form makes for a freedom of detail."

In Mr. Pound's verse, the major form is in nearly every
case visible—appearing sometimes as a clear pure melodic
line, as in the earlier verse—sometimes as a stem from which
flowers and leaves spring in abundance. I must, however,
confess that greatly as I admire the major part of *The Cantos,*
some of them do seem to me to resemble the lost luggage
office at a railway station, with the trunks strewn about but
carefully labelled. Mr. Pound has not, to the same degree,
Mr. Eliot's supreme power of fusion ; for in many of *The
Cantos,* although time that has been dead five hundred years
ago lives again for us, it cannot be said that the events have
the same simultaneity ; or, perhaps it would be more accurate
to say that many of the events seem to have only a local or
a temporary importance, and to be unconnected, excepting

rhythmically, with the line. In fact, in them "a pedantic insistence upon detail tends to drive out major form." This complaint, however, only applies to a few of the Cantos.

It is easy enough to see why the general public—but not the public practised in reading poetry—might have failed to understand *The Cantos* if they had appeared before *Personæ* and *Ripostes,* but it is impossible to guess why these should have been found difficult. The poems in *Personæ* and *Ripostes* are exquisitely balanced, and have the pure melodic line which is only to be found in the greatest lyric poetry, sometimes pausing and sinking—as a fountain pauses and sinks before springing afresh—sometimes growing like a flower. This growth, which seems so inevitable, is in reality the result of a miraculous art. How beautiful and how significant, for instance, are the varying pauses—like those of one who is about to "come again" (be re-incarnated) in this fragment from *Na Audiart.* The song seems some lonely air, strange with age, heavy with dew, drifting through the gaps in a ruined castle wall :

> Yea, though thou wish me ill,
> > Audiart, Audiart,
> Thy loveliness is here writ till,
> > Audiart,
> Oh, till thou come again.
> And being bent and wrinkled, in a form
> That hath no perfect limning, when the warm
> Youth dew is cold
> Upon thy hands, and thy old soul
> Scorning a new, wry'd casement,
> Churlish at seemed misplacement,
> Finds the earth as bitter
> As now seems it sweet,
> Being so young and fair
> As then only in dreams,
> Being then young and wry'd,
> Broken of ancient pride,

Thou shalt then soften,
Knowing, I know not how,
Thou wert once she
           Audiart, Audiart,
For whose fairness one forgave
           Audiart,
Audiart
        Que be'm vols mal.

If we contrast this with the poignant sharpness of the first
verse of *The Spring* in *Lustra*, we shall have some
idea of Mr. Pound's subtlety of hearing and of touch in these
earlier poems.

Cydonian Spring with her attendant train,
Mælids and water-girls,
Stepping beneath a boisterous wind from Thrace
Throughout this sylvan place
Spreads the bright tips,
And every vine-stock is
Clad in new brilliancies.
           And wild desire
Falls like black lightning.
O bewildered heart,
Though every branch have back what last year lost,
She, who moved here amid the cyclamen,
Moves only now a clinging tenuous ghost.

The sharpness of the first verse in this beautiful poem—a
sharpness which is like that of the "bright tips" on the
vine-branches—is caused partly by the bright sound of
"train", with its assonances "Thrace" and "place"
("sylvan place" being naturally softer, because of the soft
S and C sounds), partly by the strangeness of the assonances
"tips", "is", "brilliancies", and by the clearness of the
sound of "water-girls". The S's in "Stepping", "boisterous", and the C in "Thrace" in the third line, slow it

40

down very faintly, as the boisterous wind plays with the draperies of the attendant train, and the sound of "throughout" in the next line, echoes the sound of the wind.

In the lines :

> And wild desire
> Falls like black lightning.
> O bewildered heart,

the movement is much slower, mainly because whereas in the first three lines the word "train", in the first, was echoed by the assonance "Thrace" in the third line, and by its rhyme "place" in the next—this giving it movement and swiftness—in these later three lines there is neither assonance nor rhyme, only the long double-edged sound of "desire"—a word that has long echoes after its two syllables and a half are over—the higher sound of the first I in "lightning" (falling again to earth in the second syllable), and the rather dead sound of "O bewildered heart". After these three lines, however, we have a wandering movement :

> Though every branch have back what last year lost,
> She, who moved here amid the cyclamen,
> Moves only now a clinging tenuous ghost.

The wandering slowness of the movement of this is due partly to the "ch" in "branch" with the two S's in "last" and "lost", and partly to the fact that "lost" is a dark sinking echo of "last", and that the word which ends the last line, "ghost", is a dissonance of "lost", which ends the next line but one above it. "Ghost", however, has a longer echo than "lost".

In such poems as these we find much to delight the ear and the visual sense ; but it is a little difficult to know why the "mobile placidity" of the public was disturbed, unless it were by the fact that Mr. Pound lives, obviously, in eternity and not in time as we know it. Audiart, Eleanor of *The*

Cantos, the various Italian tyrants who inhabit these, are as
living as Steffan who jostles them in their new life. This fact
of giving life to the dead, especially in the later works, might
perhaps disconcert those who do not believe in re-incarnation
upon this earth, but in the earlier works the re-incarnation
appeared easier. The reason for the fear felt in the presence of
Mr. Pound's earlier poems may, perhaps, be found in the
fact that " In the nineteenth century "—as William Morris
pointed out in *News from Nowhere*—" there was a theory
that art and imaginative literature ought to deal with contemporary life ; but they never did so ; for, if there was any
pretence of it, the author always took care . . . to disguise
or exaggerate, or idealise—in some way to make it strange ;
so that, for all the versimilitude there was, he might just as
well have dealt with the time of the Pharaohs ".

To Mr. Pound, however, persons who had been dead for
a thousand years appeared as his contemporaries, whilst the
accidental accompaniments of our present life—motor-cars,
say—are as important as, but no more important than, those
of a thousand years ago. This, I imagine, is responsible for
some of the embarrassment felt before Mr. Pound's earlier
poems. In addition to this, there was the fact of his extraordinary learning—the fact that to the unlearned, influences
could be felt in his work, but could not be traced to their
source. There was, for instance, the influence of what Mr.
Eliot calls " the exact and difficult Provençal versification ".
But there were, as well, easily recognisable influences, such
as that of Mr. Yeat's technique, of William Morris, and of
Browning. But Mr. Pound's rhythms are not roughly muscular like those of Browning ; they are subtle and sensitive
to an almost unparalleled degree, and the muscular system
of these is the result of sensibility and is highly trained,
whereas Browning's was not.

In the midst of many technical influences—which were,
in the end, to form one of the most highly-individual techniques of our time—Mr. Pound's way of seeing was always
his own. Now, one of the reasons why the pioneers in the

arts are so much disliked is that the public has got into the way of thinking that man has always seen as he sees now. This is wrong. Not only has he seen with different eyes, but it is impossible that we should all see alike at the present time, although the crowd would prefer uniformity of sight. The modern artist gives us the great chance of exerting an individuality in seeing. The older beauty, the beauty of the Old Masters, is in the beauty of species and of mass ; the new beauty is highly individualised and separate. The modern artist is not concerned with things in the mass, he is passionately interested in the fulfilling of the destinies of the single individuals that make up the mass—whether those individuals are men, or leaves, or waves of the sea. The great quality of the Old Masters in all the arts is force, used in the scientific sense of the term—the binding together of the molecules of the world. That is partly what makes their sense of design so tremendous. The great quality of the modern masters is an explosive energy—the separating up of the molecules— exploring the possibilities of the atom. This is at once the quality and the danger of pioneer poetry. One technical aim of the more accomplished of the modernist poets is to reconcile this necessity of exploring the possibilities of the atom with the necessity for logical design and form.

In this aim Mr. Pound has been peculiarly successful, attaining to the highest degree of expressiveness and uniting a rare power of compression with an extraordinary flexibility.

The other great technical problem of the poetry of today is that of the proper use of speech-rhythms, but speech-rhythms made dynamic, not lowered in vitality or slipping down hill. Mr. Pound in his *How to Read* has said that " Great literature is simply language charged with meaning to the utmost degree." In producing this, Mr. Pound shows what Mr. Eliot has claimed to be his " complete and isolated superiority as a master of verse-form." Mr. Pound has written of this matter of dynamic language in *A.B.C. of Reading*[1] (Routledge), a work of much importance :

1. This book is being re-issued by Messrs. Faber and Faber.—Editor.

The changing of language is done in three principal
ways : You receive the language as your race has left it,
the words have meanings that have ' grown into the race's
skin '; the Germans say ' wie in den Schnabel
gewachsen ', as it grows in his beak. And the good writer
chooses his words for their ' meaning ', but that meaning
is not a set cut-off thing like the move of knight or pawn
on a chess-board. It comes up with roots, with associations, with how and where the word is familiarly used,
or where it has been used brilliantly or memorably. . . .
You have to go almost exclusively to Dante's criticism
to find a set of objective categories for words. Dante
called words ' buttered ' and ' shaggy ' because of the
different Noises they make. Or ' pesca et hirsuto ',
combed or hairy.

Mr. Pound's sensibility to these differences was always
singularly acute, and must have appeared shocking and
strange to those readers who were accustomed to the debility
and meaningless texture of the poems which were most prevalent in the first decade of the twentieth century. This intense
life pulsated through all the early poems, taking many different forms, until, in *Mauberley,* it found perfection.

In *Hugh Selwyn Mauberley (Life and Contacts)* we
have fixed for all time what is, at once, the complete record
of the life of an individual and " the document of an era ",
to quote Mr. Eliot's preface. The series of poems form a
comprehensive whole, and each poem is, to a certain extent,
dependent psychologically and rhythmically upon the others.
By this I mean that the extraordinary flexibility of the
rhythms can only be apprehended to the fullest extent if the
poems are regarded not as separate poems, but as parts of a
complete poem.

This record of an age was first broken into fragments by
the different degrees of the pressure of heat and cold which
lay, or surged, beneath the surface of the lines ; it was then
welded into a whole by the artist's supreme mastery over his

material. I use the word "welded" and not "fused" deliberately. The "broken images" of Mr. Eliot's *The Waste Land* were fused into a whole, and therein lies one of the differences between the two poems. But the difference does not lie in this alone, nor in the fact that *Mauberley* is the life story of an individual person and at the same time "the document of an era", whereas *The Waste Land* is not the record of an individual, it is the life of all mankind. The difference lies, too, in the fact that whereas *Mauberley* is the record of an age, *The Waste Land* is a world, and not the record of a world ; the seemingly dispersed fragments bear within themselves "correspondences", as Swedenborg has expressed it, as the symbols which nature shows bear correspondence one with another, as the six-rayed snowflake resembles the six-rayed crystal. It is true that this world has been shattered ; but the genius of the poet has fused the fragments into an indivisible whole once again.

The power over the material of poetry shown by Mr. Pound is nothing short of astounding. All expression is welded into an image and not removed into a symbol, or squandered in a metaphor, since these, as a means of expression, are necessarily looser and more leisurely. The whole poem is expressed in a variety of tuneless and broken rhythms, sometimes hesitating and dropping, sometimes hurrying aimlessly ; and these convey the life of a figure moving adversely in a world where the natural rhythms of life have broken down.

> For three years, out of key with his time,
> He strove to resuscitate the dead art
> Of poetry ; to maintain ' the sublime '
> In the old sense. Wrong from the start—
>
> .   .   .   .   .
>
> His true Penelope was Flaubert,
> He fished by obstinate isles ;
> Observed the elegance of Circe's hair
> Rather than the mottoes on sundials.

Unaffected by ' the march of events ',
He passed from men's memory in ' l 'an trentiesme,
De son eage '; the case presents
No adjunct to the Muses' diadem.

In this first poem he has, therefore, summed up by the use of images strongly welded together, all the interests of this artist's life. These images, with the exception of one— " He fished by obstinate isles "—need no explanation. But it is interesting to know that this, to me, rather difficult phrase has been explained by some critic—I think, by Dr. Leavis— as conveying " his inveterate eclecticism, his interest in various periods and cultures: Provençal, Italian, Chinese, and so on".

The phrase " The mottoes on sundials " is a deliberately withered and small understatement of the passage of time, of the passing of an age, of the gathering of the shadows of a new era.

In the second and third poems of *Mauberley* we have a concentrated essence of the present age, the age of machine-made mass-production (which, though they are formed by the inevitable rhythms of machines of durable steel, have, themselves, no rhythm—have no durability), the age of the stunting and standardising of the spirit, the age which has decreed that the giant cannot reach to heights beyond the stretch of the dwarf, that the dwarf cannot explore crevices and hiding-places that are unknown to the giant.

This age is produced before our eyes by the most miraculous control of technique, which allows for all looseness, all heightening and slowing of speed in the medium. Indeed, what appear, at first, to be the ordinary and careless rhythms of speech are, in reality, the result of an extraordinary sensibility of technique ; the poet produces, by the deliberate tunelessness, and by the variation between lamed, guttering-down, or over-hurried and feverish rhythms, this age which, mass-produced by a too-mechanical rhythm, has, in itself, no rhythm.

The age demanded an image
Of its accelerated grimace,
Something for the modern stage,
Not, at any rate, an Attic grace ;
Not, not certainly, the obscure reveries
Of the inward gaze ;
Better mendacities
Than the classics in paraphrase !
The ' age demanded ' chiefly a mould in plaster,
Made with no loss of time,
A prose kinema, not, not assuredly, alabaster
Or the ' sculpture of rhyme '.

The crumbling sandstone-like sound of " age ", finding its
refuge in " image " (its echo), then crumbling down into
the still softer echoes of their assonances in the next line :
" accelerated . . . grimace . . ." (the softness is that of
something which should be hard, but which has decayed into
softness)—the significance of these sounds is deliberate. And
the echo of these sounds is heard again in the next verse :
" gaze ", " paraphrase "; and the sound is less persistent
than that of " age " or of " image ", more persistent than
that of " grimace ", " grace ".

In the next poem, in the fifth verse, we have a muffling,
thickening arrangement of F's, with one slightly longer V,
and these sounds convey the thickening of human
sensibilities :

Faun's flesh is not to us,
Nor the saint's vision.
We have the Press for wafer ;
Franchise for circumcision.

The fourth poem is an almost unbearably moving record
of the war—an evocation of the men who arose from the
dead, only to walk " eye-deep " once more, into the new hell
that the old men had prepared for them.

47

... Died some, pro patria,
                non ' dulce ' non ' et decor ' ...
walked eye-deep in hell
believing in old men's lies, then unbelieving
came home, home to a lie,
home to many deceits,
home to old lies and new infamy ;
usury age-old and age-thick
and liars in public places.
Daring as never before, wastage as never before.
Young blood and high blood,
fair cheeks, and fine bodies ;
fortitude as never before.
frankness as never before
disillusions as never told in the old days,
hysterias, trench confessions,
laughter out of dead bodies.

In this great poetry (I have only quoted part of the section
from which it comes), the springs of the rhythm are broken ;
the beginning of each line starts up as a broken automaton
might start up, at the opening of each new day, to begin its
mechanical gamut of meaningless and useless toil. Then the
line struggles to its close—sometimes moving stiffly and automatically as if the spring still controlled it :

> ('' Young blood and high blood,
>   fair cheeks, and fine bodies ; '')

Sometimes sinking into nothingness :

> ('' Daring as never before, wastage as never before '')

Sometimes stretching hopelessly outward.

In the sixth poem, *Yeux Glauques*, we have gone back
to the spiritual preparations for the present time, and to the
discordance (since this is the history of an artist) between

the particular morality of Gladstone, Ruskin and " fœtid Buchanan " and that of Swinburne, Rossetti and Burne-Jones. It is, I think, one of the least interesting poems in the sequence. In the next, *Siena Mi Fe; Disfecemi Maremma,* we have the age that resulted from this—the amalgamation of the two moralities in the eighteen-nineties imaged in the death of Lionel Johnson, who . . .

> . . . showed no trace of alcohol
> At the autopsy, privately performed—
> Tissue preserved—the pure mind
> Arose toward Newman as the whisky warmed.

This crumbling, shrinking, into the dry sound of the last verse,

> M. Verog, out of step with the decade,
> Detached from his contemporaries,
> Neglected by the young,
> Because of these reveries.

The rhythm of the ninth poem, *Mr. Nixon,* has a miraculously sure poise and certainty, reproducing, as it does, the different fat stretches of self-assurance conveyed in Mr. Nixon's conversation—stretches which fall now and then into a pause, as Mr. Nixon reflects on his less certain past, when he, too, was obliged to

> Consider
> Carefully the reviewer.

The rhythm of this section differs greatly from the timed hesitancies of No. XII, where the poet, awaiting " the Lady Valentine's commands ", realises the place of poetry in the cosmos.

> Poetry, her border of ideas,
> The edge, uncertain, but a means of blending

With other strata
Where the lower and higher have ending ;
A hook to catch the Lady Jane's attention,
A modulation toward the theatre,
Also, in the case of revolution,
A possible friend and comforter.

Then, after the beautifully formed, but less intrinsically interesting *Envoi*, we come to the section called *Mauberley*, which is a quintessence of the poems which precede it. In the first section, an extra emphasis is laid on

His true Penelope
Was Flaubert,

and from this emphasis we gather that the poet passed his life in pursuing or returning to art for the sake of art—Flaubert being the symbol of the pure artist.

The lines :

And his tool
The engravers.
Firmness,
Not the full smile,
His art, but an art
In profile ;
Colourless
Pier Francesca,

concentrate, in one image, his devotion to the pure outline of art, and, in its reference to " art in profile " explains his attitude towards life.

The firmness and exquisiteness of the " profile " has changed, however, in the next poem, to weakness, to hesitation. It is a poem whose verses cannot be separated from each other with any success, or the sense of " bewilderment " conveyed by the drifting movement, the interweaving of the

thin strands of sound would be lost. The *Thirty-Three Cantos*
present far greater difficulties than *Mauberley*—at least to a
reader who, like myself, has not the advantage of a classical
education.

In some cases we have the difficulty presented by the
extreme intricacy of the interweaving of events, growing out
of each other according to the laws of nature ; in others, we
are presented with a still greater difficulty, that of events
which are, actually, echoes of each other separated by gaps
in time. These gaps in time have been abolished by the poet,
and echo and original have been welded into what Mr. Yeats,
writing of *The Cantos* in *A Packet for Ezra Pound*, has
called " an Archetypal Event "—present the appearance of
simultaneity—all time is welded into the present time.

We have, also, the problem of the presence of Archetypal
Persons—of the building up into one body of various characteristics that have persisted, throughout many ages, in many
bodies ; as an example of this simultaneity, we may point to
the fusion of the idea of the banking-house of Kahn with
the idea of Kubla Khan. Sometimes, again, we find splinters
of these Archetypal Persons, called by many different names,
and these again are splintered up into many still thinner
wedges of personalities expressing themselves by sound.

It will, no doubt, be possible in the course of time to realise
the design of this monumental work as a whole ; at the
present, this realisation is difficult. Mr. Yeats, in his *Packet
for Ezra Pound*, has given us the most valuable help that
could be found, in his record of a conversation that he had
with Mr. Pound. . . . "*He explains that it will, when the
hundredth Canto is finished, display a structure like that of a
Bach Fugue. There will be no plot, no chronicle of events, no
logic of discourse, but two themes, the descent into Hades from
Homer, a Metamorphosis from Ovid, and mixed with these
mediæval or modern historical characters. He has tried to produce
that picture Porteous commended to Nicholas Poussin in ' Le
Chef d'œuvre Inconnu ', where everything rounds or thrusts
itself without edges, without contours—conventions of the intel-*

*lect—from a splash of tints and shades, to achieve a work as
characteristic of the art of our time as the paintings of Cezanne,
avowedly suggested by Porteous, as 'Ulysses' and its dream association of words and images, a poem in which there is nothing
that can be taken out and reasoned over, nothing that it not part
of the poem itself. He has scribbled on the back of an envelope
certain sets of letters that represent emotions or archetypal events
—I cannot find any other adequate definition—A B C D and then
J K L M, and then each set of letters repeated, and then A B C D
inverted and this repeated, and then a new element of X Y Z,
then certain letters that never recur, and then all sorts of com-
binations of X Y Z and J K L M and A B C D and D C B A
and all set whirling together. He has shown me upon the wall
a photograph of a Cosimo Tura decoration in three compartments, in the upper the Triumph of Love and the Triumph of
Chastity, in the middle Zodiacal signs, and in the lower certain
events in Cosimo Tura's day. The descent and the metamorphosis
—A B C D and J K L M—his fixed elements, took the place of
the Zodiac, the archetypal persons—X Y Z—that of the Triumphs,
and certain modern events—his letters that do not recur—that
of those events in Cosimo Tura's day.*

*"I may, now that I have recovered leisure, find that the
mathematical structure, when taken up into imagination, is more
than mathematical, that seemingly irrelevant details fit together
into a single theme, that here is no botch of tone and colour—
Hodos Chameleontos—except for some odd corner where one
discovers beautiful detail like that finely modelled foot in
Porteous' disastrous picture."*

Here, then, we have *The Cantos* as seen through the eyes
of a great poet, and one who has been in constant communion
with Mr. Pound.

In the review of *The Cantos* which appeared in *Hound and
Horn* (Winter, 1931), and which has been quoted by Dr.
Leavis, we are told that "*Mr. Pound's documentation is a device,
a technic. History and literature are for him a mine of images,
and his purpose is to fix certain of these images in a lasting,
orderly design, without reference to a philosophy or to any system*

of teleological principles. Now whether the historical fact, the Image, be the blowing of apricot-blossoms from east to west, or a narcotic charge preferred against Frank Robert Iriquois of Oklahoma City, or the departure of Anchises from Troy, it is a detail of supreme importance to the frieze, a note of supreme importance to the melos, which is the poem as a whole. The poet, as I have observed, uses images precisely as another poet would use metaphors or, even more simply, chromatic words. These images have no 'hidden meaning'. Malatesta, Frank Robert Iriquois, the apricot-blossoms, are no more "puzzling" than Shakespeare's "encarnadine" in the verse about the multitudinous seas. It is true that if you have enough Latin to be able to associate "encarnadine" with "flesh", "carnation" and the other rich warm "carn" words, you will derive more enjoyment from the verse than will X, who knows only that "encarnadine" is a euphemism for "redden"; but you will "understand" the verse not a whit better than your less-informed friend. Therefore, the criticism that XXX Cantos is incomprehensible is a false criticism ; and I have gone into it at some length because it seems to be the objection that is being most strongly urged against the poem. The Cantos will baffle persons who are willing to be baffled, but this is so in the case of any considerable poem.

"The Cantos may be described as an epic of timelessness. That is to say, the poem represents Mr. Pound's endeavour to manage an arrest of time. Roughly the method is that of identification or fusion of image."

The reviewer in *Hound and Horn* does, I think, under-rate the difficulties to be found in Mr. Pound's many allusions to rather obscure current events of no particular intrinsic interest. Mr. Pound cannot, however, be blamed because his profound scholarship leads the reader of no great classical education into other difficulties. But neither must the average reader be blamed for not knowing, for instance, that the first Canto is a paraphrase from the translation of Homer, accomplished in about the year 1530 by Andreas Divus. Mr. Pound, means this, evidently, to form a bridge between the cultures of the two ages.

Those readers who are acquainted with Golding's translation of the eighth book of the Metamorphosis, or who have read Mr. Pound's *Pavannes and Divisions*, will recognise the otherwise mysterious " Schœney " in *Canto II* : Helen, the unnamed menace, is spoken of as having the voice of Schœney's daughters :

> And poor old Homer blind, blind, as a bat,
> Ear, ear for the sea-surge, murmur of old men's voices :
> ' Let her go back to the ships,
> Back among the Grecian faces, lest evil come on our own,
> Evil and further evil, and a curse cursed on our children,
> Moves, yes she moves like a goddess
> And has the face of a god
>   And the voice of Schœney's daughters,
> And doom goes with her in walking,
> Let her go back to the ships,
>   Back among Grecian voices '.

Schœney is Schœnus, the father of Atalanta, and in Golding's translation of the eighth book of the Metamorphosis we find the lines :

> Atlant, a goodly Ladie one
> of Schœneys daughters. . . .

The passage that I have quoted from the *Thirty-Three Cantos* is an especially beautiful and significant one. In the sound, in the echo of the second one-syllabled word, " sea-surge ", of " murmur of old men's voices ", we are given an evocation of the fact that the sea-surge is immemorially old, has an immemorable wisdom echoing through time. The " sea-surge " and the " murmur of old men's voices " are then separate entities, but they have come together, and are one, or at least are scarcely separate in the ear of age and wisdom. The whole passage has the movement, the majestic sound of waves breaking in all their different splendour :

And doom goes with her in walking.

In that great line we have the whole sound, gathered throughout the ages, of the sea.

Part of the magic conveying the sound of the sea is obtained by the echoes which come from time to time ; the sound of " surge ", for instance, is echoed, three lines further on, by the less-long sound of " curse ", and repeated twice, like the sound of a wave gathering itself and spreading outwards :

Evil and further evil, and a curse cursed on our children,

and the sound of " moves " in the line :

Moves, yes she moves like a goddess,.

has the far deeper echo of " doom " after the interval of a line, a sound which contains all the hollowness and reverberation of the sea-depths. There is an echo, too, at the end of the lines :

And the voice of Schœney's daughters
And doom goes with her in walking.

The whole sound is that of the sea, with all the sea's depth.

The first two Cantos are a magnificent achievement. The wide stretch of the sea, the scarcely perceptible movement of the ripples, the clear sea-airs, are all conveyed by means of the fluctuating lengths of the opening lines of the first Canto, and by the shifting of the first accent from the first syllable to the second syllable of the line ; and by the fact also that the second line is only part of a phrase and is therefore part of a terrific sweeping movement, with a pause wherein the wind gathers :

And then went down to the ship,
Set keel to breakers, forth on the godly sea, and
We set up mast and sail on that swart ship,
Bore sheep aboard her, and our bodies also
Heavy with weeping, and winds from sternward
Bore us out onward with bellying canvas,
Circe's this craft, the trim-coiffed goddess.

The Canto's first line finds us sailing over a sea (the Canto begins where my quotation begins), and if there is a more terrific sweeping-onward of movement (that is yet perfectly smooth) to be found in all English poetry, I have yet to find it.

A small wave comes in the middle of the sixth line, with the faint stresses, placed in immediate juxtaposition, of " out onward ", breaks beneath the ship, and the ship sweeps on again.

Both these opening Cantos have the most strangely accurate, sharp, acutely observed visual impressions, like the portrait of the seal in the second Canto :

Sleek head, daughter of Lir,
   eyes of Picasso,
Under black fur-hood, lithe daughter of Ocean ;
And the wave runs in the beach-groove.

The movement of the ship seems to grow faster, in the second Canto, with the shortening of the lines, and with the tight effect of the one-syllabled ending of some of the lines, followed by the strong accent on the first syllable of the next line, alternating with the loosening caused by certain female endings :

Ship stock-fast in sea-swirl,
Ivy upon the oars, King Pentheus,
  Grapes with no seed but sea-foam,
Ivy in scupper-hole.

Indeed, the whole of these two Cantos may be said to be a miracle of the transfusion of sense into sound ; or rather, of the fusion of the two.

In the first part of the second Canto, the first accent of the lines shifts its place perpetually, though the movement is not elaborately contrapuntal :

> And where was gunwale, there now was vine-trunk,
> And tenthril where cordage had been,
>> grape-leaves on the rowlocks,
> Heavy vine on the oarshafts,
> And, out of nothing, a breathing,
>> Hot breath on my ankles,
> Beasts like shadows in glass,
>> a furred tail upon nothingness.
> Lynx-purr, and heathery smell of beasts,
>> where tar smell had been,
> Sniff and pad-foot of beasts,
>> eye-glitter out of black air.
> The sky overshot, dry, with no tempest,
> Sniff and pad-foot of beasts,
>> fur brushing my knee-skin,
> Rustle of airy sheaths,
>> dry forms in the æther.
> And the ship like a keel in ship-yard,
>> slung like an ox in smith's sling,
> Ribs stuck fast in the ways,
>> grape-cluster over pin-rack,
>> void air taking pelt.
> Lifeless air become sinewed,
>> feline leisure of panthers,
> Leopards sniffing the grape shoots by scupper-hole,
> Crouched panthers by fore-hatch,
> And the sea blue-deep about us,
>> green-ruddy in shadows,
> And Lyæus, ' From now, Acœtes, my altars,
> Fearing no bondage,

> Fearing no cat of the wood,
> Safe with my lynxes,
> feeding grapes to my leopards,
> Olibanum is my incense,
> the vines grow in my homage '.
> The back-swell now smooth in the rudder-chains,
> Black snout of a porpoise
> where Lycabs had been,
> Fish-scales on the oarsmen
> And I worship.
> I have seen what I have seen.
> When they brought the boy I said :
> ' He has a god in him,
> though I do not know which god.'
> And they kicked me into the fore-stays :
> I have seen what I have seen :
> Medon's face like the face of a dory,
> Arms shrunk into fins. And you, Pentheus,
> Had as well listen to Tiresias, and to Cadmus,
> or your luck will go out of you.
> Fish-scales over groin-muscles,
> lynx-purr amid sea . . .
> And of a later year,
> pale in the wine-red algæ,
> If you will lean over the rock,
> The coral face under wave-tinge,
> Rose-paleness under water-shift,
> Ileuthyeria, fair Dafne of sea-bords,
> The swimmer's arms turned to branches,
> Who will say in what year,
> fleeing what band of tritons,
> The smooth brows, seen, and half seen,
> now ivory stillness.

The reason for the more-embodied and hard-outlined movement, for its condensation, may be found in the lines :

Void air taking pelt.
Lifeless air become sinewed.

In this miraculous poetry Mr. Pound, by some enchantment, fuses the sense of the beasts with the sense of the oncoming tempest.

The rhythms have an extraordinary variety, a lovely flexibility and inevitability that is sometimes like "the feline leisure of panthers," or like the fluctuating, flowing, waving sound of the airs coming from some immortal sea. The echoes indeed, and the sounds that originate them, vary, as do the sounds and echoes in certain of Milton's songs, from sea-air to sea-air, from wave to wave, as the beauty of the line lengthens and then runs back again.

At the end of the second Canto we have an example of this consummate power of variation. For after the plunging forward of the ship, after the embodying of the beasts, beasts with fur as thick and dark as clouds, with movements like sinewed lightning, in an air "without tempest", we have this sudden dew-laden peace that is not the result of association alone, but also of the lengthening of the line, the scarcely perceptible beat of the accents, and of what is practically an absence of Cæsura :

> And we have heard the fauns chiding Proteus
> in the smell of hay under the olive-trees,
> And the frogs singing against the fauns in the
> half-light,
> And . . .

Now let us take the strange and subtle rhythm of the first two lines in the fourth Canto :

> Palace in smoky light,
> Troy but a heap of smouldering boundary stones,

in which part of the strangeness and mournfulness is brought about by the assonance-dissonance scheme, and by the length of the dark vowel-sounds in "smoky", "smouldering", "stones", changing to the high breaking sound of "Troy", and its high chilly dissonance, the first vowels in "boundary" that sinks again into the long stretch of sound in the word "stones".

Then, shortly afterwards, we have the strange circling, windy sound of these lines :

> And by the curved, carved foot of the couch,
>   claw-foot and lion head, an old man seated
> Speaking in the low drone . . .
>   Ityn !
> Et ter flebiliter, Ityn, Ityn !
> And she went toward the window and cast her down,
> All the while, the while, swallows crying :
>   Ityn !
> ' It is Cabestan's heart in the dish.'
> ' It is Cabestan's heart in the dish ?
> ' No other taste shall change this ! '

In this extremely beautiful and poignant fragment we are given by rhythm and by the use of certain vowels, the cry of the swallows, and their swift and circling movements, and the very strangeness of these sounds embodied in human speech give us the strangeness and the poignancy of the tragedy.

Mr. Pound lives with the men on the ships at Scios and with Cabestan, whose heart was in the dish, and with his lady . . . but the modern financiers and grafters who appear in the Canto seem like figures in a tapestry. And the tapestry is not, to this reader, of any superlative interest.

Mr. Ronald Bottrall, in a very finely-reasoned essay on *The Cantos*, in *Scrutiny*, explains that "after the account of the Austrian commercial representative living in America as an agent for raw material and munitions of war, there follows a commentary on the Carranza regime in Mexico and the

problem of mineral and mining rights. Next comes an incident
related by Lamont (Tommy Baymont) to Steffens (this part
of the Cantos is founded on the Autobiography of Lincoln
Steffens) to indicate the limits of power of the Morgan firm
when confronted by the gangster activities of ' Diamond Jim
Brady '. . . . Another passage seems to deal with a meeting
of the Morgan partners, but the key is missing ".

Now, the raw material of this passage does not, in itself,
form interesting reading. The speech-rhythms are easy, but
even this easiness does not convey any pleasure to this reader,
at any rate. The lines are excellently constructed, but do not
give that extreme shock, that awakening of the intelligence
or the sensibility, or both, that is given by great poetry.
Coleridge, in *Biographia Literaria*, says that " There are
. . . poems . . . replete with every excellence of thought,
image, and passion, which we expect or desire in the poetry
of the milder muse, and yet so worded that the reader sees
no one reason either in the selection or the order of the words
why he might not have said the very same in an appropriate
conversation, and cannot conceive how indeed he could have
expressed such thoughts otherwise, without loss or injury
to their meaning."

This might, by modern critics, be taken as supreme praise ;
but we must remember the inclusion of the word : "Yet . . ."

In the passage to which I refer, the voice is not that of
one speaking " above a mortal mouth ". But in the superb
fusion of inspiration, image, and sound of, say, the first two
Cantos, of the IV Canto, and of the two appalling Cantos
about the material hell of this modern world, the voice does
speak above a mortal mouth.

The following lines, however, to my mind would not be
interesting in prose. They are no more interesting in poetry :

> Governed. Governed the place from a train,
> Or rather from three trains, on a railway,
> And he'd keep about three days ahead of the lobby,
> I mean he had his government on the trains,

And the lobby had to get there on horseback ;
And he said : ' Bigod it's damn funny,
Own half the oil in the world, and can't get enough
To run a government engine ! '
And then they jawed for two hours,
And finally Steff said : ' Will you fellows show me a
    map? '
And they brought one, and Steff said :
' Waal what are those lines? ' ' Yes, those straight lines? '
' Those are roads.' And ' what are those lines,
The wiggly ones ? ' ' Rivers.'
And Steff said : ' Government property? '
So two hours later an engine went off with the order :
How to dig without confiscation.
And Tommy Baymont said to Steff one day :
' You think we run it, lemme tell you,
We bought a coal mine, I mean the mortgage fell in,
And you'd a' thought we could run it.
Well I had to go down there meself, and the manager
Said " Run it ? Of course we can run it,
We can't sell the damn coal."
So I said to the X and B Central
—you'd say we boss the X and B Central ?—
I said : " You buy your damn coal from our mine."
And a year later they hadn't ; so I had up the directors,
And they said . . . well anyhow, they couldn't buy the
    damn coal.
And next week ole Jim came, the big fat one,
With the diamonds, and he said : " Mr. Baymont,
You just must charge two dollars more
A ton fer that coal. And the X and B will
Take it through us." ' '

The argument may be put forward that here we have the
record of the new state of the world ; the defence may be
put forward that here is a perfect balance of the depredations
of the Italian tyrants—of the trade-voyages of the Venetians :

that, perhaps, Steffens is a modern counterpart of the Doge.
Or again, it may be said that the

> Ear, ear for the sea-surge, murmur of old men's
>   voices —

> changing and withering to the
>   rattle of old men's voices.
> And then the phantom Rome,
>   marble narrow for seats

changing again, through the lolling sound of the first two
lines of the XII Canto :

> And we sit here
> under the wall,

to the dead rattling sound of

> Arena romana, Diocletian's, *les gradins*
>   quarante-trois rangées en calcaire.
> Baldy Bacon
>   bought all the little copper pennies in Cuba :

finds another, and horrible disfiguring metamorphosis in the
voice of Steffens and his confederates. It may be said, too,
that at last all vain human ambition, sounding so hideously
through the blustering voices of the modern emperors of in-
dustry, is ennobled and transmuted into these great lines—
linked up, as they are, with the themes of the first two Cantos:

> Feared neither death nor pain for this beauty :
> If harm, harm to ourselves.
> And beneath : the clear bones, far down,
> Thousand on thousand.
>   What gain with Odysseus,
>   They that died in the whirpool.
> And after many vain labours,
> Living by stolen meat, chained to the rowing bench,
> That he should have a great fame

And lie by night with the goddess ?
Their names are not written in bronze
    Nor their rowing-sticks set with Elpenor's ;
Nor have they mound by sea-bord.
    That saw never the olives under Spartha
With the leaves green and then not green,
    The click of light in their branches ;
That saw not the bronze hall nor the ingle
Nor lay there with the queen's waiting maids,
Nor had they Circe to couch-mate, Circe Titania,
Nor had they meats of Kalupso
Or her silk skirts brushing their thighs.
    Give ! What were they given ?
    Ear-wax.
Poison and ear-wax,
    And a salt grave by the bull-field,
neson amumona, their heads like seacrows in the foam,
Black splotches, sea-weed under lightning ;
Canned beef of Apollo, ten cans for a boat load ?
Ligur' ' aoide '.

These arguments may be put forward, and there is much
to be said for them. But the fact of this balance in design
does not convert the Steffens lines into the equal of the
magnificent passage just quoted. The passage about Steffens
and Baymont seems like an ordinary conversation taken down
by a secretary on the typewriter. It is a flat record, and that
is all.

If we compare these lines with any, taken at random, from
the huge appalling smoky and Tartarean horror of Cantos
XIV and XV, we shall see the difference between great poetry
and an uninspired record :

        howling, as of a hen-yard in a printing-house,
            the clatter of presses,
        the blowing of dry dust and stray paper,
        fœtor, sweat, the stench of stale oranges,

dung, last cess-pool of the universe,
mysterium, acid of sulphur,
the pusillanimous, raging ;
plunging jewels in mud,
                and howling to find them unstained ;
sadic mothers driving their daughters to bed with
        decrepitude,
sows eating their litters,

Or these deliberately shambling lines :

The slough of unamiable liars,
                bog of stupidities,
malevolent stupidities, and stupidities,
the soil living pus, full of vermin,
dead maggots begetting live maggots, slum owners,
usurers squeezing crab-lice, panders to authority,
pets-de-loup, sitting on piles of stone books,
obscuring the texts with philology,
                hiding them under their persons,
the air without refuge of silence,
                the drift of lice, teething,
and above it the mouthing of orators,
                the arse-belching of preachers.

These passages, and such lines as

Flies carrying news, harpies dripping shit through
        the air

are great poetry, and a living evocation of the modern hell,
the final state of the world which is cursed by

the old man sweeping leaves
Damned to you Midas, Midas lacking a Pan.

In these two lines, this great poet has indeed shown us the
state of our modern world—that shallow covering for the hell
of the *XIV* and *XV Cantos*.

EZRA POUND

by Allen Tate [*1936*]

I

> and as for text we have taken it
> from that of Messire Laurentius
> and from a codex once of the Lords Malatesta. . . .

One is not certain who Messire Laurentius was; one is not very certain that it makes no difference. Yet one takes comfort in the vast range of Mr. Pound's obscure learning, which no one man could be expected to know much about. In his great work one is continually uncertain, as to space, time, history. The codex of the Lords Malatesta is less disconcerting than Laurentius; for more than half of the *Thirty Cantos*[1] contain long paraphrases or garbled quotations from the correspondence, public and private, of the Renaissance Italians, chiefly Florentine and Venetian. About a third of the lines are versified documents. Another third are classical allusions, esoteric quotations from the ancients, fragments of the Greek poets with bits of the Romans thrown in; all magnificently written into Mr. Pound's own text. The rest is contemporary — anecdotes, satirical pictures of vulgar Americans, obscene stories, evenings in low Mediterranean dives, and gossip about intrigants behind the scenes of European power. The three kinds of material in the cantos are antiquity, the Renaissance, and the modern world. They are combined on no principle that seems in the least consistent to a first glance. They appear to be mixed in an incoherent jumble, or to stand up in puzzling contrasts.

This is the poetry which, in early and incomplete editions, has had more influence on us than any other of our time; it has had an immense "underground" reputation. And deservedly. For even the early reader of Mr. Pound could not fail to detect the presence of a new poetic form in the individual *Cantos*, though the full value and intention of this form appears for the first time in the complete work. It is not that there is any explicit feature of the whole design that

1. *A Draft of XXX Cantos* by Ezra Pound. Farrar & Rinehart, New York, 1933.

is not contained in each Canto ; it is simply that Mr. Pound must be read in bulk ; it is only then that the great variety of his style and the apparent incoherence turn into implicit order and form. There is no other poetry like *The Cantos* in English. And there is none quite so simple in form. The form is in fact so simple that almost no one has guessed it, and I suppose it will continue to puzzle, perhaps to enrage, our more academic critics for a generation to come. But this form by virtue of its simplicity remains inviolable to critical terms : even now it cannot be technically described.

I begin to talk like Mr. Pound, or rather in the way in which most readers think Mr. Pound writes. The secret of his form is this : conversation. *The Cantos* are talk, talk, talk ; not by anyone in particular to anyone else in particular ; they are just rambling talk. At least each Canto is a cunningly devised imitation of a casual conversation in which no one presses any subject very far. The length of breath, the span of conversational energy, is the length of a Canto. The conversationalist pauses ; there is just enough unfinished business left hanging in the air to give him a new start ; so that the transitions between *The Cantos* are natural and easy.

Each canto has the broken flow and the somewhat elusive climax of a good monologue : because there is no single speaker, it is a many-voiced monologue. That is the method of the poems—though there is another quality of the form that I must postpone for a moment—*and that is what the poems are about.*

There are, as I have said, three subjects of conversation— ancient times, Renaissance Italy, and the present—but these are not what *The Cantos* are about. They are not about Italy, nor about Greece, nor are they about us. They are not about anything. But they are distinguished verse. Mr. Pound himself tells us :

And they want to know what we talked about ?
  " *de litteris et de armis, præstantibus ingeniis* ",
Both of ancient times and our own ; books, arms,

And men of unusual genius
Both of ancient times and our own, in short the usual
    subjects
Of conversation between intelligent men.

II

There is nothing in *The Cantos* more difficult than that.
There is nothing inherently obscure ; nothing too profound
for any reader who has enough information to get to the
background of the allusions in a learned conversation. But
there is something that no reader, short of some years of hard
textual study, will understand. This is the very heart of *The
Cantos*, the secret of Mr. Pound's poetic character, which
will only gradually emerge from a detailed analysis of every
passage. And this is no more than our friends are constantly
demanding of us ; we hear them talk, and we return to hear
them talk, we return to hear them again, but we never know
what they talk about ; we return for the mysterious quality
of charm that has no rational meaning that we can define.
It is only after a long time that the order, the direction, the
rhythm of the talker's mind, the logic of his character as distinguished from anything logical he may say—it is a long time
before this begins to take on form for us. So with Mr. Pound's
Cantos. It is doubtless easier for us (who are trained in the
more historic brands of poetry) when the poems are about
God, Freedom, and Immortality, but there is no reason why
poetry should not be so perplexingly simple as Mr. Pound's,
and be about nothing at all.

The ostensible subject of *The Cantos*—ancient, middle, and
modern times—are only the materials round which Mr.
Pound's mind plays constantly ; they are the screen upon
which he throws a flowing quality of poetic thought. Now in
conversation the memorable quality is a sheer accident of
character, and is not designed ; but in *The Cantos* the effect is
deliberate, and from the first canto to the thirtieth the set
tone is maintained without a lapse.

It is this tone, it is this quality quite simply which is the meaning of *The Cantos*, and although, as I have said, it is simple and direct, it is just as hard to pin down, it is as hidden in its shifting details, as a running, ever-changing conversation. It cannot be taken out of the text ; and yet the special way that Mr. Pound has of weaving his three materials together, of emphasising them, of comparing and contrasting them, gives us a clue to the leading intention of the poems. I come to that quality of the form which I postponed.

The easiest interpretation of all poetry is the allegorical : there are few poems that cannot be paraphrased into a kind of symbolism, which is usually false, being by no means the chief intention of the poet. It is very probable, therefore, that I am about to falsify the true simplicity of *The Cantos* into a simplicity that is merely convenient and spurious. The reader must bear this in mind, and view the slender symbolism that I am going to read into the cantos as a critical shorthand, useful perhaps, but which when used must be dropped.

One of the finest cantos is properly the first. It describes a voyage :

> And then went down to the ship,
> Set keel to breakers, forth on the godly sea, and
> We set up mast and sail on that swart ship,
> Bore sheep aboard her, and our bodies also
> Heavy with weeping, and winds from sternward
> Bore us out onward with bellying canvas,
> Circe's this craft, the trim-coifed goddess.

They land, having come " to the place aforesaid by Circe " —whatever place it may be—and Tiresias appears, who says :

> Odysseus

> Shall return through spiteful Neptune, over dark seas,
> Lose all companions." And then Anticlea came.
> Lie quiet Divus. I mean, that is, Andreas Divus,
> In officina Wecheli, 1538, out of Homer.

And he sailed, by Sirens and thence outward and away
And unto Circe.

Mr. Pound's world is the scene of a great Odyssey, and
everywhere he lands it is the shore of Circe, where men " lose
all companions " and are turned into swine. It would not do
at all to push this hint too far, but I will risk one further
point : Mr. Pound is a typically modern, rootless, and inter-
nationalised intelligence. In the place of the traditional super-
naturalism of the older and local cultures, he has a cosmopolitan curiosity that seeks out marvels, which are all equally
marvellous, whether it be a Greek myth or the antics in Europe
of a lady from Kansas. He has the bright, cosmopolitan
savoir faire which refuses to be " taken in ": he will not
believe, being a traditionalist at bottom, that the " perverts,
who have set money-lust before the pleasures of the senses ",
are better than swine. And ironically, being modern and a
hater of modernity, he sees all history as deformed by the
trim-coifed goddess.

The Cantos are a book of marvels—marvels that he has
read about, or heard of, or seen ; there are Greek myths,
tales of Italian feuds, meetings with strange people, rumours
of intrigues of state, memories of remarkable dead friends
like T. E. Hulme, comments on philosophical problems,
harangues on abuses of the age ; the " usual subjects of
conversation between intelligent men ".

It is all fragmentary. Now nearly every canto begins with
a bit of heroic antiquity, some myth, or classical quotation,
or a lovely piece of lyrical description in a grand style. It
invariably breaks down. It trails off into a piece of contemporary satire, or a flat narrative of the rascality of some
Italian prince. This is the special quality of Mr. Pound's
form, the essence of his talk, the direction of these magnificent
conversations.

For not once does Mr. Pound give himself up to any single
story or myth. The thin symbolism from the Circe myth is
hardly more than a leading tone, an unconscious prejudice

about men which he is not willing to indicate beyond the barest outline. He cannot believe in myths, much less in his own power of imagining them out to a conclusion. None of his myths is compelling enough to draw out his total intellectual resources ; none goes far enough to become a belief or even a momentary fiction. They remain marvels to be looked at, but they are meaningless, the wrecks of civilisation. His powerful juxtapositions of the ancient, the Renaissance, and the modern worlds reduce all three elements to an unhistorical miscellany, timeless and without origin, and no longer a force in the lives of men.

III

And that is the peculiarly modern quality of Mr. Pound. There is a certain likeness in this to another book of marvels, stories of antiquity known to us as *The Golden Ass*. *The Cantos* are a sort of *Golden Ass*. There is a likeness, but there is no parallel beyond the mere historical one : both books are the production of worlds without convictions and given over to a hard pragmatism. Here the similarity ends. For Mr. Pound is a powerful reactionary, a faithful mind devoted to those ages when the myths were not merely pretty, but true. And there is a cloud of melancholy irony hanging over *The Cantos*. He is persuaded that the myths are only beautiful, and he drops them after a glimpse, but he is not reconciled to this æstheticism : he ironically puts the myths against the ugly specimens of modern life that have defeated them. But neither are the specimens of modernity worthy of the dignity of belief :

> She held that a sonnet was a sonnet
> And ought never to be destroyed
> And had taken a number of courses
> And continued with hope of degrees and
> Ended in a Baptist learnery
>   Somewhere near the Rio Grande.

Ezra Pound

I am not certain that Mr. Pound will agree with me that he is a traditionalist; nor am I convinced that Mr. Pound, for his part, is certain of anything but his genius for poetry. He is probably one of two or three living Americans who will be remembered as poets of the first order. Yet there is no reason to infer from that, that Mr. Pound, outside his craft (or outside his written conversation) knows in the least what he is doing or saying. He is and always has been in a muddle of revolution; and for some appalling reason he identifies his crusade with liberty—liberty of speech, liberty of press, liberty of conduct—in short, liberty. I do not mean to say that either Mr. Pound or his critic knows what liberty is. Nevertheless, Mr. Pound identifies it with civilisation and intelligence of the modern and scientific variety. And yet the ancient cultures, which he so much admires, were, from any modern viewpoint, hatched in barbarism and superstition. One is entitled to the suspicion that Mr. Pound prefers barbarism, and that by taking up the rôle of revolution against it he has bitten off his nose to spite his face. He is the confirmed enemy of provincialism, never suspecting that his favourite, Lorenzo the Magnificent, for example, was provincial to the roots of his hair.

The confusion runs through *The Cantos*. It makes the irony that I have spoken of partly unconscious. For as the apostle of a humane culture, he constantly discredits it by crying up a rationalistic enlightenment. It would appear from this that his philosophical tact is somewhat feminine, and that, as intelligence, it does not exist. His poetic intelligence is of the finest: and if he doesn't know what liberty is, he understands poetry, and how to write it. This is enough for one man to know. And the thirty *Cantos* are enough to occupy a loving and ceaseless study—say a canto a year for thirty years, all thirty to be read every few weeks just for the tone.

HOMAGE TO EZRA

by Ernest Hemingway [*1925*]

An editor has written me asking me to write an appreciation of
Ezra Pound, to be written as though Pound were dead. One
does not write appreciations of dead men but only of their
work. Dead men themselves are most uncomfortable to have
around and sooner or later one buries them or walks behind
them to where others bury them or reads about their funeral
in the newspaper and perhaps sends telegrams in which it is
impossible to avoid clichés. And if one tries to write about
dead men who were one's friends one fails for one reason or
another and it is no good.

Stylists can do it because they have a way of wrapping
things around in their style like *emballeurs* or the men who
wrapped mummies in Egypt. Even stylists though do it only
to their own satisfaction. No one else is very pleased.

So thank God Pound isn't dead and we don't have to write
about him as though he were.

Ezra Pound devotes perhaps one fifth of his working time to
writing poetry and in this twenty per cent. of effort writes a
large and distinguished share of the really great poetry that
has been written by any American living or dead—or any
Englishman living or dead or any Irishman who ever wrote
English. I do not mention other nationalities because I do not
know the poetry of other nationalities nor do I know Gaelic.
There is only one living poet who ranks with Pound and that
is William Butler Yeats. Some of Pound's later manner is
done better by T. S. Eliot. But Eliot is, after all, a minor
poet. Fine poetry is written by minor poets.

Pound happens to be a major poet just as Yeats is and
Browning and Shelley and Keats were. What is the difference?
It seems hardly necessary to point it out but it is easier to do
through the case of Eliot. All of Eliot's poems are perfect and
there are very few of them. He has a fine talent and he is very
careful with it and it is doing very well thank you. Whitman,
on the other hand, if a poet, is a major poet.

The most perfect poem to me in the *Oxford Book of English*

73

Verse was written by Anonymous. Yet I have to consider Anonymous a minor poet because if he were a major poet there would have been a name to him. That may sound like Dr. Frank Crane. But take A. E. Housman. There is the perfect case of the minor poet. He did it once and did it perfectly with the *Shropshire Lad* but when he tried to do it again it wouldn't come off and the trick of mind all showed through and it imperilled the poems in the first book. One more book would have killed off all the poems. They proved to be unimportant.

Minor poets do not fail because they do not attempt the major thing. They have nothing of major importance to say. They do a minor thing with perfection and the perfection is admirable. Ezra has written great poetry.

This is an appreciation rather than a critical article. If it were the latter I would have to stop here and go up to Paris to verify quotations. There ought to be quotations if this were to prove anything. Fortunately an appreciation does not have to prove anything.

So then, so far, we have Pound the major poet devoting, say, one fifth of his time to poetry. With the rest of his time he tries to advance the fortunes, both material and artistic, of his friends. He defends them when they are attacked, he gets them into magazines and out of jail. He loans them money. He sells their pictures. He arranges concerts for them. He writes articles about them. He introduces them to wealthy women. He gets publishers to take their books. He sits up all night with them when they claim to be dying and he witnesses their wills. He advances them hospital expenses and dissuades them from suicide. And in the end a few of them refrain from knifing him at the first opportunity.

Personally he is tall, has a patchy red beard, fine eyes, strange haircuts and is very shy. But he has the temperament of a *toro di lidia* from the breeding establishments of Don Eduardo Miura. No one ever presents a cape, or shakes a muleta at him without getting a charge. Like Don Eduardo's product, too, he sometimes ignores the picador's horse to pick off the man and no one goes into the ring with him in safety. And though they can always be sure of drawing his charge yet he gets his quota of bull-baiters each year.

Many people hate him and he plays a fine game of tennis. He would live much longer if he did not eat so fast. Young men in the years after the war, coming over from America where Pound was a legendary person, to Paris where they found him with a patchy red beard, very accessible, fond of tennis and occasionally playing the bassoon, decided there could not be anything in the Pound legend and that he was probably not a great poet after all. As the army rhyme used to say : hence criticism in America.

Like all men who become famous very young he suffers from not being read. It is so much easier to talk about a classic than to read it. There is another generation, though, in America, that is replacing the generation that decided Ezra could not be a great poet because he was actually alive and kicking, and this generation is reading him. They come to Paris now and want to meet him. But he is gone to Italy.

As he takes no interest in Italian politics and does not mind Italian cookery he may stay there some time. It is good for him to be there because his friends cannot get at him so easily and energy is thus released for production. Pound, among other things, is a composer, and has done a splendid opera on Villon. It is a first rate opera. A very fine opera.

But I feel about Ezra and music something like about M. Constantin Brancusi and cooking. M. Brancusi is a famous sculptor who is also a very famous cook. Cooking is, of course, an art, but it would be lamentable if M. Brancusi would give up sculpture for it or even devote the major part of his time to cookery.

Still, Ezra is not a minor poet. He has never been troubled with lack of energy. If he wants to write more operas he will write them and there will be plenty of force left over.

As this is an appreciation there is one thing to be emphasised about Ezra. He has never been a pitiful figure. He has fought his fights with a very gay grimness and his wounds heal quickly. He does not believe that he came into the world to suffer. He is no masochist and that is one more reason why he is not a minor poet.

THE CANTOS

A NOTE APPENDED TO HIS TRANSLATION OF THREE CANTOS

by George Seferis [*1939*]

As the sections of *Finnegan's Wake* were published at first
under the general title " Work in Progress ", so the long
poem which seems to have concentrated for many years now
the whole effort of Ezra Pound is published without a title
in successive volumes, which are distinguished by the number
of " songs " or " rhapsodies "—by the number of Cantos
which they include.

Up to the present three such volumes have appeared, the
first containing thirty Cantos, the second eleven and the third
ten. The work has not yet been completed.

Pound has called his *Cantos* a " poem of some length ".
Eliot, who has been the close friend and the best critic of the
poet, regards it, as I explain more fully later on, as a
presentation of a kind of contemporary Hell, with the shortcomings which contemporary works have for him. It is, one
could add, an epic of man of today, without plot, without
myth, tending to present, in a unity which is purely poetical,
an endless number of the ingredients, spiritual or historical,
which go to make up the life of man. Tragic clash or cathar-
sis, analysis of feelings, action : none of these exist, at least
as we are accustomed to follow them in literary works. Only
the *episode* exists—it does not matter what episode : it is
enough that it is able to mobilise the rhythmic expression
of the poet—the episode which is detached from its, for us,
normal surroundings, in order to be placed, very often in its
raw state, in the poem. Thus Pound's *Cantos* convey, on first
reading, the impression of a huge mosaic. The reader, turning
the pages, becomes dizzy, noting the successive insertions of
foreign texts ; of incidents or of conversations, very often in
foreign languages ; of persons known from history or entirely
unknown, whose unexpected presence he cannot explain ; of
landscapes which transfer the classical age into the Renaissance, into our age, or the other way round. It is difficult to
make an analysis of the text in front of one and it is, I think,

purposeless to attempt such an analysis before one becomes familiar with the climate of this poetry. It is perhaps better to have in mind, at first, that Pound uses the poetical metaphor in the correct way, as a conveyance which transfers into his work everything which the dockyards of a gluttonous spirit have been able to collect—a spirit which has assimilated a great number of the elements that form our actual life, whether they be Greek or Roman texts, texts of the Middle Ages, or of the Renaissance, or of the pre-Dantesque Provençal poetry. And he transfers them with, as almost sole guide, his feeling for verbal expression, anxious, untamed, despotic, accepting hardly a single prescribed order, hardly a single arrangement, and having no other hierarchy except the hierarchy, if it can be called that, of a rhythmic beat.

It is purposeless to demand from such a poetry, where the important and the trivial have the same value, historical or chronographical link. The only link which exists is the link of the poetical language. The first Canto, for example, beginning with a paraphrase of the XIth book of the *Odyssey*, ends with the words "so that". But the second Canto speaks to us, without any other transitive link, of Sordello :

> Hang it all, Robert Browning,
>   there can be but the one ' Sordello '.
> But Sordello, and my Sordello !
> Lo Sordels si fo di Mantovana.

The view which one must accept, if one feels it worth while to follow this epic, is that, when all is linked in the consciousness of the " rhapsodist ", the absence of historical link is unimportant ; and that a conjunction " then " is sufficient to transfer us from the conversation of Odysseus with Tiresias, to the Italy of Sordello or Sigismundo Malatesta, where the quotations of the period, almost by themselves, in the language in which they were written, come to complete the scene :

George Seferis

SIGISMUNDUS HIC EGO SUM
MALATESTA, FILIUS PANDULPHI, REX PRODI-
TORUM,
DEO ATQUE HOMINIBUS INFESTUS
SACRI CENSURA SENATUS IGNI DAMNATUS.

And the accusation in Italian :

Lussurioso, incestuoso, perfide, sozzure ac crapulone,
assassino, ingordo, avaro, superbo, infidele
fattore di monete false, sodomitico, uxoricido

and that the same can happen where the war of '14-'18 is
concerned :

C'est le corr-ggras, le corps gras,
  leurs trains marchaient trois kilomètres. à l'heure,
Et ca criait, ça grinçait, on l'entendait à cinq kilomètres.
(Ca qui finit la guerre.)
Liste officielle des morts 5.000.000.

Or Byzantium :

" Et omniformis ", Psellos, " omnis
  Intellectus est ". God's fire. Gemisto :
  Never with this religion
  Will you make men of the Greeks. . . .

Or Mozart, or Napoleon, or the American bankers, or any
incident in the life of humanity.
  From this point of view the word epic loses its meaning
as a form of literature in order to keep much closer to its
original meaning of sentence, word, speech, and becomes the
symbol of a liturgy which makes use of everything, which
changes everything into expression, and which vivifies everything within the framework of a wider unity. It could of
course be pointed out that such a great ambition cannot but
be accompanied by proportionate dangers.

Never perhaps has poetic material been collected so indiscriminately. Here should begin the criticism which, in these few bare informative lines, I do not intend to make. It is enough for the time being to note that T. S. Eliot has written of Pound that he is " the most important living poet of the English language ", and that he considers *The Cantos* his major work. And since I have spoken of Eliot, it is in place to mention also, very briefly, the following remark of his, which is, indirectly, a further observation on the poetry of *The Cantos*.

" With the vanishing of the idea of original sin "—writes the poet of the *Waste Land*—" and of strong moral struggle, the works of contemporary literature (he means the best works) tend to become increasingly less real. The same happens also to the society of men that Pound sends to his Hell : the exploiters of any kind, the liars, the imbeciles, the pedantic and all those ' who preferred the debauchery of money to the enjoyment of the senses '. It is a Hell without dignity, without tragedy, and it presupposes a Paradise without dignity."

I think that Eliot talks about Hell because he has in mind an implied comparison between *The Cantos* and the Inferno of Dante, who, in the framework of the *Divina Comedia*, a framework given by the theology of his time, constructed a remarkable and a unique hierarchy of human types and feelings. But as much as we find links with the poem of the Florentine, both in the title (Canto) and in the introduction (The Book of the Dead), and even more in the great number of characters and incidents which occur in the poem of Pound, I do not think we can talk about Hell without modification of Dante's meaning. Pound, if we regard him from the point of view from which Eliot regards him, has written an epic very often caustically satirical in tone—not as a Catholic, for whom no action can be understood without divine sanction, but as a man without religion who has, perhaps, Puritan antecedents. Eliot's criticism means, au fond, that every punishment that is not based upon a theology is a punishment without dignity, and about that one could argue at length. But such a discussion would lead us outside literature and the literary value of the work of Pound, "who has not spoken of life after death" (Canto XII).

It may be interesting to note that Pound was among the first to make known systematically to the Anglo-Saxon public the modern French Symbolist writers of the early part of the century.

Everyone will notice that Canto I is almost up to the end a paraphrase of Book XI of the *Odyssey*. This introduction is surprising only in the last lines with the appearance of the —for me at least—unknown Andreas Divus. This Divus worried me a lot. I found out who he was quite unexpectedly, reading a study[1] by Pound himself about old translations of Homer. Here is the relevant passage :

"In the year of grace 1906, 1908, or 1910 I picked from the Paris quais a Latin version of the *Odyssey* by Andreas Divus Justinopolitanus (Parisiis, in Officina Christiani Wecheli, MDXXXVIII), the volume also containing the *Batrachomachia*, by Aldus Manutius, and the *Hymni Deorum* rendered by Georgius Dartona Cretensis."

And he gives a piece of that Latin by Divus, adding that he has been using it for the third (which later became the first) Canto :

> At postquam ad nauem descendimus, et mare,
> Nauem quidem primum deduximus in mare diuum,
> Et malum posuimus et uela in naui nigra : etc.

As well as the beginning of the Hymn to Aphrodite by the Cretan Georgius Dartona :

> Venerandam auream coronam pulchram Venerem
> Canam, quæ totius Cypri munimenta sortita est
> Maritimæ ubi illam zephyri uis molliter spirantis
> Suscitauit per undam multisoni maris . . .

1. *Make it New* by Ezra Pound (London, 1934), p. 137 ff.—Editor.

Capite uero super immortali coronam bene constructam
   posuere
Pulchram, auream : tribus autem ansis
Donum orichalchi aurique honorabilis
Collum autem molle, ac pectora argentea
Monilibus aureis ornabant. . . .

Noticing the above quotations, the reader will have all the
materials which Pound used to finish his first Canto. But
Divus presented me with a problem of translation. I saw that
I had to translate a piece from Homer for the third time.
Translation of the Greek text into Latin, translation of the
translation of Divus into English (let it be remarked that
Pound knows ancient Greek); finally translation of Pound's
translation by me. These successive deposits of the translators moved me. But I had to deal with a subject which
threw light, very strangely, on the problem of the translation
of the poems. If I believed without any reservation the
classical theory according to which the translator must try
to give to his reader the emotion which the reader of the
original feels, I should have had to go back to Homer and
have translated him. As it was, I preferred the opposite way.
Translating Pound's text, I forgot Homer as much as I
could. I should have translated Homer in quite another way.
   Canto XIII is a discussion between Confucius and his
disciples. In many places it refers to *Chung Yung*, the third
book of the teaching of the Chinese philosopher. It is note-
worthy because here one can detect certain precepts which
have become values for the poet himself where his art is
concerned—a kind of ethic for his poetical way ; and they
shed light on the noblest characteristics of Pound's portrait,
" il migliore fabbro ", as Eliot has named him, in dedicating
to him his *Waste Land*. For example :

> Anyone can run to excesses
> It is easy to shoot past the mark,
> It is hard to stand firm in the middle.

Or—

> And even I can remember
> A day when the historians left blanks in their writings,
> I mean for the things they didn't know
> But that time seems to be passing.

Or again—

> And Kung said 'Without character you will be
>   unable to play on that instrument
> Or to execute the music fit for the Odes'.

And finally this, which every critic would do well to think on :

> And Kung said, 'They have all answered correctly
> That is to say, each in his nature'.

[*Translated by Philip Sherrard*]

NEW SUBTLETY OF EYES

by Hugh Kenner [*1949*]

pouvrette et ancienne   oncques lettres ne lus
I don't know how humanity stands it
    with a painted paradise at the end of it
    without a painted paradise at the end of it.

Pound tells us in the seventy-fourth Canto of the Emperor who held empire "as if not in a mortar with it, nor dazzled thereby". His own incalculable services to English poetry (by whose parochial mutations he was assuredly not dazzled) have depended upon a like detachment. Nothing is more difficult than to formulate the relation of such a poet to the tradition in which and with which he works ; our received analogies of "influence", "indebtedness" and "discipleship" connote almost Newtonian laws of action and reaction, container and thing contained, thunder and echo, as Mr. Eliot perceived in writing *Tradition and the Individual Talent* thirty-three years ago. According to such analogies art constantly improves as each generation of poets takes its acrobatic stance on the shoulders of its predecessors. At the bottom of the current English pyramid, we were given to understand, stood Shakespeare-and-Milton, grown after two centuries relatively immobile, rigid (to change the simile) as the fakir's long-uplifted arm in the hand of which singing birds have at length condescended to nest. At the top, as of 1890, stood in a swaying horizontal line the entire romantic generation.

This was the posture of events when in 1910 Pound suddenly postulated Milton's "complete ignorance of things of the spirit", and its resultant God, "a fussy old man with a hobby". He carried on (1915) with the critique of Milton's language, "clause structure modelled on Latin rhetoric, borrowed and thrust into sonorities which are sometimes most enviable". A few years later he commenced *The Cantos,* a whole dimension of which belongs to the attack on Milton ; better, attack is there modulated into correction, a

84

re-doing of what the critic's eye discovered Milton to have botched.

"The man who formulates any forward reach of co-ordinating principle is the man who produces the demonstration. . . . I think it will be found that the work outruns the formulated or at any rate the published equation, or at most they proceed as two feet of one biped." It needs to be insisted, in correction of much anecdotal emphasis, that Pound's major service to English letters has consisted less in advising men now more automatically revered than in writing *The Cantos*. The multivalent ameliorative force that revised *The Waste Land*, got *Prufrock* and *Ulysses* into print, and presided over the transformation of Yeats, proceeded—must have proceeded —from an assured centre of creative achievement. It seems in fact not ridiculous to propose that *The Cantos* constitute the first comparably seminal poem in English since *Paradise Lost*.

Pound in his long poem has provided the point of depar-ture, mythopœic as well as technical, that the eighteenth and nineteenth centuries found in Milton. There is no way of telling whether future poets will avail themselves of it ; it takes two, we have recently been reminded, to make an influence, and no one, least of all the critic, is in a position to say what the creative writers of the next century or two will want to do. It seems likely that if they do not use Pound's work they will merely have to do it all over again. In any case, the excitement with which *The Cantos* can fill a contemporary reader is largely due to his apprehension of this infinitely realisable fertilising potentiality : not merely have we in our hands a poem of inestimable independent worth, we are reading, we feel, in potency if not yet in act, *semina motuum*, the poetry of generations to come.

This argument would be easier to sustain if more use had been made of *The Cantos*—not just of Pound's services—by other poets. So far, except for Mr. Eliot's *Coriolan*, there is little to point to. But one forgets, so far off seem the twenties now, how recently this as yet unfinished poem began to appear. It is too soon to look for currents of indebtedness just yet. The claim we are making is no more intrinsically absurd than would have been a statement, about 1674, that *Paradise Lost*, then just entering its second edition, would dominate the poetic alignments of the next quarter-millenium.

This judgment of Pound's importance has three components : the critique of Milton's technique, the critique of Milton's myth, and the achievement of *The Cantos*. The first is in a critical tradition, nearly as old as *Paradise Lost* itself, which it suited the generation immediately preceding our own to disregard.[1] The second is in some respects as old as Blake. The third belongs to Pound alone.

It is first of all worth extricating the twofold critique of Milton from the form which the last thirty years' dialectic of events has given it. The first opinion of Pound's early adverse judgments was that a brash urchin had begun chucking firecrackers at a moment which demanded the utmost concentration from all the acrobats ; as the human pyramid of interlocked indebtedness rises to its fifth or sixth generation, muscles tense, feet are locked, alignments are more and more rigidly preserved. (Hopkins, whose reading of Milton led him to "admire and do otherwise", had to be temporarily excluded from the act by Dr. Bridges for this reason.) The second phase of opinion focussed itself, guided by Mr. Eliot's practical demonstration, on questions of language. The return of poetry to speech (if not song) was applauded, certain Miltonic intricacies became "period", the new grand style modelled itself on the tautness and resonance of the first part of *The Waste Land*, with a corollary demand that every image should not merely underscore but advance the action of the poem. The quasi-peripeteia of Mr. Eliot's 1945 lecture has spread dismay on this front ; correct opinion may, however, when it settles down, be expected to echo his dictum that we are now sufficiently free from Milton (no longer in

1. Dryden had his doubts as early as the Preface to *Sylvæ*. Pope's gibe about God as School-Divine is familiar. Landor's lengthy analysis of Miltonic versification in his dialogue with Southey is of the utmost contemporary interest, yet remains virtually unknown.

the mortar with him) to learn from him (Pound indicated his awareness of Milton's "real merits" almost every time he assailed the Miltonic incubus.)

These mutations of climate have been cued rather by *obiter dicta* than by a grasp of the realised body of contemporary poetry which has displaced Milton from the shrine where preceding generations, guided by their own contemporary poetry, were constrained to place him. Certain aspects of his work have been superseded ; he remains, now that we have had the Eliotic corpus, *Ulysses,* and *The Cantos,* a uniquely solitary personality, a master of a certain number of blank verse techniques, a point of reference to which alone large masses of succeeding poetry can be said to stand in intelligible relation—status enough, surely, for any man —but no longer the accredited quarry of serious " effects ", and no longer (a related function) the inescapable arbiter of moral and emotional hierarchies in poetry.

Which brings us to the critique of the myth : not necessarily a Bible-smashing enterprise. English poetry since the Restoration has been obsessed by the Fall, for reasons not entirely theological. The garden as paradisal, the city as corrupt and corrupting, is a motif latent even in Augustan citification and notoriously predominant in Wordsworth and his successors. There are psychological reasons, of course, for this concern, and economic, religious and philosophical reasons behind or beside the psychological. Usury and the industrial disease, the mechanistic imbalance of Cartesian and Lockeian epistemology, the decay of the feeling for architecture and town planning by which the Augustans had manifested a poise maintained in some departments of the spirit, the historical wound of the Civil War, all these met to condemn by association whole congeries of images, perceptions, modes of thinking and feeling. The matter should be put in some such way to avoid misunderstanding of the rôle the literary historian must assign to Milton. How far Milton's idiosyncratic Christianity imposed itself on a succession of disciples, how far the Miltonic emphases, his dispositions of approval and disapproval, were articulations of a coarsening indigenous to his age and so in their context inevitable, is not germane to this inquiry. But at the level of poetic sensibility, after *Paradise Lost* no one could read Scripture any longer except through Miltonic eyes. (Since the English poet's ethical vocabulary is scriptural, the consequences of this were far from being confined to the professedly Hebraical. Byron was infected ; Swinburne was infected. Chaucer, for instance, could write,

> And of thy light my soule in prison lighte,
> That troubled is by the contagioun
> Of my body, and also by the wighte
> Of erthely lust and fals affeccioun,

with a meaning in each of the terms ; Puritan ethical shrillness warps such modalities of speech into virulent contempt for the flesh. To recapture the finesse of Chaucerian ethical statement, Pound has had to invent new forms of language based on the metaphorical immediacy of Confucian ideograms.)

Milton took, as it were, the side of Jove against Prometheus, yet obliquely accorded his devil Promethean status ; stigmatised the multiform modes of heroic energy as diabolical ; and drew a Satan whom later generations were to have no difficulty in apotheosising (not without an embarrassed bravado—Milton, from whom their configurations are borrowed, possessing so much the admonitory aspect of his own Great Taskmaster—that has inhibited tragic art ever since), a God as impossible to be loved as he was implacably just, and archangels so little corresponding to superhuman currents of volition that they are scarcely remembered, except as shadowy ambassadors, an hour after the book has been closed ("enlarged men with wings", as Pound put it). Landor challenges "any reader, who is not by many degrees more pious than poetical," to say " whether he felt a very great interest in the greatest actors of *Paradise Lost*, in what is either said or done by the angels or the Creator ''. Landor's genuine awe of what Milton did do carries the more weight for this huge qualification.

Some effects of these dislocations on the practice of later poets will be noted later. That the reader may more easily see the relevance of such an inquiry, it is worth noting first the extraordinary way in which Pound's epic recapitulates that of his predecessor. *Paradise Lost* is essentially a definition of terms ; the outline of the story was *ex hypothesi* familiar ; Milton's task (justifying the ways of God to man) was to orient the reader's will and affections by defining what was lost, and by what perversion, and through what agency, and with what precedent and consequent misalignment of thought and feeling. How far his ideogram of the good differs from that of Pound's master Dante was exposed by Pound in *The Spirit of Romance,* his first prose work. *The Cantos* undertakes a comparable task of definition. It is an account of *paradise lost* (and in some modes regainable) at many levels : the epic includes history, but its subject is not history. Its subject, the Fall, is rendered without theological accessories—

The empty armour shakes as the cygnet moves

—so rendered as to emerge, the controlling form, from amid the hundreds of discrete particularisations afforded by dozens of analogous actions and interactions :

And all that day
Nicea moved before me
And the cold grey air troubled her not
For all her naked beauty, bit not the tropic skin,
And the long slender feet lit on the curb's marge
And her moving height went before me,
We alone having being.
And all that day, another day :
Thin husks I had known as men,
Dry casques of departed locusts

> speaking a shell of speech . . .
Propped between chairs and table . . .
Words like the locust-shells, moved by no inner being ;
> A dryness calling for death.   (VII)

The Miltonic lexicon could contain neither of the components of this collocation ; the first would have been improper, the second simply uninteresting.

Pound is not dealing with a chronological scheme corresponding to the Genesis story, nor with a single action moving forward and downward in time, though action in time, as in Cantos LII-LXI, forms part of his design. One way of thinking of his poem is as a great lexicon of volitional states, modes of action and passion, qualities and orientations of thought and feeling, each edged and focussed by its unique tonality, rhythm, and imagery, each evalued, like the ideological motifs in *Guide to Kulchur,* by adroitly calculated juxtaposition. The need for a poem of this kind is contingent on the mess into which definition and evaluation of such material has fallen. The first seven cantos in particular are explicitly such a lexicon (" These fragments you have shelved [shored]"). *The Pisan Cantos* build their mosaic out of fragments very small and very sharply defined indeed, and the hierarchic arrangement is everywhere explicit :

> And Margherita's voice was clear as the notes of a
>   clavichord
> tending her rabbit hutch,
>   O Margaret of the seven griefs
> who hast entered the lotus.

> ' Trade, trade, trade . . .' sang Lanier
>   and they say the gold her grandmother carried
>   under her skirts for Jeff Davis
>   drowned her when she slipped from the landing
>   boat ;
> doom of Atreus

(O Mercury, god of thieves, your caduceus
is now used by the american army
   as witness this packing case)

Born with Buddha's eye south of Mason and Dixon
as against :

   Ils n'existent pas, leur ambience leur confert
      une existence . . . and in the case of
Emanuel Swedenbourg . . . ' do not argue '
   in the 3rd sphere do not argue
above which, the lotus, white nenuphar
Kuanon, the mythologies
we who have passed over Lethe.   (LXXVII)

The eighty-fourth canto leads up to its close with :

   quand vos venetz al som de l'escalina
                              ἦθος gradations
   These are distinctions in clarity

   ming 明   these are distinctions

And one of the running morals of the work is summed in
LXXIV :

         Le Paradis n'est pas artificiel
   but spezzato apparently
   it exists only in fragments unexpected excellent sausage
         the smell of mint, for example,
         Ladro the night cat. . . .

" Beauty," as Pound wrote about 1915, "is a brief gasp
between clichés."
   Pound's timeless frieze contains an enormously wider range
of discriminations than Milton's arrangements of high-styled
narrative and heavy conversation ; Milton, it is by now
widely realised, did not altogether benefit his poem by his

heroic determination to play everything on the diapason.
Milton, furthermore, did not succeed in realising his motifs
in articulate flexibility. It is much remarked how his shifts
of tone seem not quite within his control ; how often, as he
comes to a sunlit Arnoldian patch of Hellenism, the sap suddenly flows—the fall of Mulciber, for example, or the lines
on Proserpine's rape " that cost Ceres all that pain ", contain
a pathos with which he was unable to invest the backstairs
politics of Adam's lapse from grace. As the *locus classicus*
of long-current dissatisfactions may stand Mr. Empson's
shrewd surmise (*Some Versions of Pastoral*) that Milton was
not writing plumb from the centre of himself, that his use of
the pagan descriptions of Elysian fields implied a parallel
between the Satanic destruction of Eden and the Christian
destruction of paganism by which the official Milton would
have been embarrassed ; that " the fall from paganism is like
the fall from paradise ". One need push these observations
only a little further to find a defect of sincerity at the very
heart of the poem ; and this is what levels down so much
of it to cantankerous speechifying.

In *The Cantos* Pound for all his incidental didacticism moves
unembarrassed by the contradictory *schemæ* that bedevilled
Milton. No one ever knew his own mind more clearly. Indeed
the didactic gestures emerge naturally from the storehouse
of volitional forms ; the assault against *usura* ("contra
naturam") grows out of the many passages celebrating the
abundance of nature ; the laudation of the *condottieri* joins
hands with the praise of Odysseus which in turn is related
to the inspired opportunism of the artist's voyage toward
Tiresias. Gesell and Douglas are sub-cases of the distribution
of abundance ; Confucius articulated a world of moral forms
which generated the Chinese civilisation as the form seen in
the air engenders the statue ; as nations know their founders,
so we are shown

> stone knowing the form which the carver imparts it
>   the stone knows the form.

Pound's principal achievement, or one way of stating it,
is that he has discovered ways of making his materials co-
exist : classical myths, Christian virtues, Confucian insights,
violence and contemplation, casual anecdotes, historical
exempla. Stalin and Arthur Symons get into one poem without mutual devaluation. It will not be easy to discover, in
his anatomy of the *directio voluntatis,* either components missing or components ill-fitted. His heroic figures, Odysseus,
Malatesta, the great Emperors, function with a sane exuberance, his modes of passion cover a very long scale without
gap or overlap, from

> Helios
> Lord of the Light's edge, and April
> Blown round the feet of the God   (XXIX)

to the miniature descent of an infant wasp—

> The infant has descended,
> from mud on the tent roof to Tellus,
> like to like colour he goes amid grass-blades
>   greeting them that dwell under XTHONOS ΧΘΟΝΟΣ
> ΟΙ ΧΘΟΝΙΟΙ ; to carry our news
> εἰς Χθονιους to them that dwell under the earth,
> begotten of air, that shall sing in the bower
> of Koré Περσεφόνεια and have speech with Tiresias,
> Thebæ'' (LXXXIII)

We have only to compare the wit of this last vignette with
the magniloquent inflexibility with which Milton habitually
encrusts both terms of an extended comparison, or the
Poundian sharpness—

> with the veil of faint cloud before her
> Κύθηρα δεινὰ as a leaf borne in the current
> pale eyes as if without fire

with the Miltonic half-realised metaphor—

> . . . meanwhile murmuring waters fall
> Down the slope hills, disperst, or in a Lake,
> That to the fringed Bank with Myrtle crownd,
> Her chrystall mirror holds, unite thir streams . . .

(the Lake as *femme de toilette* hopelessly at odds with the Lake as receptacle of streams) to understand how Pound's flexibility belongs to an inwardness of linguistic manœuvre, a scrupulous response to contemplated existences. It is no wonder that he has spent over forty years growing into a technique the externals of which an Auden could learn to counterfeit in two.

The importance of Pound's unscrambling of what was botched in the Miltonic enterprise cannot be over-estimated. The epic undertakes to be encyclopædic, to fix its hundreds of details in a hierarchy ; it was by furnishing such a compendium of ethical and affective paradigms that Homer became the educator of Greece. Milton has been in the same way the schoolmaster of post-Renaissance England ; since the publication of *Paradise Lost* it has been virtually impossible to intuit not only the Genesis story but any moral drama except in his terms. *Paradise Lost* has presented itself to poet after poet as *the* inescapable fact, alternately accepted and rebelled against from Addison to Swinburne, but never evaded. It is the frame of reference for events so diverse as the mythology of Blake, the personality of Byron, the *Idylls* of Tennyson, the nature-cult of Wordsworth, and the " classicism " of Robert Bridges. Blake's equations are essentially Milton's with the signs exchanged ; Byron's personality is that defined by Milton for the rebel against irreclaimable respectability ;[1] Tennyson's *Idylls* were assimilations of the

---

1. Or as a Thief bent to unhoord the cash
    Of some rich Burgher, whose substantial dores,
    Cross-barrd and bolted fast, fear no assault,
    In at the window climbes, or o're the tiles ;
    So clomb this first grand Thief into Gods Fould.   (IV-188/192.)
    Raffles and Mr. Charteris' " Saint " are nascent here. The effect of such collocations as the " rich Burgher " with God in fixing the poetic status of the middle class (rocks of virtue but a fair mark for the Bohemian) shouldn't be overlooked. Milton's heaven exhibits the frigid paternalism of the nineteenth-century factory town ; it was not for nothing that Macaulay found him so congenial.

Miltonic negative goodness with Victorian ethical earnestness;
Wordsworth's Nature is Milton's Eden ; the " classicism "
of the Augustans when at their worst and of men like Bridges
when at their best depended on an ideal of faultless correct-
ness which depended in turn on actions being split down the
middle, as in Milton's myth, into the energetic on the one
hand and the unblemished on the other.

Another important aspect of the Miltonic heritage in art
is its perversion of the symbolic value the City has had for
the West from St. Augustine through Dante to Shakespeare.
Wordsworth rejected the city for the country, but insofar as
his rejection is validly symbolic rather than idiosyncratic the
terms were prepared for him by Milton. The *Prelude* contains
curious echoes of *Paradise Lost* (" The world is all before
me " he exults on the first page) which illustrate this fact.
Wordsworth is passing up with relief his chances of a safe
career in the Miltonic heaven ; like Adam and Eve, he elects
rather to make over unregenerate nature into a disciplined
analogue of the animistic Eden of boyhood. This is only to
say that the City, as Blake saw, had been turned, by events
corresponding to the Miltonic imagination, from a New
Jerusalem into a well-policed mill-town. The Augustan
urbanity (*urbs, urbis*), it is well known, is not inseparable
from a certain smugness ; after that interregnum of the Elect,
we are confronted by a succession of poets, from Cowper
onward, picturing London as the archetype of the asphaltic
detestable, polarised by Elysian visions of Windsor Forest,
Tintern Abbey, the Asia of Shelley, the Calydon of Swinburne's *Atalanta*. The City has only resumed its Augustinian
and Apocalyptic rôle with *Ulysses* and *Finnegans Wake*, with
Pound's exhortation

> to build the city of Dioce whose terraces are the colour
> of stars,

and with his account of how the Doges

> built out over the arches
> and the palace hangs there in the dawn, the mist,
> in that dimness.   (XXV.)

In his use of the imagery of stone alone Pound's poem marks a significant peripeteia. The cut and squared stones of Romantic death become at his hands invariably factive positives :

> The grey stone posts,
>   and the stair of grey stone,
> The passage clean-squared in granite. . . .   (XVI)

> .   .   .

> . . . I sleep, I sleep not, I rot
> And I build no wall.
>   Where was the wall of Eblis
> At Ventadour, there now are the bees,
> And in that court, wild grass for their pleasure
> That they carry back to the crevice
> Where loose stone hangs upon stone.
> I sailed never with Cadmus,
>   lifted never stone above stone.   (XXVII)

The distrust of the imagery of the City which stems from Milton's inability to focus his civic positives goes with the complete absence of social and moral context for his actions to occur in. (The background went out of portrait painting at about the same time, to be replaced by Rembrandtian *trompe d'œil* of shadow.) His wars are carried on between naked personalities ; his world is not one of hierarchic modalities of vision, but of irritated personal relationships. Adam's agony after the Fall recalls in its purely individual predication the squirming of a spotlit third degree victim, isolated in a darkened room alike from his torturers and from the world in which the crime is supposed to have taken place. Satan rebels against a priggish old man, Adam fusses about placat-

ing him and then forgets to, the sinners are led by the hand
by the expelling angel. It is not an order that is maladjusted
by sin, but a jealous deity that is offended ; he feels snubbed
and protests his own rectitude :

> Whose fault?
> Whose but his own? ingrate, he had of mee
> All he could have ; I made him just and right,
> Sufficient to have stood, though free to fall. . . .

These tones are exactly echoed by the outraged father of
nineteenth century melodrama ("Never darken my doorstep
again"); indeed, the melodrama with its inflexible parent
and its innocent victim who doesn't understand about mort-
gages, exhibits a thoroughly Miltonic cast ; its top-hatted
villain is simply the dashing Satan seen through audience's
eyes of horrified respectability.

The melodrama grows comic because its conflicts occur
within a framework of manners, not of morals ; only the
more assured rhetoric of Milton, Byron and Tennyson has
prevented their conceptions from dating in quite the same
way. They manipulate no analogical tensions, social, moral,
and metaphysical ; their actions are always starkly diagram-
matic. None of them has any conception of a society. Wordsworth's heroes stride about wrapped in mists, playing out
moral dramas (*Michael*) as stark as Samson's solitary *agon*
in Gaza. The London of Dickens makes contact with his
human grotesques, but not with his blank heroes and centri-
fugally outrageous villains ; Tennyson's *Arthur* comes across
neither as the wronged husband nor as "ideal manhood
clothed in real man" simply because in this anti-political
world of exposed nerves and hurt feelings there is no possible
bridge from the instance to the symbol ; his intolerably Phari-
saic closing address to the grovelling Guinevere could have
been stomached only by an audience accustomed, under
Miltonic ægis, to hazy idealisation of any priggish nastiness.
And only the total absence of civic context could conceal the
perversity with which a Byronic hero and a Miltonic Samson

alike (Samson has odd affinities with Satan) manifest virtue solely in acts of destruction, and the destruction of a City at that. Miltonic virtue and nineteenth century virtue alike consist in acts of destruction or renunciation ; between Prospero and the heroes of Pound the cult of factive intelligence is dormant.

The factive intelligence has been little honoured in Anglo-Saxondom. Though most people would agree that Prospero is a mask of Shakespeare, little thought is given to the significance of his dukedom in Milan. The parthenogenetic "magic" of poetry is thought to have little to do with rule. It should be remembered that the epic poet and the city founder of classical and Renaissance theory were alike in employing many provinces of rhetoric, the statesman and the poet analogously related to their material and analogous in their grasp of a world of mental forms, giving Caliban speech and Ariel liberty. James I of England writes to his son in this vein, and he was near the end of the tradition ; Milton was to present its modalities, in *Paradise Regained*, as diabolical temptations ; the only City that is built in his works is "Pandemonium, the high capital of Satan and his peers".

In his respect for an ordered civic wisdom, as in so much else—his sense of natural abundance, his harmonies between the human and the superhuman, his respect for the reality of trans-sensuous knowledge, Pound is in the Chaucer-Shakespeare line. He got there by going to China, Provence, Tuscany. He went around the world to get home. He went around the "Chinese Wall" of John Milton. If he has never ceased to be a mid-western American, he has also never ceased to be a contemporary of Mencius, Guido, and Arnaut Daniel. He is for this reason the only poet since Pope (to whom much of the prelapsarian lucidity remained) who has been able to learn from Chaucer, and his *A.B.C. of Reading* contains the most comprehensive tribute to Chaucer ever written.

That he has learned from Chaucer and from so many

others is built into the vision of *The Cantos*. Nothing is commoner than the supposition that Pound's intense concern for the craft of verse marks a separation between form and content, technique and sensibility (journalist's version : "he can only translate"). So it is not surprising that the revaluation of Milton with which his name is connected should be thought of as occurring at the level of technique alone, the only level at which Pound is supposed to work. But the dichotomy between myth and treatment belongs to the Miltonic ethos and not to the Poundian. "Finding the exact word for the inarticulate heart's tone," as Pound translates a Confucian node of meaning, inevitably expands into every department of volition with an analagous sincerity. "Orthography is a discipline both of *morale* and of morals." For the poet to expand this discipline into as many fields of consciousness as possible is to bring to an honest self-awareness the sensibility and intelligence of his time ; it is part of the undertaking represented by *The Cantos* that in the world of articulate forms there projected, distinctions between theme and treatment, thought and feeling, the poetical and the unpoetical, the contemplative and the factive, should become factitious. If criticism persists in behaving toward *The Cantos* as though these distinctions were real, criticism is spinning webs out of its own inside without looking at the poem.

THE ITALIAN BACKGROUND TO *THE CANTOS*

by John Drummond [*1949*]

As an example of the kind of difficulty *The Cantos* present to the reader, and to perceive how far it hinders his understanding of the meaning or lessens his appreciation of the poetry, consider the following lines from Canto LII :

> Between KUNG and ELEUSIS
> Under the Golden Roof, la Dorata
> her baldacchino
> Riccio on his horse rides still to Montepulciano
> the groggy church is gone toothless
> No longer holds against *neschek*.

The poetic effect is immediate, and yields little more when all the references are explained. Read in their context the first line and the last two present no difficulties (baldly, KUNG stands for order and moderation, ELEUSIS for violence against nature and art as punished, together with usury (*neschek*), in Circle 7, Ring 3, of the *Inferno*). But "la Dorata" and the "Golden Roof"? And Riccio riding to Montepulciano? The latter allusion will probably be familiar to anyone fairly conversant with Trecento painting : it is to Simone Martini's fresco in the Palazzo Publico at Siena. And if he has an encyclopædic mind he will perhaps spot a typically Poundian blunder, for Guido Riccio is riding to Montemassi, not Montepulciano, quite indifferent to Mr. Pound's scansion. But it is impossible to pretend that the allusion to la Dorata will be understood by anyone who is not either a Cavalcanti specialist or one who has made a special study of Pound's writings. La Dorata is the church of la Daurade at Toulouse, mentioned by Cavalcanti in his seventh Ballata, and rendered by Pound in his 1912 edition as "the golden roof". Thus it is clear that we cannot *know* everything about *The Cantos* until we have read not only everything that Pound has written, but everything he has read as well. If this requirement were also essential for our understanding of the significance of the poetry, it would be an unanswerable objection, and one might as well put the volume to some such useful purpose as propping up a window with a broken sash cord. But this is surely not the case, as the above quotation should make clear ; once the theme is grasped, ignorance of the particular object referred to does not necessarily prevent our perfectly understanding the function it has in the context.

Yet there is much in *The Cantos* where the meaning cannot be so readily appreciated without our knowing something of the actual matter that is being referred to. This is partly due to the fact that Pound ranges over fields unfamiliar to most of us, and instead of bringing us back dry erudition (which we could have got for ourselves out of plenty of dull textbooks if we had wanted) he gives us the treasures he has discovered in a condensed, ideogrammatic form essential to the intensity of his poetic vision but not adaptable to a systematic and Aristotelian exposition of his ideas, for which he is not temperamentally equipped in any case. If the poetry is good enough and the ideas important enough, we must want to know something of the background from which they spring, and it is on the assumption that they are that these notes have been compiled. It is hoped that insofar as the Italian background to *The Cantos* is concerned they will help towards a freer enjoyment of the poetry and a quicker understanding of the meaning.

There is one difficulty, however, that they can do little to alleviate : it derives from the ever-present problem of communicating relevant private experience that hinges on contingent circumstances without clogging it up with redundant explanations. Many instances of this occur in the reminiscent passages of *The Pisan Cantos*. For instance : a shadowy scene in the Café Dante, Verona, "by the arena", in Canto LXXVIII but echoed from the very earliest Cantos, with some decayed nobleman who wore (rather dirty) lace cuffs ; and an enigmatic line in Canto LXXVI, "la scalza : Io son' la

luna ", occurring elsewhere in *The Pisan Cantos* with variations : " the barefooted girl : I am the moon "—a mystery,
unless one should happen, one day, to hit on the clue.

Italy, in *The Cantos,* begins with Sordello. In fact, *The
Cantos* were originally conceived as Pound's *" Sordello "*,
and the influence of Browning in the now discarded draft of
Cantos I-III is very evident. In the present version " So
that : " at the end of Canto I and the openings of Cantos II
and III preserve the allusions to Browning's poem.

The story of Sordello's elopement with Cunizza da Romano
(called Palma by Browning) has significance for Pound in
that Dante placed her in Paradise in spite of her past. In
1265, the year of Dante's birth, she executed an act of manu-
mission, freeing her slaves. This took place in the Cavalcanti
home at Florence, and the famous lady's visit must have
made a strong impression on the youthful Cavalcanti, and
on Dante, too, at second hand. (Cantos VI and XXIX.)
In later life Sordello was in the service of the Count of Anjou
(afterwards Charles I of Naples), whose defeat of Manfredi
at Benevento (1266) re-established the Guelf predominance
in Italy. In that year Sordello was a prisoner of war at
Novara, and the Pope remonstrated with Charles for being
negligent about paying his ransom. Later Charles gave him
some castles in the Abruzzi. (Canto XXXVI.)

The study of Cavalcanti has been a constant preoccupation
for Pound, from the bilingual edition of the *Sonnets and
Ballate* published in 1912 to the ill-starred edition, with
photographic reproductions of manuscripts, eventually published in a truncated form at Genoa in 1931, after the
" failure " of the English publisher when the work was half
printed.[1] The substance of this edition, except for the texts
and translations of the *Sonnets and Ballate,* but including
those of the Canzone, " Donna mi Prega ", is to be found in
Make it New, and is a great help to the understanding of the

---

1. Three Canzoni not included in this edition, from the Codex 1.IX.18 in the
Biblioteca Comunale, Siena (see *Make it New*, p. 372, note), are now published,
with facsimiles of the MSS., as No. XIX of the " Quaderni dell'Accademia
Chigiana " (Ticci, Siena, 1949).

references in *The Cantos* to mediæval philosophy before the
advent of "fat-headed Aquinas" (Avicenna, Averrhoes,
Albertus Magnus, etc.): the intellectual climate that pervades
"Donna mi Prega". The first part of Canto XXXVI is an
improved translation of this Canzone which it is interesting
to compare with the more interpretative translation given
in the Genoa edition. Scraps of the Italian text of the Canzone, in italics, occur frequently in the Adams Cantos
(LXII-LXXI). The line "che fa di clarità l'aer tremare",
mentioned two or three times in *The Pisan Cantos,* is from one
of the Sonnets, and refers to a question of textual criticism.
Some MSS., followed by the Giuntine edition, have "che fa
tremar di chiaritate l'are", a reading which Pound considers
"blasphemous". Carducci, it seems, didn't, and the only
texts now in print still follow Carducci—which might have
something to do with Italian "competenti" declaring the
Genoa edition to be "monstrous".[1] In Italy today, Dante is
adored rather than read, and the mention of any other name
in the same breath as that of the Master is almost considered
a sacrilege. And when Pound explains his critical position in
these "few words" (in his Italian preface), "that Guido is
not inferior to Dante in quality ; that these two gave the poetry
of the world something that did not exist, and does not exist,
elsewhere, and that for the six centuries after their exiles
Italian poetry has not reached their level", the sacrilege
becomes almost an insult, leading the gentleman whose name
we have mentioned in the footnote to the wilful misrepresentation that Pound "maintained that Italian poetry finished
with Guido Cavalcanti ". If the Genoa edition has certain imperfections, due to the circumstances of its publication, and
also to the fact that Pound is too much of a poet to assume the
rôle of the pedantic textual critic whose only concern is to
"obscure the text with philology" (Canto XIV), it is none
the less true that for the last forty years, at least, Cavalcanti
has been disgracefully neglected by his own countrymen and
no other modern critical edition of his works exists.

1. Or so at least says E. Montale, *Corriere della Sera,* 3rd March, 1949.

The relevance of Dante to *The Cantos,* and his importance to Pound, is too obvious or too readily studied to require elaboration here. After Dante Italian literature has little to interest Pound: we note only a scene from a *Novella* (No. 137) by Franco Sacchetti, a younger contemporary of Boccaccio (end of Canto XXII), and allusions, towards the end of Canto V, to Sannazaro and various poetasters of the time of Leo X. One of the latter, Baraballo, was induced to so high an opinion of himself that he made formal application to be crowned with laurel on the Capitol. The request was granted for the fun of the thing; the laureate was to ride in triumphal procession on the Pope's elephant (a present from the King of Portugal), but the poor beast was so frightened by the fireworks and laughter that it refused to budge.

The craftsman par excellence, Pound has always been especially interested in the point at which an art, or a new phase in the history of an art, springs into life. It is consistent, therefore, that his interest in Italian literature is focussed on the turn of the thirteenth and fourteenth centuries, in art on the Quattrocento (and slightly later in the case of the Venetians), in architecture on the proto-Christian, the Romanesque and the early Renaissance. We hear nothing of Raphael or Michelangelo in *The Cantos*: plenty of Mantegna (Cantos III and XLV), Botticelli, Jacopo Sellaio, Agostino di Duccio, etc. (XX, etc.), Cosimo Tura and Francesco del Cossa (XXIV, and several times in *The Pisan Cantos* LXXVII-IX), Pisanello (XXVI), commissioned to buy horses because he could paint them, Giovanni Bellini (XXV and XLV), Carpaccio (XXVI), Titian (XXV), etc.; nothing about Renaissance architecture after L. B. Alberti, plenty about the cathedral of Ferrara, where "the perfect measure took form" (XXVII), San Zeno at Verona, being the "church of cut stone signed: *Adamo me fecit*" (XLV, LXXIV, LXXVIII), and the sculpture of Pietro and Tullio Lombardo in Santa Maria dei Miracoli at Venice (XLV and LXXIV). Many of the descriptive passages throughout the *Cantos* can only be fully appreciated in terms of Quattrocento painting.

Canto XLV, cited above, is the Usury Canto, and is echoed in Canto LI. Pound maintains that decadence in art, obscurantism in literature, sterility in nature, and injustice in economics, are all symptoms of the same malady. Compare Chapter 16 of the *Guide to Kulchur,* where he states : " I have not deflected a hair's breadth from my lists of beautiful objects, made in my own head and held before I ever thought of usura as a murrain and a marasmus "; and Canto XLVI : ". . . look, if you can, at St. Peter's . . . 1527. Thereafter art thickened. Thereafter design went to hell. Thereafter barocco, thereafter stone-cutting desisted."

The aspect of the Humanism of fifteenth-century Italy most relevant to *The Cantos* is its neo-Platonism. Long before the foundation of the Platonic Academy, before Marsilio Ficino (Canto XXI) was born, and before the fall of Constantinople, the first wave of Platonism broke upon Italy with the visit of the Byzantine Emperor and the Patriarch of Constantinople for the Council to effect a reconciliation between the Greek and Latin Churches. The Emperor and his suite arrived at Venice at the beginning of 1438, where they were given a sumptuous reception, then proceeding to Ferrara, where Eugenius IV already awaited them. (Canto XXVI.) The following year the Council transferred to Florence (Canto VIII). Gibbon gives a colourful and characteristic account of the whole affair in his Chapter LXVI, citing in a footnote " The Latin vulgar was provoked to laughter at the strange dresses of the Greeks, and especially the length of their garments, their sleeves, and their beards . . .", which eighteenth-century phraseology may be compared with Pound's twentieth-century idiom on the same subject. But the Council brought Gemistus Plethon to Florence, and Gemisto reintroduced Platonism to Italy, after which he returned to the Peloponnesus, where he died in 1451, and where his body was acquired in 1465 by Sigismondo Malatesta, that it might take its place among the worthies in the sacrophagi ranged along the side of the Tempio Malatestiano at Rimini.

The Tempio represents the highest achievement of Humanism ; Sigismondo Pandolfo Malatesta, its creator, was the most representative personality of his time, and he remains the dominating personality of *The Cantos*. He lived from 1417 to 1468. A professional *condottieri*, he already, at the age of eighteen, commanded the Papal armies in Romagna and the Marches, and he took part in all the wars in Italy for the next thirty years, first in the service of one *signoria*, then of another, making war in between times on his own account against his life-long rival, Federigo, Duke of Urbino. Imbued with all the enthusiasm of the age for the new learning and the arts, he spent all his spare cash and energy on the construction and embellishment of the Tempio, assembling the best artists of the time, in the face of continual difficulties. His vicious moral character has probably been largely exaggerated, owing partly to the personal animosity of Aeneas Silvius Piccolomini (Pius II) and partly to the propaganda of the Church that was out to despoil him of his possessions. An heroic and pathetic figure, always fighting a losing battle against fate, he died with nearly all his territories lost to him, and a half-finished edifice—that remains, nevertheless, the most eloquent monument of its epoch.

Sigismondo's personality is presented in Cantos VIII-XI, with a few references scattered elsewhere throughout *The Cantos*. Before dealing with his story directly, it will be best to give a brief summary, based mainly on Muratori's *Annali d'Italia*, of the historical events of the time.

The main powers to be reckoned with in the Italian peninsula around the year 1440 were : the Duke of Milan, Filippo Maria Visconti ; the Republic of Venice ; the newly-established *signoria* of the Medici at Florence ; the Pope, Eugenius IV, with an insubordinate Council of Basle on his hands ; and Renato (René) of Anjou and Alfonso V of Aragon, warring for the succession of the Regno of Naples after the death of Queen Joanna II (1435). Smaller states adopted a see-saw policy with powerful neighbours (e.g., Nicolò III, Leonello, and Borso ("Keep-the-peace") d'Este, of Ferrara), or their rulers hired themselves out as *condottieri* to whichever of the larger powers paid best, hoping to acquire something for themselves on the side (e.g., Francesco Sforza, Niccolò Piccinino, Sigismondo, and Federigo d'Urbino).

The warfare of these years turned on the perennial struggle between Venice and Milan. Florence's settled policy supported Venice against Milan, and the Veneto-Florentine League, captained by Sforza, favoured the Angevin cause in the Regno against Alfonso, who, with Visconti's encouragement, was always ready to attack Tuscany or Sforza's territories in the Marches. Sforza was the ablest *condottiere* in Italy, and the Duke of Milan could never make up his mind whether it were safer to have him as his ally or his enemy. In 1441, however, he took the plunge, made peace with the League, giving his daughter Bianca to Sforza, with Cremona and Pontermoli in dowry—and then regretted it almost immediately.

Sforza, thrown on his own resources during the following years of peace between the greater powers, had to withstand the attacks of Alfonso (who had finally ousted Renato), the Pope, Niccolò Piccinino (his old rival and Visconti's general, now ostensibly fighting on his own account), and the malicious intrigues of his father-in-law. He was at his last gasp in 1446, when the situation was saved by a new outbreak of war between Venice and Milan, both sides bidding for his services. He declared for his father-in-law—who died in the following year. After playing his cards artfully, first as general of the Milanese against the Venetians, then with the Venetians against Milan, and then, for a remarkable moment, with them both allied against him, he besieged Milan, which surrendered and acclaimed him as Duke in 1451.

After a year of peace, war broke out again. Florence had now changed sides, and the new line-up was Milan and Florence against Venice and Alfonso. Sforza had to appeal to the French, promising to support the Angevin cause in the Regno. The arrival of Renato's French troops, with their barbaric methods of warfare, so terrified the population of

Lombardy that they declared for Milan, and the peace of
Lodi was negotiated in 1455. The appeals of Nicholas V,
eager to organise a crusade following the fall of Constantinople, had also been a factor in the peace.

The next Pope, Calixtus III, broke with Alfonso owing to
the latter's being much keener on crushing the Genoese than
crusading against the Turks, and he refused to recognise his
successor, Ferrante the Bastard, when he died. But the Pope
died too (1458), and Pius II soon made friends with Ferrante. While Pius II was more seriously trying to organise a
crusade at Mantua, in the following year, Ferrante was having trouble with rebellious barons, and with the Angevins, led
by Giovanni d'Anjou, Renato's son, joined in 1460 by Giacomo
Piccinino, son of Niccolò, who had died in the meantime.

In 1457, Genoa, to save herself from Alfonso, had put herself under the protection of Renato. Now, in 1461, the Genoese
drove the Angevins out of the city, not without the approval
of the Duke of Milan, who was now glad to get rid of the
French. The Angevin cause, opposed by Milan and the Pope,
also collapsed in the Regno, and Piccinino transferred his
services to Ferrante (1463). The Pope was now free to get
on with his crusade, but he died in 1464 when he was about
to lead the fleet in person from Ancona.

To return to Sigismondo—he "was twelve at the time"
(end of Canto VIII) of his uncle's death in 1429, when the
inheritance passed to the three brothers (all illegitimate, incidentally, but legitimised by Martin V—Renaissance popes
seem to have done a brisk trade in legitimising the bastards
of Renaissance princes) : Galeotto, who "went pious" and
died in 1432 ; Sigismondo ; and Domenico, better known as
Malatesta Novello ("Novvy" to Pound), Lord of Cesena,
where he founded the Biblioteca Malatestiana. The end of
Canto VIII and the beginning of Canto IX refer to Sigismondo's struggles to defend his inheritance, and other events.
The aged Emperor Sigismund knighted the two brothers on
his way back from being crowned at Rome in 1433.

In the early 'forties, in the service of the Venetians, he

operated in close alliance with Sforza. In 1442, with peace in Lombardy, Sforza and his bride passed through Rimini "to the wars southward" (Canto VIII) on an ill-fated campaign to recover his possessions that Alfonso had grabbed while he had been fighting in the north. He was accompanied by Sigismondo, who had that year married Sforza's daughter Polissena. He continued a wavering ally of Sforza during his declining fortunes of these years, finally breaking with him over the affair of Pèsaro and Fossombrone in 1445. Sigismondo had been trying to get these cities away from Galeazzo and Malatesta, and he expected Sforza to help him. Sforza, however, through some wangle with Sigismondo's sworn enemy, Federigo d'Urbino, obtained that Galeazzo sold Pèsaro to his brother, Alessandro Sforza, and Fossombrone to "Feddy". (Cantos VIII and IX.) To get his revenge, Sigismondo went over to the Pope, in alliance with Alfonso against Sforza.

The next passage in Canto IX refers to his breaking his contract in 1448 with Alfonso, who had hired him to make war against Florence. But when the Florentines offered him better terms he changed sides immediately, pocketing the thirty or forty thousand *scudi* he had had from the King.

In 1449 we find him besieging Crema in the service of the Venetians in their war against Milan, but with his mind more on the Tempio which he had already begun building— whence, perhaps, his employers' query : "Did he think the campaign was a joy-ride?" (Canto IX). The letter to Giovanni de' Medici dated "In the Field", at the beginning of Canto VIII, shows this pre-occupation. The identity of the *Mæstro dipentore* is not known ; it is unlikely to have been Pier della Francesca, who painted the fresco in the cella delle Reliquie showing Sigismondo kneeling before the Emperor Sigismund ; it might have been Filippo Lippi, but in any case the idea of frescoes for the chapels was given up in favour of sculpture. He withdrew from Crema before a superior relieving force just when the city was on the point of surrendering.

In the following year the Venetians sent him to help the Milanese, besieged by Sforza ; but he failed to achieve anything, and as soon as the city surrendered in February he scampered back over the Adda and destroyed the bridge. This was followed by the affair of the " German-Burgundian female " (Canto IX), a beautiful noblewoman who was passing through Verona on her way to Rome for the Jubilee. She was assaulted and let herself be killed rather than submit to the libidinous desires of her seducer. The crime was popularly attributed to Sigismondo, but Muratori, though believing him capable of it, is careful to add : " Whether he was really guilty of this outrage I am unable to say, for in spite of all the investigations made by the sagacious Venetians, they were unable to discover the culprit ". However, as a result of these real or alleged shortcomings, both on and off duty, the Venetians gave him the sack.

This was the busiest period of the work on the Tempio, and much of his time was taken up with scrounging marble, some of which he filched from S. Apollinare in Classe, Ravenna (Canto IX), supervising builders, masons, carpenters, etc. In 1452 he entered the service of the "most magnificent commune of the Florentines" (Canto VIII), victims of Aragonese aggression, and in 1454 he was appointed captain-general of the Sienese troops in one of their perennial wars with the Counts of Pitigliano (see also opening of Canto XXIX). In August he besieged the Count Aldobrandino Orsini (an instrument of Florence and/or Alfonso) in Sorano, and the siege dragged on into the winter. The Sienese suspected him of secret intelligence with the enemy, and, in fact, Pitigliano had sent him the letter paraphrased at the beginning of Canto X. To get evidence against him they intercepted his mail, and the letters " found in the post-bag ", still preserved in the archives at Siena, have proved the most valuable documentation, not of his dealings with Pitigliano, but of the identity of the artists employed on the works of the Tempio.

Extracts from these letters are given in Canto IX.[1] Pound's

1. The full texts are given by Charles Yriarte, *Un Condottiere au XVe Siècle*, Paris, 1882.

renderings, which are translations from century to century as well as from language to language, are mostly self-explanatory, but the following few comments may clarify. The first extract is from a letter from the architect Matteo Nuti. Luigi Alvise (Alwidge) was the carpenter, and Giovanni, writer of the second extract, his son. "Mr. Genare" is Pietro di Genari, Sigismondo's secretary, and writer of the last letter about the consignment of the marble from Verona, etc. (In this letter, "aliofants" stands for "elephants", and Agostino is the sculptor Agostino di Duccio.) The letter beginning "Monseigneur" was dictated, if not actually written by Isotta herself. Yriarte's conclusion, on the basis of this, that Isotta was illiterate cannot be accepted.[1] It refers to a peccadillo of Sigismondo's with a young girl. The two letters about the bay pony require no gloss. The gentleman who presumed to "offer counsels to Hannibal" was Sigismondo's court poet, Servulo Trachulo, and this part of the "damn'd epistle" is mentioned in the next Canto.

In 1457 Sigismondo's fortunes began the catastrophic decline from which they never really recovered. Alfonso, still smarting over the trick Sigismondo had played on him when he went over to Florence in 1448, incited Federigo d'Urbino and Giacomo Piccinino against him. By 1459 they had reduced him to such straits that he had to appeal to the new Pope, Pius II (holding his Crusade Council at Mantua) to make peace, which he did, on pretty stiff terms for Sigismondo. The latter part of Canto X covers this period. His and Federigo's sentiments for each other, as manifested on an occasion when Borso d'Este had tried to effect a reconciliation between them, are alluded to on the second page of the same Canto : " I'll soon slit yer belly up for yer ! "—" I'll cut the guts out of *you* ! " (as the Italian might be freely translated), and recalled years later in Canto LXXXI.

Offended with the Pope for declining his proffered services, Sigismondo started hostilities against the Church in 1460, and

---

1. See Corrado Ricci's monumental work, *Il Tempio Malatestiano*, Milan-Rome, 1925. Yriarte's book, the main source of Pound's information, contains several inaccuracies, some of which are reflected in these Cantos.

in the following year associated himself with the Angevin cause against King Ferrante, who was supported by the Pope. After initial failures, he administered a sound defeat to the papal troops at Castello Leone in July (Canto XI). His temporal arms having failed him, the Pope now opened up with all his spiritual artillery : ". . . the anger and hate which the pontiff Pius conceived against him, Sigismondo, beggars description ; so he began issuing excommunications and put all his cities and territories under interdict, and represented him as a traitor to the States of the Church" (Muratori). Every possible accusation was raked up, or invented, against him ; the Cardinal of San Pietro in Vincoli was appointed *rapporteur,* and found him guilty on every count ; and he was condemned to be burnt as a heretic, but as they couldn't obtain his person they burnt him in effigy on the steps of St. Peter's (Canto X).[1]

However, in August 1462 (continuing with Canto XI), Sigismondo, on his way to help the Angevins, was defeated by Federigo and the Papal troops at Mondolfo, and his son, Roberto, after gallantly holding Fano for four months against Federigo by land and a Papal navy by sea, had to surrender, owing to the defection of the citizens, in September 1463. After the Mondolfo débacle, Sigismondo had gone by sea to Taranto to see if the Angevins could do anything for him, but he found them down and out too. On his return, having lost all but Rimini and a few castles, and with " that nicknosed s.o.b. Feddy Urbino "[2] exultant over his misfortunes, there was nothing left for it but to ask the Venetians (who had already been secretly helping him—Canto XXVI) to appeal to the Pope on his behalf. Pius, after imposing " de mos' bloody rottenes' peace ", " forgave " Sigismondo.

1464-5 was the year of the unsuccessful campaign against the Turks in Morea. On his return he hoped that the new

1. According to the Pope's own rather shamefaced account, in which he tries to shift the responsibility for this undignified piece of tomfoolery onto the cardinals. From other more circumstantial accounts it appears that there were actually three stakes in different parts of the city.
2. The literal accuracy of this description will be appreciated if one recalls the well-known portrait by Pier della Francesca in the Uffizi, and bears in mind the Duke of Urbino's very dubious parentage.

Pope, Paul II, who had wanted to call himself "Formosus", might do something for him, but in vain. In his anger he even went to Rome with the intention of stabbing the Pope, but his spirit failed him when he found himself in the august presence. He died in 1468.

Canto X contains references to Giacomo Piccinino, who had become the best *condottiere* in the peninsula, and his death, which was the result of a particularly perfidious piece of work by Sforza and Ferrante. Suspecting that Ferrante was thinking of liquidating his most dangerous collaborator, he appealed to Sforza for protection. Sforza welcomed him to Milan, and gave him his long-promised daughter, Drusinia, in marriage. He then sent the couple on a goodwill mission to Ferrante, who, after entertaining them lavishly for a month, had Piccinino strangled and his body thrown out of a window, giving out that he had fallen out by accident (1465). The unsuspecting decoy, Drusinia, was then sent back home. The Duke had sent him to slaughter, the King had been the butcher, it was said.

Other episodes of Italian history of the fifteenth and sixteenth centuries referred to in *The Cantos* are : the adultery of Parisina Malatesta, wife of Niccolò III of Ferrara ; and two famous assassinations—of Giovanni Borgia and Alessandro de' Medici.

The story of Parisina is the subject of a poem by Byron and a drama by D'Annunzio. Niccolò discovered her intrigue with his bastard son Ugo, and had them both beheaded (1425). (Canto XXIV, and stray allusions in Cantos VIII and XX.)[1]

In 1497 the Duke of Gandia, Giovanni Borgia, the eldest son of Alexander VI, was murdered one night and his body thrown into the Tiber near the church of S. Girolamo degli Schiavoni. A witness described how the cloak floated and the assassins threw stones on it to make it sink. The body was fished up later. The authors of the crime were never dis-

---

[1]. The story is adequately related in Chapter III of *Ferrara* by Dora Noyes (Mediæval Towns series).—Editor.

covered, but writers hostile to the Borgia attribute the responsibility to his brother Cesare.

The assassination of Alessandro de' Medici in 1539, which resulted in the passing of the *signoria* from one branch of the family to another, remains an enigma of history, it being impossible to say whether Lorenzino ("Lorenzaccio") was a patriotic hero or a psychopathological case. Pound, however, is mainly interested in Varchi's account of the affair : [1] his efforts to discover the truth, and his scrupulously refraining from passing judgment on what he knew he couldn't be sure about.[2]

The theme of these two assassinations, bracketed together, is introduced in Canto V, that of Lorenzaccio recurs in Canto VII, while his death, eleven years later, is the occasion of a letter given in Canto XXVI. The "click of hooves on the cobbles by Tevere", towards the end of Canto LXXIV, again recalls the death of Giovanni Borgia.

Further glimpses, largely based on original documents, of Italian states in the later Middle Ages and the Renaissance, sometimes mingled with contemporary impressions, are given in the following Cantos : XVII (Venice), XXI (the Medici), XXIV (the d'Este of Ferrara, including Niccolò's trip to the Holy Land), XXV-VI (Venice and Venetian painters), and XXX (Fano, where Girolamo Soncino set up a printing press in 1501).

The latter part of the sixteenth, and the seventeenth, century in Italy, the period of the Mannerists, the Baroque, and the Counter-Reformation, are of no interest to Pound for their art and literature. But one event to which he attaches great significance in this period is the foundation of the Monte dei Paschi, the Sienese bank, a subject which, together with a contemporary eye-witness account of the preparation of the Carroccio for the Palio—Siena's horse-race for the *drappellone* still kept up with mediæval pageantry—and a few

---

1. Benedetto Varchi, *Storia Fiorentina*, Lib. XV.
2. Cf. Canto XIII   "And even I can remember
         A day when the historians left blanks in their writings
         I mean for things they didn't know."—Editor.

miscellaneous items from the public archives, is fully treated in Cantos XLII and XLIII. The Palio is referred to again in Canto LXXX, together with an allusion to the restoration of Bibbiena's Teatro dei Rinnovati, where Pound first met the operatic composer, Bruno Barilli, who in his critical writings has agitated for a no less urgent restoration of Italian opera to its best traditions.

With Cantos XLIV and L we enter Tuscany during the period of the Grand Duchy under the house of Lorraine, interrupted by the changes of the Napoleonic period. After a deplorable interval following the extinction of the Medici, when the country was ruled by an agent like an Austrian province, Pietro Leopoldo was nominated Grand Duke at the age of eighteen and came to rule in person (1765). His honest administration and liberal reforms greatly benefited the Duchy. He succeeded to the Empire in 1790 and was packed off to Vienna, but his son, Ferdinando III, continued the good work until he was ousted by the French in 1799. In 1808 Napoleon made his sister Elisa Grand Duchess of Tuscany; she remained until she "departed from Lucca" in 1814. Ferdinando III was restored, to be succeeded by Leopoldo II (1824-48). Pound's source for the material of these two Cantos is mainly a *Storia civile della Toscana* (Florence, 1850) by Antonio Zobi, an historian interested in economic matters and an Italian acute enough to observe "Italy for ever doomed with abstractions". The contrast between these Cantos, together with those about the Monte dei Paschi, as examples of economic and social justice, and the Usury Cantos (XLV and LI), and the examples of injustice and exploitation in Canto XLVI and elsewhere, will not escape notice.

The period of Romantic Liberalism, of Garibaldi and the Risorgimento, say from 1848 to 1915, is scarcely reflected in *The Cantos*, except for the vignette of "Prince Oltrepassimo" in Canto XXVIII, which must also be the only passage in *The Cantos* in which a typically Roman subject is treated for its own sake. The "Sacconi" are the members, recruited ex-

clusively from the "black" aristocracy, of a religious con-
fraternity whose uniform is a penitential robe made of
sackcloth covering body and head, with holes for the eyes,
skull and crossbones, etc. They go barefoot in their annual
procession on Good Friday, and are buried in their "sacconi", without a coffin, when they die. As for the Discobolus,
the best of the three in Rome belonged to the Lancelotti
family, and they kept it very much to themselves—until they
sold it to Germany in 1938. It has now been returned to the
Italian State.

The best gloss to the passages in *The Cantos* dealing with
Mussolini and Fascism is *Jefferson and/or Mussolini*, written
in 1933 (though not published until 1935). Although Pound
did not see what was coming during his visits to Italy in the
years immediately preceding the Fascist *coup d'état*, we find
him interested in Mussolini as early as 1927, in the *Exile*,
where the name is bracketed with Lenin's, while the Decennio
Exhibition, celebrating the first ten years of Fascism (Canto
XLVI), probably sharpened his interest. But there are more
cogent reasons for Pound's admiration of Fascism, such as
the obtuseness of the Marxists in all matters concerning the
financial system, and the ingrained, stultifying traditionalism
that is typical of so many strata of Italian life. Although
they have an extraordinary vitality and exuberance, a widely
diffused talent (but rare native genius) for the arts, a great
deal of ingenuity, often anti-socially applied, and a much
higher *medial* line of civilisation than one finds in Anglo-
Saxony, Italians are none the less afflicted with an unrecep-
tiveness to new ideas that, in one's most despairing moments,
almost forces one to maintain that Fascism's greatest crime
was not that it was too hard on the Italians, but that it was
not hard enough. Pound, like many others, made the mistake
of taking Fascism too much at its face value and endowing
it with his own wishful thoughts; but we owe it to him to
recognise that he did so in good faith and not for reasons of
self-interest. Future historians will probably weigh the merits

and demerits of Fascism not on an ideological basis but as
an Italian phenomenon that partook of the secular merits
and demerits of the Italian people. (It is, for instance, absurd
to pretend that administrative corruption was specifically a
Fascist institution, or that there has been any less of it in
Italy before or since.)

In *The Cantos* the subject is first introduced in Canto XLI.
The anecdote there recounted probably came from Bottai,
a Fascist Minister of Education. After Canto XLVI, mentioned above, most of the other references to Fascism occur
in *The Pisan Cantos*, which open with a comparison between
Mussolini's death and that of the founder of the Manichee
religion, whose flayed skin, stuffed with hay, was set up over
a gate of the city of Gunde-Shapur. In Canto LXXX we have
a glimpse of Mussolini after the March on Rome, and a
reference to the problem of " what to do with your gunmen "
after a revolution. In Canto LXXVIII there is an allusion
to the Salò Republic, the end, and San Sepolcro, the beginning, of the Fascist Regime. The " Programma di Verona "
was a manifesto establishing the principles of action of the
Fascist Republican Party (October, 1943). The point of style
referred to probably alludes to the sentence : " Quello della
casa non è soltanto un diritto di proprietà, è un diritto alla
proprietà."[1] A passage on the same page describes an incident
during Pound's hitch-hike north from Rome after the Armistice
(8 September, 1943).

There remains the Italy that Pound has directly known
himself : personal impressions, anecdotes, encounters, re-
actions to landscape, etc. Apart from the American and
Chinese Cantos, from the day he "sat on the Dogana's
steps " (Canto III), which must have been in about 1908, to
the relief brought by the morning sun after the night of hoar
frost that grips his tent in the American glasshouse camp
near Pisa, in the autumn of 1945, concluding *The Pisan
Cantos*, Italy is frequently the main subject of the argument,
and the Italian background is never completely lost to view.

1. " The right to a home is not only a right of property, it is a right to property."

Preoccupation with the literary content of *The Cantos* is apt to make one undervalue Pound's acute observation of nature and his sensitiveness to the surrounding scene. Anyone who is familiar with the Mediterranean landscape will not fail to appreciate the precision of the lines describing olive trees stirred by the breeze in Canto XX :

> With the leaves green and then not green,
> The click of light in their branches,

or blown white, if the wind is stronger, as at the beginning of *The Pisan Cantos.*

At Rapallo the mountains, clothed above a certain altitude with heath and ilex groves, descend steeply to the sea in olive-terraces, or in rocky crags with Mediterranean pines. Among the olive-terraces, particularly above Zoagli, are scattered farmhouses in which silk looms can often be heard at work, and an old bridle-road, the Roman via Aurelia, caterpillars over the shoulders of the hills and loops back into the valleys. Such is the landscape that forms the setting of several passages in *The Cantos,* especially Cantos XXXIX and XLVII, and is frequently alluded to throughout *The Pisan Cantos.* It is the landscape that Pound's fancy peoples with the mortals and immortals of the ancient world and other personæ of *The Cantos,* as at the beginning of Canto LXXVI. Likewise, in *The Pisan Cantos,* the coastal plain where the camp was situated, in sight of the Leaning Tower, and the distant hills towards Lucca, identified with the sacred mountains of China, is the setting in which Pound suffered the refined tortures of modern scientific savagery—yet composed some of his finest poetry. Out of all that beauty something *did* come.

THE ELLIPSE IN THE PISAN CANTOS

by Charles Madge [1949]

In hysterical poetry, the poet puts more down on paper than he has in his head. In the flux of words, the elusive substance of poetry disappears and the evocation is a fake. Poetry which has lived a long time, and which we therefore call classical, carries no such superfluity. The lines are often so bare that the greater part of the poem has to be read between them. Academic "classicists" like to pretend that the mere sententious shell of the language is all that there is to it. The classic becomes a performance which obsessional neurotics can impose on other obsessional neurotics. To make them more palatable, the successful academician is even able to suggest that certain classical authors really shared the sentimental hysteria of our own period. In one way or another, our connection with the classical writings is blocked by these falsifications. And yet when anybody is able to win access to them, to break a way through, these classics can still re-create our insight into the present and the future.

More than anyone in our time, Pound has been conscious of this situation between ourselves and the classics. He has constantly sought to rediscover the classical literatures of Europe and has explored those of China and Japan. Passionate and often dogmatic, he has pushed his way past current judgments and interpretations. Those whom the ancients themselves valued highly, Pound will often dismiss on a slender acquaintance, while in minor authors he finds unsuspected genius. All is based on a direct feeling at first-hand and governed as often as not by some compelling need of Pound's own personal history. He is the brilliantly talented child let loose in the nursery of all the ages, pulling everything out of the toy cupboard higgledy-piggledy and playing out his own games in his own way, assured in the power of his own inner fantasy. Like a child he can be wilful and destructive, but the over-riding impulse is of reparation and restitution. We have good cause to be grateful for the imagination which can restore life to the dead and we need not take up too much time in finding out whether an improvised scholarship has been adequate to so sweeping a task.

I do not pretend to understand all the allusions in *The Pisan Cantos*, and a greater knowledge would undoubtedly add to my appreciation of the poem. But even with these gaps, the work as a whole has an immense force : " with one day's reading a man may have the key in his hands." Whether a certain type of reader, given certain resistances, can ever get this key, I am not sure. But by suggesting what I myself have found, some others may be led to a similar experience.

The ellipse is the figure of speech in which a part of what is to be understood is left unstated. It necessitates the mind taking a jump across a gap. At its crudest, it is telegram language, where the sender is trying to convey as much as he can in the fewest possible words. In this sense it is one kind of economy in expression. But in the case of the poetic ellipse, evocation takes place between the words as well as in them. As a musician uses silence or a painter space, the poet uses the ellipse. In doing so he invites his reader to embody an elusive perception.

This figure (like the ambiguity in words which William Empson has demonstrated) is so inherent in poetic statement that it is widely used without any conscious theory. In fact, once one starts to compose a poem it is difficult not to produce elliptical effects and ambiguous effects. In certain poets, however, the tendency to paronomasia, or punning, is so marked that it must almost certainly have been deliberate ; and there are also examples in literature of a deliberate use of the ellipse as a convention. I am submitting that Pound's main stylistic device is an intensive exploitation of the ellipse.

Among many sources for Pound's elliptical style may be mentioned his study of Greek and Latin poets, especially where their texts are mutilated or their work has only survived in fragments, so that time itself has introduced elliptical gaps into their statements. Moreover, to Pound, as to Mallarmé, the visual appearance of his poems is of importance

—the space across which the poetic spark has to fly is an actual space on a printed page. This goes with a passion for the calligraphic Chinese ideogram. A rather exaggerated example of this visual kind of ellipse is to be found at the end of Canto LXXVII :

bringest to focus
Zagreus
ch'êng   Zagreus   ch'êng

Here the elements are a Chinese word meaning " perfect or focus " and a Greek word which is an epithet of Dionysus, Greek god of wine, in his esoteric rôle. The words are arranged so as to suggest to the eye that it should actually perform a focussing operation. This focussing act is a metaphor of the kind of focus Pound is inviting us to acquire in our contemplation of the civilisations and their existence inside as well as outside our individual selves.

A simplified demonstration of the elliptical device from his earlier work is the little poem called *Papyrus* from *Lustra* :

Spring ....
Too long ......
Gongula ......

Here Pound is suggesting that an imaginative archæologist might pick up a tiny scrap of papyrus on which these few words were written and from them reconstruct a love-affair, in a way which showed the essential similarity between our own personal lives and those of dynastic Egypt or some other remote civilisation and which therefore confirmed his own unacademic view of scholarship.

The dots in the Papyrus poem represent the gaps in the codex and the space to be filled in by the imagination—the elliptical space. They turn up again in *Mauberley* :

Drifted . . . drifted precipitate
Asking time to be rid of . . .
Of his bewilderment ; to designate
His new-found orchid . . .
To be certain . . . certain . . .
(Amid ærial flowers) . . . time for arrangements

—and so on. On a conscious level, the dots suggest that
Pound might have written a much longer poem, that he
might have been embarrassingly personal or autobiographical
and that in refraining he has arrived at a more impersonal
and more generally valid form of statement. He has simply
gone at this possible longer poem with a blue pencil or a pair
of scissors, or with the acid of the engraver.

The other function of the dots in *Mauberley* is to
suggest the activities of an unconscious censor. Pound is
indicating that there are subjects which it is painful or difficult, even dangerous, to mention. This reticence is in contrast
to the robust instruction to his poems in *Lustra* : " Go out and
defy opinion " and

Go ! rejuvenate things
Rejuvenate even " The Spectator ".
    Go ! and make cat calls !
Dance and make people blush,
Dance the dance of the phallus
    and tell anecdotes of Cybele !
Speak of the indecorous conduct of the Gods !

(Tell it to Mr. Strachey)

This attitude of " impudence " is never wholly convincing in
Pound and is not long sustained. It has the picaresque quality
which Pound likes in Catullus and Villon ; and it is "cheeky"
after the manner of little boys, with their addiction to the
joking forms of anal-sadism—references to farting and belch-
ing, for example. In certain Cantos, e.g., XIV and XV, dots
are used to express anal obscenity and malice, the " bad "

elements in Pound. But this juvenile (rather than infantile) strain is disowned by Pound in his more adult rôle. In that rôle, as is shown by *Mauberley*, he is closer to Henry James, hyper-æsthetic in his sense of conduct. The interest in Confucius extends the New England ethos. And so Pound, in spite of a resolve to be free and Pagan, is a man of scruples and inhibitions. And he admits this, in his perceptive way, by the dots in *Mauberley*. " I am the child of my time " he says in effect, " There are gaps in me which you, readers of a later generation, will have to fill in." To this extent, Pound's use of the ellipse is a kind of humility in face of the future.

The first Canto ends with a colon, like this :

> Venerandam,
> In the Cretan's phrase, with the golden crown, Aphrodite,
> Cypri munimenta sortita est, mirthful, oricalchi, with golden
> Girdles and breast bands, thou with dark eyelids
> Bearing the golden bough of Argicida. So that :

In my *New Directions* edition the remaining two-thirds of the page are blank so that one can either regard the space as a large-scale ellipse, or else as indicating a kind of continuity with the next Canto. In either case the elliptical construction of *The Cantos* is made clear. Pound often uses freak punctuation to suggest discontinuities and internal spaces within his text. At the end of the second Canto he reverts to dots :

> And we have heard the fauns chiding Proteus
>   in the smell of hay under the olive-trees
> And the frogs singing against the fauns
>   in the half-light.
> And . . .

One of Pound's elliptical devices therefore is simply to leave a phrase or sentence uncompleted. Another is to juxtapose sentences without any apparent logical connection ; take the opening of Canto II :

> Hang it all, Robert Browning,
> there can be but the one " Sordello "
> But Sordello, and my Sordello ?
> Lo Sordels si fo di Mantovana.
> So-shu churned in the sea.

There is a certain syllogistic link between the first four lines of this quotation in which Pound appears to make an ironic assertion of his own right to interpret history, in this case Italian history, and perhaps to have a better right than Robert Browning. In the fifth line, however, we are quite illogically transposed to Chinese mythology. Pound is again expressing his sense of the co-existence of cultures. He must be free, he claims, to switch from Italy to China, and from the past to the present. It is as though he were a kind of demi-urge (So-shu), in whose consciousness (the sea) there appear and disappear fragmentary insights out of all epochs and regions. The very subject-matter of *The Cantos*, taken as a whole, is elliptical in this sense, because one might indeed question why the poet had put together in one poem such apparently disconnected elements. Having stated or implied the connection between monetary theory and æsthetic integrity, he does not argue out the connection fully, but simply refers to both in successive parts of the same poem and leaves the reader to work out a connection if he can.

As well as incomplete sentences, and gaps between sentences, there are within the sentences themselves elliptical tendencies of various degree. There is a simple condensation of syntax :

> And then went down to the ship,
> Set keel to breakers, forth on the godly sea, and
> We set up mast and sail on that swart ship.

Pound often reaches for the inflected texture of Latin and Greek. He likes to leave out pronouns and articles. Sometimes, in imitation of classical drama, he cuts out words in the telegraphic manner :

And I cried in hurried speech :
" Elpenor, how art thou come to this dark coast ?
Cam'st thou afoot, outstripping seamen ?"

And he in heavy speech
" Ill fate and abundant wine. I slept in Circe's ingle.
Going down the long ladder unguarded,
I fell against the buttress,
Shattered the nape-nerve, the soul sought Avernus."

This is elliptical writing as it was understood by classical rhetoricians. It is easy to expand the words " Ill fate and abundant wine " into some such meaning as " I met my death through an accident which befell me when I was drunk ". Such expansions are often necessary in translating classical authors. At other times, the condensation is the sort one gets in a literal translation from Chinese or Japanese where the reader has to construct a syntactical sequence from the series of ideograms, for example, those running down the right-hand margin in the middle of Canto LXXVII. Literally they read, according to Pound :

not
one's own
spirit
and
sacrifice
is
flattery
bi gosh

And he elaborates this into " To sacrifice to a spirit not one's own is flattery (sycophancy)". Fascinated by such exercises in interpretation, Pound frequently lays a kind of trail made out of disconnected words and phrases.

In some cases one can appraise these elliptical effects with certainty, where for example there is compression in the phrase, as in void air taking pelt

a highly economical way of describing the magical appearance out of nothing of the lynxes and leopards summoned by Dionysus. But in other cases, where Pound has left a yawning gap in argument or syntax, it is difficult to prove that the implied statement, and its aura of feeling, is of a poetic order. The gap might simply mean that Pound did not know what to say, or could not say it, or even that there was nothing to be said. The final decision as to whether the empty space does or does not contain a living spirit is very largely a matter of testimony. I can testify to what I find in the poem, but I cannot be sure that others will find it. (Critics as different as F. R. Leavis and C. B. Bowra have found *The Cantos* worthless.)

To me it appears that Pound is bringing to the surface by a process of free association certain elements in the cultural unconscious which are painful and harmful. By so doing, he is enlarging the consciousness of a future age, but he is also provoking mental resistances which are naturally strongest in those who come nearest to his meaning.

In the first Canto, Pound set out on a voyage without knowing where it was going to end. Each Canto is in fact like a psycho-analytical session, probing the cultural unconscious of literature and history. As the analysis proceeds, events are taking place in the outer life of contemporary history and of Pound's personal history and these are referred to. Both in his life and in the poem, Pound is side-tracked. To take one instance, in Cantos IX to XIII, one seems to have got held up. This is explained by the break through in Cantos XIV to XVI of a congeries of "bad" elements which were being repressed. In the process, the poet manifests anxiety and aggression, followed by exhaustion :

> Oblivion,
>   Forget how long,
> Sleep, fainting nausea,

" Whether in Naishapur or Babylon "
I heard in the dream.
　　Plotinus gone,
And the shield tied under me, woke ;
The gate swung on its hinges ;
Panting like a sick dog, staggered,
Bathed in alkali, and in acid.

　　　　blind with the sunlight,
Swollen-eyed, rested,
　　Lids sinking, darkness unconscious.

It turns out that the nightmare that had to be faced was the murderous 1914-18 War, and the revolutions that followed.

Taking the work as a whole, it begins in the first eight Cantos with a simplicity and relatively sparing use of elliptical effects which is not regained. The main ellipse is the actual argument implied *between* the separate Cantos, rather than in them ; in other words, what sort of a story are *The Cantos* telling ? Or what story are they *going* to tell ? Because Pound does not know at the beginning of his poem how it is going to end. He decides, first, on a " descent into hell ", with the objective, later on, of " rising again ", after traversing various hells and purgatories, and perhaps eventually reaching paradise—although to start a poem with a schema whereby final paradise was certain would seem intolerably smug under modern conditions.

Anyone who undertakes an epic is conscious of forerunners. The title which Pound chooses for his poem suggests that the forerunner with whom he first identified himself was Dante. In making this comparison he no doubt had in mind that the *Inferno,* as a poetic hunting ground, has a greater variety than the *Paradiso*. But Dante set out on his progress with a strong faith in his ability to write a long poem which should be as symmetrical as a crystal and in which every facet should shine. Pound sets out with a different faith, or with the faith of no-faith which is characteristic of our own time—like Odysseus setting home for Ithaca, not knowing whether he would get there or what he would find there. More like Odysseus than like Aeneas setting out with a vague promise of later on founding Rome, or begetting its founders. Dante took Virgil as his guide, because of the famous descent into Hell in the fifth book of *The Aeneid* and because in the mediæval thought Virgil was almost Christian, a kind of prophetic link between ancient poetry and catholic faith. All this has little relevance to Pound, who goes back to Homer for the circumstance of his descent into Hell. Canto I is abstracted from the eleventh book of the *Odyssey*, the Nekuia, in which Odysseus summons the spirits of the dead by means of a blood sacrifice. Until nine lines from the end of the Canto, the Homeric original is followed in close paraphrase, though with some condensation, ending at the prophecy of the ghost of Tiresias :

> . . . he strong with the blood, said then : " Odysseus
> Shalt return through spiteful Neptune, over dark seas,
> Lose all companions."

It is with this sense of looking forward to a final homecoming, though after much disaster, that the poem opens. At the time of this beginning, Pound could not have guessed what his own homecoming would be. Already in the second Canto he is another mythological character in another ship, and thereafter the poem is built largely from short passages of paraphrase, quotation and commentary, which (as Pound seems to imply) might lead anywhere. He seems to be adopting a theory of poetic composition, and then discarding it under a more immediate inspiration. When the true afflatus comes, the sails of the ship fill up and the poem gathers momentum. At other times, theory remains for too long a space unqualified by inspiration. Then the poem relapses into prose—as in Canto IX or Canto XXXIII for example—or into passages of the kind of which it is said that " Homer nods ". When Pound begins to feel that this laborious construction has gone on long enough (and it is, after all, a replica of the

#*Charles Madge*

laborious works that make up human civilisation), he throws
in a change of key, as in Canto XXXVI :

> A lady asks me
> I speak in season
> She seeks reason for an effect, wild often
> That is so proud he hath Love for a name

and so on in an ultra-poetic paraphrase which ends :

> Go, song, surely thou mayest
> Whither it please thee
> For so art thou ornate that thy reasons
> Shall be praised from thy understanders,
> With others hast thou no will to make company.

For this ultra-poetry too, then, a place is found, a special
place among the works of men, but the awareness of the
other and more banausic works remains heavy, even in this
Canto, which before it ends has reverted to the imagery of
the tired man of action :

> "And what the hell do I know about dye-works ? ! "
> His Holiness has written a letter :
> "Charles the Mangy of Anjou . . .
> . . . way you treat your men is a scandal . . ."
> Dilectis miles familiaris . . . castra Montis Odorisii
> Montis Sancti Silvestri pallete et pile . . .
> In partibus Thetis . . . vineland
> > land tilled
> > the land incult
> > pratis nemoribus pascuis
> > with legal jurisdiction.

The argument of the poem proceeds more clearly after this
Canto for a while, or rather the argument becomes more
explicitly a political argument about the cultural implications

129

of the different attitudes it is possible to have towards money or currency abstracted from property. The solution of this political problem is in some way necessary before Odysseus can get home—here are his Scylla and Charybdis. And this problem is in some way linked with a more personal one, the problem of Circe (Canto XXXIX) who seduces him. Her magic turns out to be bad magic, but finally she is willing to release him. She is an epitome of the æsthetic and sexual magic of European capitals, but they will not always detain Odysseus from New England Penelope. With a vigorous, even ruthless programme for renovating European culture, Mussolini offers an apparent Phæacia, a resting place neither so Philistine as the U.S. nor so corrupting as Paris or London. Mussolini makes his appearance in Canto XLI. Between this Canto and *The Pisan Cantos* is a long stretch in which the ratio of the laborious to the inspired is rather high. There is an almost complete history of China (Cantos LII-LXI) and a good deal of early U.S. history (Cantos LXII-LXXI). To the criticism that this is excessively didactic, Pound has a poetic answer (Canto XLVI) :

> And if you will say that this tale teaches . . .
> a lesson, or that the Reverend Eliot
> has found a more natural language . . . you who
> think you will
> get through hell in a hurry . . .

The retort is left incomplete, but one is given to understand that the history and the near-economics are to be endured for the good of our souls, because :

> To the cave art thou called, Odysseus,
> By Molü hast thou respite for a little,
> By Molü art thou freed from the one bed
> that thou may'st return to another.
>
> (Canto XLVII.)

In a sense, *The Pisan Cantos* show that Pound's expectation of a Nostos, of a slaughter of the suitors and a regaining of Penelope, was unfulfilled. The other possible end of his epic, the attainment of Paradise, is also ruled out. *The Pisan Cantos*, which Pound wrote in the American prison camp at Pisa, bear the marks of being an emergency poem. The situation was too alarming for Pound to feel quite sure of himself. He must have felt that he was writing against time, cut off from his books and his friends. This deprivation, by making him less cocksure, makes him more human. The quotations may be more inaccurate, the reminiscences more haphazard, than usual. But tested against the severity of his ordeal, the value of these fragments was proved more thoroughly.

The final effect of the Cantos is Shakespearean in the manner of King Lear and the Tempest. But Prospero has not triumphed over his enemies even in fantasy, and the broken accents are those of Lear after the crisis of his madness and humiliation. Yet even in this predicament Pound is able to master his situation poetically and to compose it musically. Long before this, Pound had learnt that the way to purify style and to make it ready for the future is to wrestle with the immanent future in one's own life. When the time came, he was ready.

In these final Cantos, the reader will find that Pound is using the elements of his actual experience and that reality, which had faded from the earlier Cantos, has come back with shattering effect. The poem is shattered and yet the pieces lie side by side in a pattern. It is all ellipse, and yet the poetic continuity is stronger than earlier, more consecutive Cantos. The unifying element is the consciousness of the present, in which every small detail has a historical significance. The human species is personated by the black guards :

> 4 giants at the 4 corners
> three young men at the door
> and they digged a ditch round about me
> lest the damp gnaw thru my bones
>
> (Canto LXXIV)

and those negroes by the clothes-line are extraordinarily
    like the figures del Cossa
Their green does not swear at the landscape
2 months' life in 4 colours

                    (Canto LXXVIII)

      I like a certain number of shades in my landscape
as per/ '' doan' tell no one I made you that table ''
or Whiteside :
        '' ah certainly dew lak dawgs,
          ah goin' tuh wash you ''
(no, not to the author, to the canine unwilling in question)
                    (Canto LXXIX)

There are references to the sky and to a kind of composite
landscape :
                sinceritas
from the death cells in sight of Mt. Taishan @ Pisa
as Fujiyama at Gardone

                    (Canto LXXIV)

As Arcturus passes over my smoke-hole
                    (Canto LXXVII)

[Only shadows enter my tent
      as men pass between me and the sunset]
                    (Canto LXXX)

Most Poundian of all and most expressive of a visible ellipse
are the recurrent allusions to swallows seen perched on tele-
graph wires, which are interpreted by Pound as musical notes
set in the stave :

4 birds on 3 wires, one bird on one
the imprint of the intaglio depends
    in part on what is pressed under it
the mould must hold what is poured into it

in
> discourse
>> what matters is

to get it across e poi basta
> 5 of 'em now on 2 ;
> on 3 ; 7 on 4
>> thus what's his name

and the change in writing the song books
5 on 3 aulentissima rosa fresca

> > > > (Canto LXXIX)

8th day of September
> f   f
>> d
>>> g
>>>> write the birds in their treble scale

Terreus !   Terreus !

> > > > (Canto LXXXII)

the loneliness of death came upon me
> (at 3 P.M., for an instant)   δακρύων
>> ἐντεῦθεν

three solemn half notes
> their white downy chests black-rimmed

on the middle wire
> > periplum

> > > > (Canto LXXXII)

In these passages the figure of the ellipse is pushed to its
extremest point, and they seem to be expressing *through*
style a comment on style and its relation to life, to the actual.
The birds sitting on the wire express visibly and externally
the ellipse in the poet's mind.

THE CANTOS AS EPIC

by D. S. Carne-Ross [*1949*]

The term 'epic' must at least be described, even if it cannot
be defined. It is taken in this essay to mean a long poem on a
major subject. The writer of epic must, like Odysseus, have
" seen the cities of many peoples and known their ways "; he
must present, in some form or other, the most profound and
permanent aspects of human life. The structure can vary
greatly—*The Divine Comedy* is as much epic as the *Iliad* or
Paradise Lost—and the ostensible subject matter is not always a
guide. The *Odyssey*, which might seem to be simply a superb
narrative poem (like *The Ring and the Book*), is epic because
it conveys what may be called the archetypal significance of
Odysseus' adventures so profoundly that they have a permanent symbolic relevance to human experience in all times
and all places. The *Orlando Furioso*, on the other hand, is not
epic, for in spite of its wide range of theme it lacks the epic
depth and comprehension.

Pound's earlier poetry gives no obvious indication that he
was going to devote the greater part of his life to the " poem
of some length " which is *The Cantos*. Its inspiration is
extremely literary and suggests that the author has responded
to the styles of a great many different poets rather than looked
very deeply into men's minds or very widely at their actions.
Even in *Mauberley*, where he is dealing with a non-literary
event like the first world war, his response remains very partial
and secluded ; he was enraged by this maniacal combustion
which interrupted the free exchange of the arts and killed some
of his best friends, and though this led him to attempt some
evaluation of the civilisation on which he had been con-
tentedly pasturing until then, he was still chiefly concerned
with the cultural milieu and with his own problems as a poet.
Moreover, his early poems are very fragmentary ; most of
them are short—the Imagist discipline which Pound did much
to propagate incited to brevity—and even when they are
longer, they are usually composed in a series of brief spurts.

And yet we know that he was planning an epic poem some-

where before 1909 for in *Scriptor Ignotus*, a little known poem
from the volume *Personæ* which appeared in that year, he
makes his "unknown poet" speak of the moment when

> That great sense of power is upon me
> And I see my greater soul-self bending
> Sibylwise with that great forty year epic
> That you know of, yet unwrit. . . .

Re-reading the *Selected Poems* with this clue in mind, we can
see in what sense they represent Pound's 'incammination'
towards *The Cantos*. Homer is described in a Greek epigram as
"the ageless voice of the whole world", and in some form or
other this must be the description of every epic poet. It seems
eminently inapplicable to Pound until we reflect that in his
numerous 'dramatic lyrics', however thin and literary
they may look beside Browning's monologues, what
Pound is doing is *learning to become a voice* with which other
men may speak. And even when he is writing about his
ordinary young-mannish feelings, he lacks the romantic note
of unrestrained subjective immediacy which such subjects
usually incite. He is interested in his experiences, not simply
because they happen to him, but because they are the material
for poetry. The distinction is important and accounts for the
general disinterest in his work. To those who can only conceive of poetry as an intensely personal commentary on the
writer's tormented subjectivity, Pound has seemed as dull
and external as a Greek statue. Yet it is precisely this quality
which characterises most of the major poetry of the past—
which, of course, explains why it is now unread.

Nowhere is this epic ascesis more apparent than in what
Eliot has called the "steady effort towards the construction of
a style of speech"[1] which can be studied in the *Selected Poems*.
By the time he came to write *The Cantos*, his style "stopped
changing because it had attained its form", one that could be
lyrical, narrative, didactic or merely informatory, as occasion

1. *Selected Poems*, p. 14.

demanded, and could accommodate the most diverse material without losing its rhythmic line.

Most people would admit this, but they would say that the creation of a style is only half the problem, since the poet is not merely a maker but also a seer. It has been generally felt that *The Cantos* have no subject sufficiently extensive to demand the vast proportions of epic. We know that Pound wanted to write a big poem ; but what was his poem to be about ?

The choice of a subject is a difficult problem in an age which possesses no body of accepted familiar stories and no coherent system of beliefs. It is common to express this by saying that we have no great contemporary myth which unifies experience for us; but this is not quite true for, in the disintegration of Western civilisation, we possess a myth which is very fertile and all too contemporary. Pound has inevitably handled it, but he wisely decided that its extended treatment was best left to the practitioners of the Inner Gaze. In its place, he has chosen a myth which occurs in every Alexandrian age and is very potent in our own ; it may be called (somewhat ponderously) syncretistic universalism. With the dissolution of regional systems and beliefs, men's eyes range over wide horizons in the effort to discover in distant times and places what they have lost at home ; and they are led by their artists and thinkers who endeavour to construct new systems out of the most diverse materials. Anthropologists have familiarised us with the myths of all mankind, Jungian psychology has taught us that a twentieth century Londoner, an ancient Sumerian and a South Sea Islander may all repeat in their unconscious minds certain age-old world-wide patterns or archetypes, historians like Toynbee attempt to offer us a vision of all history, and journalists like Wells do the same thing on a cheaper level. Nothing less than everything will satisfy our imagination, and even the politicians, usually way behind the times, have to pretend that they are thinking in terms of the whole human race.

Did the modish public but know it, *The Cantos* are as

" contemporary ", as much " in the movement " as could be desired. Pound has called his poem " the tale of the tribe ", and the description is helpful, so far as it goes, for the subject of *The Cantos* is no less than " all history ", " all myth ", without distinction of time or place. His theme, stated at its widest, is a version of the struggle of light and darkness ; more specifically, it is the way in which the Good Life is thwarted or realised. And since every vision of history must have its special angle, he has chosen the action of money upon the affairs of men.

Pound believes that criticism should avoid general discussion and proceed by the " examination of exhibits ", so it will be as well at this point to turn to the poem itself. *A Draft of XXX Cantos* begins with a translation of some sixty lines from book eleven of the *Odyssey* which deal with Odysseus' descent to hell. To start an original poem with a long passage of translation may seem unusual but it serves a number of purposes : it presents Odysseus, one of the principal *personæ*, or characters ; it states the theme of the descent into hell and the sea-voyage, both central to the poem ; and, more dubiously, it perhaps seeks to indicate the classical culture of the Renaissance, since the translation is made not from the original Greek but from a Latin version by one Andreas Divus Justinopolitanus, published in 1538. Canto II opens with a series of references : to Browning, one of Pound's formative enthusiasms and the author of a poem about Sordello who is a type of the poet passionately concerned with contemporary politics ; to Eleanor of Aquitaine—grand-daughter of Guillaume of Aquitaine, the Provençal poet-prince who is to appear again later ; and to Helen of Troy who in turn gives way to Homer ; having briefly stated a series of themes which he will develop later, Pound devotes the rest of the Canto to a full statement of another theme, that of the transformation wrought by Dionysus on a voyage to Naxos. The passage is an adaptation of the third book of Ovid's *Metamorphoses*.

Canto III, after a brief allusion to Pound's youthful days

in Venice (a theme which reappears in *The Pisan Cantos*), introduces the Mediterranean theme :—

> Gods float in the azure air
> Bright gods and Tuscan, back before dew was shed.
> Light : and the first light, before ever dew was fallen.

This Mediterranean background is felt behind the whole poem, wherever the action may range. It is one of Pound's indisputable glories that in an era given over to Grendelian darkness he has set his scene so firmly beneath the splendours of the Mediterranean sun.

Canto IV opens with a beautiful passage which would be in every anthology were it printed as a separate poem, and then proceeds to develop the Greek-Provence relation with a pair of parallel figures, Itys and Cabestan, who were both eaten, and Actæon and Vidal who were both chased by dogs. The whole Canto shows Pound's writing at its finest : the rapidly changing scenes are presented without narrative or syntactical sequence in a series of clear, visual images.

So far there has been nothing which should very much puzzle the perceptive reader of good will, *provided that he does not obstruct his reception by asking why theme follows theme as it does*. His task is simply to receive. But the next Canto is more perplexing and seems at first sight to be merely a patchwork of beautiful or incomprehensible fragments. The city of Ecbatan appears for a moment, melts into memories of Neoplatonic philosophy which in turn gives way to adaptations from Sappho and Catullus ; a fine piece of writing follows about a Guillaume de Poicebot, one of Pound's numerous Provençal figures, then the scene moves on to Renaissance Florence with Varchi and the Cinquecento Medici. It is Cantos like this (and there are all too many of them) which have led to the belief that Pound's work is hopelessly " obscure ". All modern poetry is supposed to be obscure, but the Cantos are generally considered to carry this obscurity to impossible extremes. Many excellent people avoid them on the grounds that their perusal requires an erudition and perceptiveness far beyond anything they possess. A distinction needs to be made : obscurity of the emotion or concept (such as we find in Eliot, for example) hardly occurs in Pound, and in fact it might well be argued that *The Cantos* are insufficiently obscure, or subtle, to deal with so vast and varied a theme. What there is in Pound's poem is obscurity of reference. In a period without a common inheritance of myth or legend this is in a sense inevitable, and a great deal of difficulty could be cleared away by an adequate commentary. Take the first passage that comes to hand, the opening of Canto VI :

> What you have done, Odysseus,
>> We know what you have done. . . .
> And that Guillaume sold out his ground rents
> (Seventh of Poitiers, Ninth of Aquitain).
>> ' Tant las fotei com auzirets
>> Cen e quatre vingt e veit vetz. . . . '
> The stone is alive in my hands, the crops
>> will be thick in my death year. . . .

At first sight this may seem very confusing, yet even the most modest commentary can remove much of the difficulty. The opening lines mean that the Odysseus theme (descent into hell, sea-voyage) has already been presented ; they may also mean that the *Odyssey* is, or should be, common knowledge so that the actions of Odysseus are familiar to everyone. Guillaume of Aquitaine, who was prepared for by the reference to Eleanor in Canto II, takes over from Odysseus in line 3. It is a basic principle of *The Cantos* that all related characters can merge, or melt, into one another. (See page 149.) His action in selling out the ground rents is perhaps meant to show the just ruler pursuing a just monetary policy. The Provençal couplet which follows (it comes from the fifth of his poems in Jeanroy's edition, and could be rendered : " Tellement je les foutus, comme vous l'entendrez, cent quatre-vingt-huit fois ") shows another side of the Poundian " hero ". The

poem from which the quotation is taken is an indecorous
affair which relates how Guillaume once spent eight days
incognito with two noble ladies who, having satisfied themselves that he was dumb, encouraged him to have his way with
them to the prodigious extent indicated in the couplet. The
original context is light-hearted but the lines which follow in
the Canto ("the crops will be thick in my death year") show
that Pound's subject is much more profound, namely the
ancient religious conception of the king as a semi-divine being
upon whose potency, in every sense, the whole life of nature
depends. The king's exuberant sexuality, which is related to
the fertility of nature, is traditional, and is religious in origin ;
his sacrificial death is an even more familiar theme. The words
"the stone is alive in my hands", (in prose, "I encourage a
sound architectural style") point to the societal as against
the religious aspect of the just ruler, and involve Pound's
belief that good art can only occur in a non-usurious society.
"*With usura*", he writes in Canto XLV, "stone cutter is kept
from his stone", and again "Came no church of cut stone
signed : *Adamo me fecit.*" These lines present in a very com-
pressed form a many-faceted image of the Poundian hero,
seen as ruler of his people.

I have dealt with this passage at some length because it
illustrates the kind of obscurity to be found in *The Cantos* :
an obscurity of historical or cultural reference which can only
be elucidated by encyclopædic knowledge or an exhaustive
labour of commentary. It is not Pound's fault that he has not
got a body of known material at his disposal (though nothing
prevented him from making his references a little more appre-
hensible); and it is not the reader's fault that he is not familiar
with the history and culture of a dozen countries.

The limits of the present essay obviously make it impossible
to continue so detailed a commentary, although it is this,
rather than general discussion, that *The Cantos* most require.
However, it is essential to touch on a few more of the most
important themes in the first thirty. Cantos VIII-XI, dealing
with Sigismondo Malatesta, ruler of Rimini in the middle of

the fifteenth century, a man who has been taken as an extreme instance of the "many-sided Renaissance personality", show the Poundian historical method to advantage. Instead of attempting to offer a unified picture of Renaissance civilisation he presents it in the form of a composite image, consisting of a number of scenes taken from the life of one of its typical figures. XIII, the Confucian Canto, introduces another central theme and is in itself a singularly beautiful piece of writing. Just as XLV, the Usura Canto, explains and connects the numerous economic passages, so the Confucian Canto is intended to elucidate the Chinese component which is treated at length in Cantos LII-LXI. Cantos XIV and XV deal with the Poundian Hell which lodges the various sorts of perverts who have indulged their particular deviation from the human norm. A number of different vices are castigated —or a number of Pound's hatreds are aired; a hell that awaits lady golfers and is especially prepared for the English cannot be said to be impartial—but the root of evil in Pound's system is monetary, and the most despicably damned are the usurers.[1]

Space does not permit a more extended analysis of *XXX Cantos,* but even so bald a summary should serve to indicate the richness and the apparent incoherence of the material. Certain guiding "lines", or themes, appear, and certain characters belonging to widely separated eras clearly correspond to one another, but it is not apparent why they appear in the order they do. None the less, poetic vitality is sufficiently sustained to make the reader suspend his judgment and await enlightenment from the Cantos to come. The fact that this is exactly what has not happened, and that for every hundred people who know something about Eliot's poetry there is hardly one who knows anything about Pound's, is a damaging indictment of contemporary taste.

It would be pleasant to be able to continue on a note of ringing denunciation, but unhappily it is not possible to do so, for the expectations aroused by the first volume are sadly

1. Pound has even managed to convince himself that Dante's Hell is of this sort. V. *Polite Essays*, p. 42.

disappointed by the second, *A Draft of Cantos XXXI-XLI*. The primary objection to it is simply that it is extremely dull. In an age when people look to literature (or at least to " highbrow " literature) for what was formerly given them by religion, the use of such an adjective will seem shallow and irrelevant, but the fact remains, as Eliot has quietly pointed out, that " the first—and not one of the least difficult —requirements of either prose or verse is that it should be interesting ".[1]

These new Cantos deal primarily with American economic and social history. Whether or not this is intrinsically less adapted to poetry than the material Pound used before I will not attempt to discuss, but the indisputable fact, which can be discovered by opening the book almost anywhere, is that the poetic vitality of the writing has markedly diminished. This is a very different matter from the occasional dull passage which occurs in every long poem. The trouble with these Cantos is that for page after page Pound is content simply to versify " images " or fragmentary pieces of information from the period he is seeking to present. Whether or not they are important in themselves (and it is often very hard to believe that they are) need not for the present concern us, what matters is that they shall be felt into poetry, and again and again Pound has simply not done this. The method of writing which appears to such advantage in the Sigismundo Cantos here signally fails, and we are led to reflect that what counts is not the method, or theory, but the quality of the writing itself.

Similar objections apply to the first twenty pages of the third volume, *The Fifth Decad of Cantos,* which deals chiefly with the economic history of seventeenth and eighteenth century Italy, and to the fourth volume, Cantos LII-LXXI, which is concerned with Chinese and American history. The method is the same as before: Pound chooses a series of supposedly significant moments on which to concentrate, presumably hoping that although in isolation they may convey

[1] *Selected Essays,* p. 418.

nothing, or next to nothing, their total effect will be to build up in the reader's mind a vision, or image, of the period more complete and vital than that given by ordinary historical studies.

The reader who is not familiar with the periods Pound is covering is likely to be completely at sea, so seemingly capricious is the choice of " significant moments " and so various the range of references; while the historian will wonder if the normal way of writing history is not both clearer and more interesting. The ordinary historical book proceeds by means of narrative and exposition; what it lacks in vividness it makes up for by coherence. Pound abandons coherence but all too often he does not achieve vividness, which is not surprising since for the most part he is simply versifying passages from various historians. To take an example, it is extremely hard to see what kind of poetical life Pound believes to be inherent in a passage like the following (which is no better and no worse than a score of others) :

Towards sending of Ellsworth
and the pardon of Fries
25 years in office, treaties put thru and loans raised
and General Pinckney, a man of honour,
declined to participate
        or even to give suspicion of having colluded
deficiency in early moral foundations
                    (Mr. Hamilton's)
they effect here and there simple manners
            true religion, morals, here flourish
            i.e. Washington 4th March 1801 . . .
                        (LXIII)

Has Pound forgotten his injunction " Do not re-tell in mediocre verse what has already been done in good prose "?[1] Possibly American historians are poor stylists.

How is the reader supposed to react to this tangle of history and economics? I believe that the only possible

1. *Make it new*, p. 337.

approach is the exact opposite of that required by the best
poetry. A pair of examples will be enough to suggest the
right and wrong way of turning history into poetry. The first
example comes from *Paradise Lost* and deals with the building
of Pandemonium, which Milton describes by one of his
characteristic negative similes :

> Not *Babilon*,
> Nor great *Alcairo* such magnificence
> Equal'd in all thir glories, to inshrine
> *Belus* or *Serapis* thir Gods, or seat
> Thir Kings, when *Ægypt* with *Assyria* strove
> In wealth and luxurie.
>
> *(Paradise Lost,* I, 717 ff.)

The second comes from one of Pound's Chinese Cantos :

> For three hundred years, four hundred, nothing
> quiet.
> WALL rose in the time of TSIN CHI
> TCHEOU lasted eight centuries and then TSIN
> came
> and of TSIN was CHI HOANG TI that united
> all China . . .   (LIV)

Allowing for all the obvious differences in style, subject
and intention, what distinguishes these two passages is that
Milton has realised his subject so completely that further
information, from Verity or elsewhere, would only add dis-
tracting detail to an already completed picture ; Pound, on
the other hand, simply informs us that a wall was built—
presumably it is the famous one, but in spite of the capital
letters his reference leaves the image of the wall which we
already have in our minds quite unqualified. About the
Tcheou, and the various personages mentioned, we are told
nothing, so their effect on our minds and imagination is nil.
For enlightenment, we must refer to a book of Chinese
history.

In the light of Pound's frequent failure to turn the historical component of *The Cantos* into poetry, it may be profitable to compare his definition, or description, of epic as "a poem including history"[1] with Johnson's statement that "History must supply the writer (of epic) with the rudiments of narration, which he must improve and exalt by a nobler art, must animate by dramatic energy. . . ."[2] It is not unfair to say that the difference between the two passages quoted above is that Milton's *animates* history while Pound's merely *includes* it. The distinction is a capital one.

The reader may be inclined to attribute the failure of this part of *The Cantos* to the prevalence of an "unpoetic" subject like economics ; but this is an error, since anything that can passionately engage the human spirit is potential material for poetry. Pound himself settles the matter once and for all in Canto XLV where his sustained economic passion creates a passage of magnificent eloquence. But unhappily much more typical of his "economic poetry" is the almost unreadable accumulation of monetary information which we find in Canto XLII—to take one example out of many. What these Cantos show is not that economics is an "unpoetical" subject, but rather that Pound has not gone the right way about putting economics into verse. He should have left this mass of facts and figures—the mere raw material of his economic convictions—in the "red leather note-book" he refers to in Canto LXXXVIII and brought to his poem only the refined metal. But Pound has always had the unhappy conviction that anything he has ever read is somehow inherently significant.

Two possible objections may be made against this criticism. The first is that it would be dishonest to present one's conclusions (i.e. Canto XLV) without first presenting one's evidence (Canto XLII); but this is to equate the poet with the economist and to forget that the *poetic truth* of the Usura Canto is demonstrated by the quality of the writing.[3]

1. *Make it new*, p. 19.
2. *Life of Milton.*
3. "A . . . theory which has entered into poetry is established, for its truth or falsity in one sense ceases to matter, and its truth in another sense is proved." T. S. Eliot, *Selected Essays*, pp. 274-5.

The second objection is that I am overlooking the in-evitable co-existence of lesser and greater levels of intensity in a long poem. But it must first be demonstrated that the bulk of Pound's economic verse possesses any poetic intensity at all.

A further, more radical objection to the whole critical approach of the last few pages suggests itself. No long poem, it may be said, can be judged by the isolated literary beauty of this or that part, since the parts cannot be understood until they are seen in relation to the whole. And so far, very little effort has been made to grasp *The Cantos* in their totality.

Such a criticism has its obvious truth, but unless handled very carefully it is liable to turn into a reversal of the proper critical procedure. A passage of verse—whether it is complete in itself or simply an extract from a larger work—must be judged primarily by its purely literary qualities. Only when it has been found satisfactory by these standards does it become necessary to examine the materials which have gone to its making or the statement which it may seem to be enunciating. It is utterly untrue to say that the parts of the *Divine Comedy* or *Paradise Lost* are only significant in relation to, and because of, the theme of the whole poem. They are intensely (though of course only partially) significant in themselves, and when they are not so it is because Dante or Milton are for the moment writing badly. It would be truer to say that the whole—that is, the theological and cosmo-gonical system implied—is only poetically significant be-cause of, or in relation to, the parts. To try to reclaim all the pages of aridity or tiresomely fragmented information which *The Cantos* contain by commentary and reference, and then to assert that the poem as a whole is important because the material it contains or the *Weltanschauung* it advances are important, is a reversal of the true critical procedure. It is far better to face the fact that for long sections of *The Cantos* Pound has simply failed in his poet's job.

The Pisan Cantos, written when Pound was in a military detention camp at the end of the war, solve certain problems and raise others. They show that he had lost none of his technical skill and that his lyrical vein was as beautiful as ever. And what is even more important, they reveal an awareness, both of himself and of life in general, of which the earlier Cantos gave no sign. Sometimes it issues in moments of self-examination, like

> Tard, très tard, je t'ai connue, la Tristesse,
> I have been hard as youth sixty years.   (p. 105.)

or

> J'ai eu pitié des autres
> probablement pas assez, and at moments that
> suited my own convenience.   (pp.44-5.)

sometimes in general statements like

> nothing matters save the quality of the affection

or   (p. 51)

> filial, fraternal affection is the root of humane-
> ness.   (p. 21.)

This new note is all to the good and does something to supplement the deficiencies of the preceding Cantos, but it does not say much for Pound's spiritual development that he had to be put in the death cells to discover what other poets have known all along : that human affairs cannot be profoundly contemplated without a great sense of pity and that life cannot be profoundly conceived except in terms of tragedy. Surely some realisation of these truths should have reached him during the long years at Rapallo when he was jauntily or furiously versifying history and economics. Perhaps it did, but if so, it failed to get into his poetry.

The personal note in *The Pisan Cantos* is not due to an access of self-pity, and is perfectly consistent with the scheme of the whole poem. Pound himself was always one of the

personæ of his own poem and it is quite logical that his
experiences at Pisa should provide him with material for one
of his main themes, that of the just man suffering in his
struggle for the Good Life (as Pound conceives it). It is not
the theme but the way he handles it which is objectionable.
It takes the form of a gigantic monologue in which the various
events of his life are presented against the background of the
military prison at Pisa. The earlier Cantos passed rapidly
from one theme to another, but he usually developed each
theme sufficiently to allow it to stand coherently on its own.
In *The Pisan Cantos*, however, he breaks up his material into
a succession of tiny fragments; almost the whole volume
consists of a stream of partial reminiscences, many of which
are so trivial in themselves—not to mention being often
incomprehensible to those who have not moved in Pound's
entourage for the last thirty years or so—that it is hard to
see how he can possibly achieve his purpose, which is presumably to present a composite picture of the *mœurs du siècle*.
The final effect is simply that of an old man wandering at
random through his memories, which is a very different thing
from the seemingly artless but in fact strictly controlled flow
of mental images which we find, for example, in Mrs. Bloom's
monologue in *Ulysses*.

The fact that *The Pisan Cantos* so clearly fail in spite of the
poetical powers which Pound has lavished on them suggests
that it may be his method which is at fault. This impressive
failure invites an examination of the structural principle
underlying the whole poem. Pound has rejected coherent
architectonics in favour of a system which, it has been suggested, approximates to that of the Chinese ideogram. However this may be, the poem is in fact built up out of a series
of " themes " varying greatly in length and nature and usually
recurring, which melt into one another according to some
logic of the emotions which is to be apparent when the whole
work is finished. The most important of them is probably that
of the sea-voyage, or Periplus, the main developments of
which are the voyages of Odysseus to hell in Canto I, of

Niccolò III of Este to the Holy Land in XXIV, and of the
Carthaginian Hanno along the West Coast of Africa in XL.
Another main theme is that of the artist's position in society:
Cantos VIII and XXI show Sigismundo and Jefferson playing the part of the enlightened patron; Cantos XXV and
XXVI present the artist (Titian and Mozart) in relation to
society—a theme which the victory of the Allied Armies
gave Pound the chance of treating at length in *The Pisan
Cantos*. Canto XLV relates all these passages to each other
and to Pound's conviction that art can only flourish in a just,
non-usurious society. Another major theme is provided by a
series of key figures, like Odysseus, Sigismundo, Guillaume
d'Aquitaine, Jefferson, Adams and Pound himself, who are
all related to each other—are indeed one composite character
—by virtue of possessing more energy and vision than the
common run of men who surround them :

> Being more live than they, more full of flames and
> voices.[1]   (VII)

A theme may also consist of a single statement ("to redeem
Zion with justice/said Isaiah. Not out on interest said David
Rex" LXXIV), of an image ("In the gloom the gold/Gathers
the light about it" XVII) or of some pivotal quotation
("Pollon d'anthropon iden" XII).

At a deeper level, the poem is inspired by certain general
doctrines, sometimes defined negatively, as in the hell Cantos,
sometimes positively, as in the Confucian; they are intended
to be seen "in action" in the various historical sections. These
doctrines do not admit of very precise definition, and there is
force in Mr. Watts' objection that Pound's good is less intensely conceived than his evil.[2] However, we can see that
they include the Confucian teaching on order and the mean;
they are concerned with the Good Life as it is lived on this
earth and as it presents itself to the five senses and the intellect;

1. The whole passage—one of the finest Pound ever wrote—should be studied.
Cf. also the reference to Odysseus, " the live man among duds " in *Polite
Essays*, p. 45.
2. *Philosopher at Bay*, H. W. Watts, CRONOS, March 1948, p. 16.

they demand a respect for the natural rhythms and, above all, a social order that does not permit the various monetary practices which Pound describes as usurious.

A very detailed line-by-line study of the whole poem would be needed to show how these various binding elements operate, and until this study has been made it may seem premature to attempt a final judgment (particularly since the poem is not finished). None the less, the fact remains that whatever unity and coherence Pound's interests may possess within his mind, the general impression which *The Cantos* give is one of chaos. The absence of architectonics could have been made good by a very rigorous use of the binding elements which he has allowed himself, but unfortunately he has employed his links very sparingly. A single half-phrase, repeated hundreds of pages later, is a most inadequate way of relating two passages. Moreover, even when the links are perceived, they resemble stray grappling lines thrown from ships vaguely drifting by in the night, rather than true principles of unification.

A further difficulty is the sequence in which the themes occur. For example, various sea-voyages are described in the poem, but would it matter if Hanno's voyage preceded instead of following Niccolò's? Would it matter if any incident occurred in a slightly different place? Would it even matter if in a new edition of the poem a careless printer were to transpose a few pages or even alter the order of entire Cantos?

Until some extremely convincing Poundian exegesis has been performed, the answer to all these questions must, I believe, be negative. Pound has written in praise of order, but he has signally failed to achieve it. And he has rather given the show away by suggesting that something called " texture " may be at least as important as form.[1] The difficulty is that texture must be uniformly good if you are going to rely on it. Milton, writing within a powerfully constructed framework, can afford to nod a little every now and then, but Pound has to be at his best all the time. Unfortunately, much of the texture of Cantos XXXI-LXXI is such that it

1. In *Polite Essays*, pp. 75-6.

could only pass muster if it were seen in relation to some extremely compelling theme.

I believe that the method of *The Cantos* is radically mistaken and that Pound has tried in vain to work against the structure of the mind by requiring it to hold in pleasurable solution an almost indefinite sequence of partially or totally unrelated parts until the final moment when they are to cohere in one vast world-picture. It is not even clear what he hopes to gain by such a method of writing, or why he could not have devised some structural principle which did violence neither to his distrust of Aristotelian architectonics nor to the mind's inherent desire for order.

And yet in art no catalogue of faults need ever spell total failure; Dickens is the obvious instance of a writer who again and again wrests victory out of the jaws of seeming defeat. *The Cantos* could still succeed if their cumulative effect was of some great vision embracing all experience and all knowledge, past and present : for this is the function of epic and alone justifies its vast proportions.

Pound's theme, it has been suggested, is the struggle of light and darkness, of good and evil, of the values expressed in Canto XIII against those expressed in Cantos XIV-XV; but the point to be determined is the form which this struggle takes. Since the poem may be going to finish with a paradiso, we cannot fully define its good, but it is unlikely to differ radically from the good Pound has presented before. This has always been primarily a naturalistic good in which a just social order, care for the arts, " brotherly deference " and " filial, fraternal humaneness " take the place of an interest in " life after death " or such unsatisfactory mystical matters. His good is excellent but never radical. And his evil is of the same sort. Primarily monetary, issuing in usury and the corruption of the will which usury produces, it gives no hint of the existence of permanent essential Evil underlying this or that manifestation.[1] And yet the Vision of Evil is perhaps the

1. See the penetrating criticism of Pound's hell in T. S. Eliot's *After Strange Gods*, pp. 42-3.

most searching test of a writer's quality. "What theme had Homer but original sin?" Yeats asked. What theme has all the most profound literature, of the past and present? But it does not appear in *The Cantos*.

Their fundamental weakness is that they do not show any real religious comprehension. Lacking it, Pound has not been able to dispose of sufficiently powerful forces to move a mighty poem; he presents a vision of the good, which does not satisfy our deepest demands, checked and thwarted by an evil which is never radical enough. Thus the aspiration towards the good is not heroic; and the failure to realise it is not tragic. The one is simply admirable, the other deplorable, but it is with stronger meat that the great poets of this or any other day have fed us. A further consequence of Pound's failure in religious awareness is that it deprives his poem of the one element which might have bound it together into a satisfying whole, in spite of all the structural faults. The poet who works at a sufficiently profound level may be able to say, or rather to make the reader feel, that

> . . . whether in Argos or England
> There are certain inflexible laws,
> Unalterable, in the nature of music.

and that consequently distinctions of time and place do not matter. But this synoptic vision Pound does not possess, and its absence is all the more unfortunate since on the plane on which he moves distinctions of time and place do matter; hence his transitions from Greek myth to Provençal legend, or from ancient China to modern America, do not affect us as anything deeper than a literary device which permits him to compose poetry about the various subjects which interest him.

This critique of *The Cantos* is offered as no more than a prelude to the more adequate evaluations which the present revival of interest in Pound should bring about. Criticism has dealt so inadequately with him in the past that even his faults

—let alone his virtues—have not been properly recognised. Future critics may or may not endorse the view proposed in this essay, which is that in attempting so ambitious a work as *The Cantos* Pound has over-rated his powers, but has nevertheless written some of the finest poetry of our time. What matters is not that there should be agreement, but that the relevant texts should be examined. It is also desirable that those who wish to see Pound's work justly appreciated should not overstate their case, for in so doing they will merely win him a temporary notoriety at the cost of an even deeper subsequent neglect.

POET'S POET

by Ronald Duncan [*1950*]

". . . for the language of the great poets was regulated by form—whereas the rest merely wrote at haphazard."
—Dante : " De Vulgari Eloquio."

Many young men acquire a temporary taste for poetry whilst they are at the university; but it was almost my experience to lose my interest in literature whilst I was at Cambridge, although I had gone up there with the sole intention of reading it. If it had not been for Dr. Leavis, I should not have stayed a month. He had told me not to bother with half the Tripos lectures; but even those few I did attend bored me. My natural impatience soon turned to disgust with that academic approach to literature; the respect which is due to the dead, but is nothing to do with the living. It all smelt of the morgue. And even when the lecturer clambered out from his bog of dates, it was only to collapse into a mire of irrelevant biographical detail concerning dead poets' dead dogs. So concerned were they with the lives of the poets that a poem was seldom mentioned, and then only as an opportunity for glossary grubbing; or, as a point of departure towards some facetious speculation on whether the poem had been written at the foot or the summit of Mont Blanc.

I see that my Tripos notes on the Restoration poets contain the astounding information that Rochester died of syphilis or drink or both. But the lecturer had omitted to mention that the poet had written any lyrics. . . . The *Satire on Man* was dismissed with the comment "influenced by Boileau".

As others can confirm, the lecturers seldom mentioned a poem and, when they did, they seemed only concerned with talking about what the poem was about and never a word on *How* it was written.

There was not a single lecture on prosody. Nobody mentioned metre or method.

After wasting a year in this fashion, I could recount the names and addresses of Donne's mistresses but knew nothing

about the development of the Sonnet. . . . It was like an
Academy of Music in which nobody had bothered to learn their
notation and knew nothing of the range of an instrument. I
told Leavis that, unless he would give me some personal super-
vision outside the Tripos Curriculum, I would send myself
down from the University. He readily agreed to do this; and,
as soon as the aspiring literary detectives had left with their
notebooks packed with clues, he took me out to his orchard
and read a poem to me. It was *Hugh Selwyn Mauberley*.

My interest revived from that moment. Although this poem
had been written twenty years previously, it had not yet been
noticed by the Curators of Petty Cury. But why had I not
found it for myself? I suppose that all revolutionaries are
embarrassed by their disciples. Certainly, the Imagist Movement was profoundly misunderstood. I had read the imitators
of Pound and Eliot and, disgusted with their formless,
maudlin confessions and subjective hosannas, had not been
encouraged to seek the originals themselves. I now realised
that " vers libre " was not as free as Richard Aldington made
it; and that Pound and Eliot's revolution was, in the true
sense of the word, a turning back to a concern with the technical side of verse which made Tennyson look like a gifted
amateur.

For me, *Mauberley* was not only the key to contemporary
sensibility but the model for controlled expression contained
within the confines of a form.

And I still believe that it, and Canto LXXXI, are Pound's
highest achievements. It is a masterpiece of ironic understatement; its superb concision makes it a great tragic poem—a
tragedy without rhetoric. There is little, including dramatic
verse proper, which can compare with this in intensity.

How is his intensity obtained? One cannot analyse what is
only achieved by way of synthesis. But one can say that if ever
a poem were made by craft, here it is. The texture is tight
because the woof runs across the warp; that is, the rhythm
of the line runs against the verse-structure and *not* with it.

155

Knowing my coat has never been
Of precisely the fashion
To stimulate, in her,
A durable passion ;

If the rhythm ran with the verse structure, as Swinburne
would have written it, urbanity and ironity would be lost ;
and a mere sentimental nostalgia achieved—however much
the words "precisely" and "durable" do, of themselves,
objectify the experience.

It is not what the poem says that gives it this edge ; but
what it refrains from saying. And the content is always in
counterpoint, a method which, of course, makes the Cantos
almost an inevitable development from *Mauberley*.

Sometime after reading *Mauberley*, I sent Pound a post-
card. He invited me to enroll myself at the one man university
of Rapallo—for how many has he not done as much? The
essential seriousness and concern for literature which both
Pound and Eliot have can be gauged by the amount of
patience they show in teaching the very young.

Pound offered to be both Chancellor and lecturer and, to
these duties, I recall, two other were added : that of a bursar
who paid the pupil's fees—and proctor. . . .

(I remember arriving at Rapallo about 2 a.m. and, realising
that the hour was slightly unsuitable for calling at Pound's
flat, I approached a porter at the station and asked him to
direct me to an hotel. He pointed to a light about a couple of
hundred yards away. Feeling very tired after a long train
journey I went straight to this place and asked for a room.
An old crone led me upstairs. I thought she was asking me if
I wished to be called in the morning ; I replied that I did. My
Italian has never been very good. The proprietress lit a small
lamp ; I surveyed an enormous bed and was soon fast asleep.

But after a few minutes, I was awakened by the noise of the
door opening. A girl stood there—I immediately assumed that
the old crone had mistaken the hour at which I had asked to be
called, so I simply turned over and tried to sleep again. As I

was dozing off I recalled how inadequately the maid who had just woken me had been dressed. No doubt, I thought, she has now gone back to bed, too. I suppose I slept for another hour when I had a strange dream. The room now seemed full of some half dozen almost naked women who stood around in the most grotesque attitudes. But, eventually, these phantoms disappeared after lolling about my bed.

When I awoke—without being called at all—I remembered the fantastic figures of the night and dismissed my dream as beneath contempt. I hurried round to Pound's flat and, after a suitable time had elapsed, summoned up the courage to ask him if he could lend me the money to pay my hotel bill.

"Where did you stay?" he asked. "I'll send the money round."

"At some small hotel near the station," I replied, "but I can't recall its name."

"There isn't an hotel near there," he remarked, "so there's nothing for it but for you to take me to it."

We walked round there.

"This is the place," I said, recognising the door. Ezra raised his eyebrows imperceptibly and stalked in and paid the bill. I remained outside.

"Do you always put up at brothels?" he asked, giving me the change. It was then that I realised that the only curious thing about my dream was that it had not been a dream at all.

Ezra taught me more in one day than I had learned in a year at Cambridge. The practise of apprenticeship should be revived. He began by reading to me Guido Cavalcanti's canzone :—

> Donna mi priegha
> > perch'i volglio dire
> D'un accidente
> > che sovente
> > > e fero
> Ed è si altero
> > ch'è chiamato amore. . . .

He then gave me the book as a present. There was I with an Honours degree in English literature and I'd never even heard of Cavalcanti—let alone become aware of the form of a canzone. And, like many other student graduates at Rapallo, I have continued to have, as it were, a post graduate course by postcards from the Chancellor.

Only last week one arrived. It read : " Tell the young to read Goodwin's Greek Grammar, chapter on prosody." Incidentally, it is an excellent beginning for those interested in how poetry is made ; and one calculated to discourage many aspirants who are convinced that the writing of poetry is merely a matter of having a bright idea or an emotional puff.

Pound's concern with Provençal poetry was no idle romantic excursion ; but an attempt " to resuscitate the dead art of cantabile ". A glance at *Langue D'oc* in particular:

In orchard under the hawthorne
She has her lover till morn,
Till the traist man cry out to warn
Them. God how swift the night,

           And day comes on !

O Plasmatour, that thou end not the night,
Nor take my beloved from my sight,
Nor I, nor tower-man, look on daylight,
'Fore God, how swift the night,

           And day comes on !

Lovely thou art, to hold me close and kisst,
Now cry the birds out, in the meadow mist,
Despite the cuckold, do thou as thou list,
So swiftly goes the night

           And day comes on !

My pretty boy, make we our play again
Here in the orchard where the birds complain,
'Till the traist watcher his song unrein,
Ah God ! How swift the night

           And day comes on !

Out of the wind that blows from her,
That dancing and gentle is an pleasanter,
Have I drunk a draught, sweeter than scent of myrrh.
Ah God ! How swift the night.

                  And day comes on !

Venust the lady, and none lovelier,
For her great beauty, many men look on her,
Out of my love will her heart not stir.
By God, how swift the night.

                  And day comes on !

        Vergier : Langue D'oc IV : Quia Pauper Amavi.

                      Ezra Pound.

reminds me of Pound's question : Wrong from the start ?
Most obviously right in the end as the following lines prove :

What thou lovest well remains,
               the rest is dross
What thou lov'st well shall not be reft from thee
What thou lov'st well is thy true heritage
Whose world, or mine or theirs
               or is it of none ?
First came the seen, then thus the palpable
          Elysium, though it were in the halls of hell,
What thou lovest well is thy true heritage.

The ant's a centaur in his dragon world.
Pull down thy vanity, it is not man
Made courage, or made order, or made grace,
         Pull down thy vanity, I say pull down.
Learn of the green world what can be thy place
In scaled invention or true artistry,
Pull down thy vanity,
             Paquin pull down !
The green casque has outdone your elegance.

Master thyself, then others shall thee beare
        Pull down thy vanity
Thou art a beaten dog beneath the hail,
A swollen magpie in a fitful sun,
Half black half white
Nor knowst'ou wing from tail
Pull down thy vanity
              How mean thy hates
Fostered in falsity,
            Pull down thy vanity,
Rathe to destroy, niggard in charity,
Pull down thy vanity,
        I say pull down.

But to have done instead of not doing
           this is not vanity
To have, with decency, knocked
That a Blunt should open
        To have gathered from the air a live tradition
or from a fine old eye the unconquered flame
This is not vanity.
        Here error is all in the not done,
all in the diffidence that faltered.

                      Canto LXXXI.

Here is the achievement : language which, of its own movement, lifts itself into song with the same ease and grace that a
quickened walk becomes a run. This passage is effortless technical virtuosity, the result of fifty years at the bench.

Pound found the lyric flabby and effeminate : Nineteenth
Century and Georgian " Songs " do not sing of themselves :
they have to be set. They have no irresistible melody of their
own. Pound's technical achievement has been to give song
back its masculine rhythms and make it move again with its
own muscles. Pound's lyrics can be accompanied in the same
way as the Troubadours improvised a bass ; but the melody

is in the verse itself. These lyrics defy " setting to music " in the sense that a flat, effeminate lyric can be adapted to fit any musical line, having none of its own.

Neither Elgar, Brahms, Delius nor Schumann could have accompanied a Pound lyric—which requires the free melodic line of Purcell, Jenkins, Vivaldi or Lawes. I suspect that many composers would say that the verse was too irregular and that it even lacked a beat.

It is not that Pound's verse is irregular but that its regularity depends on weight felt in the ear and not on rule-of-thumb counting of syllables. . . .

And what has been said here on the pre-eminent nature of words to be used may suffice for everyone of inborn discernment. (De Vulgari Eloquio.)

Scansion, as taught, is—to my mind—very dangerous even for the deaf ; but, for those with ears of their own, it is a positive hindrance ; for, if a line does not *weigh* in the sensitive ear, then whether it scans or not does not matter. The quantity of syllables cannot be counted.

Nor must we omit to mention that we take feet contrary to that of the regular poets, because they said that a line consists of feet, but we say that a foot consists of lines, as appears plainly enough. (De Vulgari Eloquio.)

You cannot write music with a metronome. In the last analysis, what makes Pound the brilliant technician that he is, is not his range of scholarship but the sensibility of his ear —and without which, nothing.

The base for all Pound's translations and adaptations— whether from Arnault Daniel or Rihaku is—" make it new !"

Compare his Villonaud *Ballad of the Gibbet* with Swinburne's translation: " Men, brother men, that after us yet live." And look at the beautiful canzon of *The Yearly Slain* :—

III

The faint damp wind that, ere the even, blows
Piling the west with many a tawny sheaf,
Then when the last glad wavering hours are mown
Sigheth and dies because the day is sped ;
This wind is like her and the listless air
Wherewith she goeth by beneath the trees,
The trees that mock her with their scarlet stain.

IV

Love that is born of Time and comes and goes !
Love that doth hold all noble hearts in fief !
As red leaves follow where the wind have flown,
So all men follow Love when Love is dead.
O Fate of Wind ! O Wind that cannot spare,
But drivest out the Maid, and pourest lees
Of all thy crimson on the wold again !

> Canzon : The Yearly Slain.
> Selected Poems by Ezra Pound.

and compare it with Manning's " Kore ".

Not every poet can make a sestina ; and few indeed whose style can survive the limits of this exacting form. Under most people's hands, the Sestina becomes a flat exercise of no more interest than a crossword puzzle. But the high priest of so-called " vers libre " was able to produce in *Altaforte* a boisterous vitality within the confines of the form :—

II

In hot summer have I great rejoicing
When the tempests kill the earth's foul peace,
And the lightnings from black heav'n flash crimson,
And the fierce thunders roar me their music
And the winds shriek through the clouds mad, opposing,
And through all the riven skies God's swords clash.

> Sestina : Altaforte.
> Selected Poems by Ezra Pound.

Pound's personal idiom survives the imposition of any form
which is proof of his technical capabilities. Here the Sestina is
animated. The internal rhythm is not dominated by the line
but carries over. It is not lamed by the rhyme. Compare
Altaforte with :—

I

I saw my soul at rest upon a day,
   As a bird sleeping in the nest of night,
Among soft leaves that give the straight way
   To touch its wings but not its eyes with light,
So that it knew, as one in visions may,
   And knew not as men waking, of delight.

II

This was the measure of my soul's delight :
   It had no power of joy to fly by day,
Nor part in the large lordship of the light ;
   But in a secret moon-beholden way
Had all its will of dreams and pleasant night,
   And all the love and life that sleepers may.

Sestina by Swinburne.

There is all the difference between writing *in* a form and
writing *against* a form. The bore of a hose pipe does not by
itself make the water spurt—the pressure is produced by the
head of water being confined to the pipe.

Swinburne has no thrust carrying over the line. He clutches
at each rhyme and his Sestina dies another death on each one.

My point concerning the difference between writing to a
form and writing against it can be examined by comparing
Donne's sonnets with almost anybody else's—except (pace
Ezra) Hopkins'. Pound's translations of Cavalcanti's sonnets
are no mere renderings. If you compare his translation of :—

S'Io priego questa donna, che pietate
Non sia nemica del suo cor gentile

If I should pray this lady pitiless
That mercy to her heart be no mere foeman

with Rosetti's :—

If I entreat this lady that all grace
Seem not unto her heart an enemy . . .

I think my point is made. Incidentally, I suppose Pound's *Cavalcanti Rime* (Edizioni Marsano) is probably the most honest and competent piece of editing that I have ever come across.

The Cantos are not, as superficial critics maintain, a departure from Pound's concern with form—the apparent freedom of the Cantos is obtained because the discipline lies behind them. There are more varieties of verse technique in this one poem than there are in the whole book of Oxford English Verse.

People who will not read the Cantos because they cannot swallow Pound's philosophy or politics, and dare not taint themselves with the work of one whom they say is not a true democrat—would be well advised to make sure that Dante was also a true democrat before risking the contagion of *The Inferno.*

Whatever blocks may be put in the way, the Cantos must inevitably roll into place as a great English Epic. By what can we measure it ? We are forced back and must use the Florentine as a rule ; for there is no other.

It is not for nothing that there now exists what might be called " The Scattered Tribe of Ezra " just as there was once " The Tribe of Ben ". For Pound and Jonson have much in common. Each is a poet's poet. Both are superb craftsmen whose technical abilities depend, not on their scholarship but on an exquisite ear.

POUND'S CRITICAL PROSE

by Marshall McLuhan [1949]

The Senecal or Jonsonian vigour and precision of Mr. Pound's critical writing has been too much the foil for the urbane sinuosities of Mr. Eliot's prose—a fact which reflects on the twentieth century reader and not on these writers. Mr. Pound is the only writer of our time whose prose achieves the effect of actual conversation as it occurs among those who exist in an intense focus of complex interests. It shocks again and again with the dramatic stress of the spoken word, and yet amidst all that has been said of " salty Yankee speech " it has not been recognised for what it is. Mr. Pound has incorporated in his prose the radical individualism of generations of sea-board Yankees—not the mannerisms only but the entire move-ment of mind—the intensity, the shrewdness, and the passion for technical precision. And these are just the qualities which he brought to bear on the reshaping of poetry in London in 1908-1922.

By contrast with Pound's sharp and alert sentences the gentle rhythms of Eliot's paragraphs are a balm for minds which find only distress in the violence of intellectual penetra-tion. Mr. Eliot has said the same things, for example, about Dante and the French Symbolists as Mr. Pound. They share an immense interest in verbal technique and poetic structures. But whereas Mr. Pound has been vehement and explicit about these things, Mr. Eliot has been unobtrusive and casual. Mr. Eliot has adjusted the "frequency modulation" of his prose so that it causes little perturbation in foolish ears, but Mr. Pound insists on his readers' attention even where no likeli-hood of understanding is present. And for this he has not been forgiven by the literate. With entire Yankee optimism he has insisted on the universal import of his interests, while Mr. Eliot's sceptical wisdom has led him to soothe the literate and to seek understanding only from a few. Mr. Pound brought to letters the evangelical public-spirit of the American town-meeting. It thus never occurred to him to apologise for having serious intellectual and literary interests at a time when such things were of even less general account than they now are. And he has likewise omitted the various rituals of self-flagellation which our world still exacts from the literary man who ventures to present his views directly:

> It appears to me quite tenable that the function of literature as a generated prize-worthy force is precisely that it does incite humanity to continue living; that it eases the mind of strain, and feeds it, I mean definitely as *nutrition of impulse*. . . . It has to do with the clarity and vigour of "any and every" thought and opinion . . . the individual cannot think and communicate his thought, the governor and legislator cannot act effectively or frame his laws, without words, and the solidity and validity of these words is in the care of the damned and despised *literati*. When their work goes rotten—by that I do not mean when they express indecorous thoughts—but when their very medium, the very essence of their work, the application of word to thing goes rotten, i.e., becomes "slushy" and inexact, or excessive or bloated, the whole machinery of social and of individual thought and order goes to pot. This is a lesson of history, and a lesson not yet half learned.

It is also the lesson of *The Cantos*. Human association, it is implied, depends on the utmost fidelity of sensuous and intellectual discrimination. Let there be complete humility in the presence of the actual diversity of things and absolute intolerance of the obtuscators of language. This is an existential philosophy which makes Mr. Pound impatient with the average degree of human apathy and confusion. So that in the drama of human history he finds as little to admire as did Gibbon. His roots are in the America of Adams and Jefferson, who also sought to make things new and whose limitation was also to see past and present as no more than philosophy, teaching by examples.

However, the America which Mr. Pound left about 1908 gave him a great deal which he translated into literary perception and activity. It was the technological America which

Siegfried Giedion has been the first to explore in *Space, Time and Architecture* and in *Mechanization Takes Command*. It is also the America which appears obliquely in Henry James's prefaces and in his notes on the technique of the novel. Commenting on James's notes to *The Ivory Tower* Mr. Pound says,

> I give this outline with such fullness because it is a landmark in the history of the novel as written in English. It is inconceivable that Fielding or Richardson should have left, or that Thomas Hardy should leave, such testimony to a comprehension of the novel as a "form". . . . The Notes are simply the accumulation of his craftsman's knowledge, they are, in all their length, the summary of the things he would have, as a matter of habit, in his mind before embarking on composition.

In the America of 1908 the most authentic æsthetic experience was widely sought and found in the contemplation of mechanical tools and devices, when intellectual energies were bent to discover by precise analysis of vital motion the means of bringing organic processes within the compass of technical means. Mr. Pound records in his *Gaudier-Brzeska* the delight of his young contemporaries in examining and commenting on machinery catalogues, "machines that certainly they would never own and that could never by any flight of fancy be of the least use to them. This enjoyment of machinery is just as natural and just as significant a phase of this age as was the Renaissance 'enjoyment of nature for its own sake', and not merely as an illustration of dogmatic ideas." The impersonal concerns and impatience of Mr. Pound's critical outlook are everywhere associated with this passion for technical excellence: "The experimental demonstrations of one man may save the time of many—hence my furore over Arnaut Daniel— if a man's experiments try out one new rhyme, or dispense conclusively with one iota of currently accepted nonsense, he is merely playing fair with his colleagues when he chalks up his result."

This fascination with technological discovery co-existing

with erudition and sensitivity in language and the arts was what gave Mr. Pound his peculiar relevance in London, 1908. It was a combination of interests indispensable to anybody who wished to undertake the task of importing into English letters the achievement of the French from Stendhal to Mallarmé. (It may not be irrelevant to consider that this same combination of interests which also appears in Edgar Poe's *Philosophy of Composition* had helped to guide those very French developments which in turn Mr. Pound did so much to introduce into English.) As Mr. Pound saw it, the job was to acclimatise seventy years of French discovery within a single decade. And with the assistance of Wyndham Lewis, T. E. Hulme, T. S. Eliot, and Joyce, that job was mainly done by 1922. But it could not have been done without Mr. Pound's intense concern for technique:

> Later it struck me that the best history of painting in London was the National Gallery, and the best history of literature, more particularly of poetry, would be a twelve-volume anthology in which each poem was chosen, not merely because it was a nice poem or a poem Aunt Hepsy liked, but because it contained an invention, a definite contribution to the art of verbal expression.

The *ABC of Reading* was a later issue of this project. The exactitude of the dissociations of style and technique which appear in the selections and comments of that small book give it the distinction of being at once the shortest and the most heavily freighted account of English poetry. The short section on Chaucer is the only appreciation he has received since Dryden that relates him to the mind of Europe or that indicates, in contrast, the defects of Elizabethan culture.

Mr. Pound's technical interests exist in so sharp a focus that they have had a decisive impact only on those who shared them in equal measure. So that while Joyce, Yeats, and Mr. Eliot have never stinted their tributes to him for his direct effect on their work, no critical comment has so far risen to that level of perception where this influence could be evaluated. Perhaps such criticism cannot be conducted without literary and rhythmic analysis as severe as they themselves directed, especially to Dante and the French Symbolists. At any rate this advent of rigour after a long period of slackness in English letters was mainly owing to Mr. Pound. Now this rigor which is everywhere apparent in his prose criticism has long passed current as the irresponsible and scornful expression of a hasty mind. If there is any critical prose more exact, more pointed, more weighted with perception it may be found in the last essays of Mallarmé, but nowhere else in English. For English letters depth of perception has tended to be associated with opacity and suggestiveness. So that the values of plastic hardness and precision in Chaucer and Ben Jonson are readily overlooked in favour of the rich associations of Shakespeare. Not unrelated to this preference for psychological atmosphere to the exclusion of other qualities in poetry is our related expectation that prose is obliged to carry the reader forward by the appearance at least of casually connected conceptions. But in both poetry and prose Mr. Pound has not only disappointed such ordinary expectation, he has resolutely avoided any such means of effect. They are not the means pursued by anybody whose tool is the engraver's or whose presentation is analogical.

Thus when he says that *Sweeney Agonistes* contains more essential criticism of Seneca than Mr. Eliot's essays on English Senecanism we have a typical observation whose form is that of exact juxtaposition. It is not a casual statement but an ideogram, a presentation of an analogical proportion depending on a precise analysis of Seneca, on one hand, and of *Sweeney Agonistes*, on the other. Syntactically elaborated it would fill many pages. But Mr. Pound seldom translates himself into ordinary prose. And anecdotes and reported conversations which enrich his essays are, in the same way, never casually illustrative but ideogrammatic. In the language of the schoolmen, for whose precision of dissociation Mr. Pound has so frequently expressed his admiration, the ideogram represents the "copula of agglutination". That is to say, the copula of

existential reality and not the copula which connects enuncia-
tions and conceptions in rationalistic discourse. And it is the
consequent solidity and sharpness of particularised actuality
(in which the Chinese excel) that baffles the reader who looks
for continuous argumentation in Mr. Pound's prose and verse
alike.

So that if there is one theme which emerges everywhere in
Mr. Pound's critical prose it is the seeking out of those
qualities and techniques in a writer which lead to the
economical rendering of complex actualities. Writing of Henry
James he says:

> 1907. *The American Scene*, triumph of the author's long
> practice. A creation of America. . . . I know of no such
> grave record, of no such attempt at faithful portrayal as
> *The American Scene*. Thus America is to the careful
> observer.

Implied, of course, is the absolutely bracing effect of such an
artistic realisation. Greater in scope than *The American Scene*
and much more exacting in execution, Mr. Pound's *Mauberley*
is "The London scene" for the same period, and *The Cantos*
are the human scene for a long period. This may be said, at
least, by way of illustrating the mode in which any poet's prose
criticism directs the keenest possible ray on his own poetic
practice. And it is the neglect of close study of Mr. Pound's
prose which has deprived *The Cantos* of due understanding.
His *Guide to Kulcher* is the inevitable prose companion of
The Cantos, constructed like them without any overlayering
or underlying concepts but existing by the affirmation of the
proportions which are present in the juxtapositions of persons,
places, things. Yet *Kulcher* offers only a preliminary training
in perception which is presumed to be fully developed in the
contemplator of *The Cantos*.

Mr. Eliot has held the interest of a whole generation of
readers by making basic concessions in his prose to their
demand for dialectic and persuasive charm. What he has to
say, however, is neither dialectical nor charming, but pro-

foundly analogical and even unpleasant. Mr. Pound's prose
on occasion follows the procedure of Mr. Eliot's poetry when
it is for most readers extremely obscure, just as the organisation of the sections of *The Waste Land* employs the analogical
"music" of *Mauberley*. It is "to live in the wink", in the
concentration of those timeless moments when the eye of
mankind has been most open to intelligible form. And this
method of proportionality is "symbolic" in the strict sense of
the Greek. It dispenses entirely with syntax and rhetoric and
leaves the reader naked to the diversity of existence. Mr.
Pound's poetry has finally swallowed his prose. But it remains
essentially a critical prose, always carrying the method of
direct comparison and contrast of specific qualities to a point
of decisive discrimination.

Permettre à ceux qui en valent la peine d'écrire franchement
ce qu'il pense—seul plaisir d'un écrivain.

POUND: MASKS, MYTH, MAN

by G. S. Fraser [*1950*]

I

This will not be the kind of essay that Ezra Pound himself would approve of. I am writing on the passenger deck of a vessel bound for Japan, the books I want to quote from are in the hold, and so I shall have to talk around him, and around him, digging up what illustrative tags I can from my memory. That is not his own way of criticising. It is perhaps not quite true of him, as John Crowe Ransom says it is of Eliot, that he "never lifts his nose from the page"; he has forcible opinions on a hundred subjects, and his critical essays are full of all sorts of pungent "asides"; but on the whole he is at his best as a critic when he opens a book, thrusts it at you, and says "See for yourself". What you have to *see*, generally, is not an illustration of some favourite thesis but a poem on a page, worth looking at for its own sake. He exposes you to impacts. Some of his best critical essays —that on French poetry, for instance—are not so much even close examinations of texts as little anthologies, with just enough commentary to let the reader get to grips on his own. And in the essays illustrated by translations, those on Provençal poets or on Cavalcanti's *Donna mi prega*, the prose setting of the translations has often the air of acute, but disconnected, notebook jottings. And Pound's best criticism, no doubt, *is* in his translations. He makes ghosts walk again, in their habit, as they lived ; yet his ghosts, paradoxically enough, have a common aspect ; we know them by their gait, and the gait is Pound's. *Homage to Sextus Propertius*, for instance, will send you (if you have the kind of schoolboy smattering of Latin I have) to Propertius, looking for a wry humour, which is perhaps only Pound's, or which anyway no one would have seen in Propertius until Pound had read it into him. He gives things his own flavour ; but I am not, in this essay, attempting to give him *my* flavour. I am trying to arrive at a tentative judgment of him as he is in himself.

Such versions, or such handlings, rather, as *Homage to Sextus Propertius*, are what Pound calls *personæ*, as he might say masks or maybe rôles. But the puzzle for his readers is, of, say, Pound and Propertius, which is the actor and which is the part : is it a question of Garrick as Hamlet, or Hamlet as Garrick ? Perhaps we should think of neither of these simple alternatives ; Pound's Propertius is more an antique Roman than a Yank, but just sufficiently a Yank to be not too stuffily an antique Roman. This is perhaps Pound's great gift as a poet of rôles—his power of forcefully combining partial inadequacies into a not at all inadequate whole. Propertius, for instance, needs re-interpretation, even distortion, to bring him within our own framework ; but we must also re-interpret and distort that framework (we must correlate two variables, in fact) to come to terms with *him*. This is why both Pound's rage against academic scholars, and the rage of academic scholars against Pound, are largely critically irrelevant. Academic scholars are able to get an objective view of a text by dissociating it as far as possible from their own contemporary sensibility, which is what the poetic critic and translator—who for that very reason can never get a wholly objective view—dare not do. The scholar must not, and the poet must, project himself into the text. A kind of amateur scholarship has, perhaps, been a stumbling-block to Pound. It is right for a poet, making the first draft of a translation, to guess, guess all the way—to use his in-tuition about how a poem of a certain kind *must* be built up —but I think he should then check his guesses with a good dictionary or a reliable crib. His guesses will be brilliant but not necessarily accurate. Pound, I feel, has too often omitted this checking ; he has more of the spirit of scholarship than many scholars, but, after all, the letter counts too. On the other hand, it is this schoolboy eagerness that has kept him, for so many years, so wonderfully fresh as a man and a poet.

The sensibility, then, of Propertius, or Li Po, or Bertrans de Born, is one variable that Pound has had to adjust in shaping his masks ; another variable has been his own raw, quick, exceedingly American sensibility. That, in isolation, has its inadequacies, too. Pound's emphasis, for instance, on the notion of "culture" is very American, and there is that little early poem (not one of his best) where he imagines American life strangely transformed by a general study of "the Classics". I think that for the intelligent American reader today—for the intelligent reader almost everywhere, for that matter—one trouble is that there are too many "Classics" altogether. The point about somebody like Jefferson was not that he had read a great deal (the eighteenth-century novel, for instance, which for us is a "classic", for him was an unwholesome distraction), but that what he had read was what most educated gentlemen of his time, in England and France as well as in Virginia, would have read too. That age demanded of a gentleman a wide, clear, and superficial range of knowledge over a known range of subjects; Lord Chesterfield, for instance, told his son that a young man should know about architectural styles, but not about building materials, for the latter kind of knowledge was not "liberal" but "mechanical".

A great deal of what was once liberal knowledge has today become mechanical in that sense; even literary criticism has today its quite elaborate technical jargon. But our liberal knowledge, the part of our knowledge that is still genuinely liberal, has no longer the cohesion that it had in Jefferson's day. There are more books worth reading than we shall ever read, and more arguable points of view than we shall ever come to terms with. Let us imagine that Pound could dictate a course of reading in "general literature" for the leading American universities; it would be a drop in the bucket, it would leave the general cultural confusion richer, perhaps, but also more thick and sticky than ever. Our reading today is rather, in fact, like an American salad—cheese, gherkins, nuts, lettuces, pears, endives, perhaps a slice of pineapple and a rub of garlic—and one needs a bottle of thick mayonnaise to mask the contrasting flavours, and the name of the mayonnaise, in the United States, is "culture".

"Culture", as most Americans use the word, covers anything that is not obviously practical or pleasurable; like
visiting, for instance, Stratford-on-Avon. In this sense, the
notion of culture can become a blanket smothering individual
taste and discrimination—and this, of course, is not, one would
never dare hint it, exactly Pound's sense of culture. But his
sense has something, at least, in common with what the
American humanists, Irving Babbitt and Paul Elmer More,
understood by culture; and what they understood was in a
sense the opposite of what an anthropoligist understands by *a*
culture; they understood not something that could be encouraged to grow out of the habits and perceptions of daily
American life, but something that had to be protected from
these. Their humanism was an admirable notion, but it had
no roots in the American soil, and so produced no flowers or
fruits there. On the contrary, one would be tempted to say
that some of the best and most racy American writing
(*Huckleberry Finn, Fiesta, Soldiers' Pay, The Thin Man*)
springs from the soil of a sensitive philistinism; poetry,
too, William Carlos Williams' poetry of red brick houses,
suburban wives, cheerful standardised interiors. It was
a weakness, an amiable and typically American weakness
in Pound, that he was too eager to make everybody else read
his own favourite authors and too hopeful about the changes
that would spring from such a reading. It is not so much
what people read, as *how* they read, that can make them
startlingly and pleasantly different.

Our point, however, is the poetry. In these masks or rôles
of Pound's, the inadequacies of an eager American eclecticism, and of various primitive or archaic attitudes, not
easily revivable in contemporary terms, do seem to combine,
after all, as something poetically adequate. This whole question of the triumphant combination of inadequacies becomes
peculiarly fascinating in the unique case, before *The
Cantos—Hugh Selwyn Mauberley*—where the *persona*, the
mask, the rôle, is not the old empty armour that begins
to shape, and clank, and move as if it had life in it, as Pound's

swan passes on the stream—I am making an allusion, there,
to the opening of one of the early *Cantos*—but, on the
contrary, a rôle, a contemporary rôle, rather like Pound's
own. I say "rather like" for *Mauberley* is not *exactly* Pound.
He is, one gathers, a minor poet of genuine talent, high, frail
ambition, and classical tastes : a sort of Landor *de ses jours,*
but with a wistfulness and an irony that are more like
Laforgue. The poem has the smell of its time. When we read,
for instance, of Mr. Nixon advising the poet to "take a
column", and "butter reviewers", warning him that the
"nineties tried your game, but died of it", we cannot help
thinking of Arnold Bennett, playing the part of the Card in
life as in literature.

In such a discouraging atmosphere, Mauberley can only
drift, collect fugitive impressions, remember the 'nineties
and the pre-Raphælites, bitterly note decay,

> In that thoroughfare
> The sale of half-hose has
> Long since superseded the cultivation
> Of Pierian roses.

In the end he vanishes to a euphoric death in the South Seas :

> I was
> And I no more exist ;
> Here drifted
> An Hedonist.

Mauberley, in his passivity, is in some degree inadequate as
a person, though not in the least so as a *persona* (Dr. Leavis,
if I remember rightly, though a passionate admirer of this
poem, has something sniffy to say about the "merely æsthetic"
attitude implied in it). Pound himself was made of tougher
stuff. He did not drift to the South Seas, but instead started
to study economics and to write the longest readable poem
of our time, *The Cantos*. This was a move from the lyrical

scale to the epical ; and it implied, at the same time, a move
from the lyric mask to the epic myth.

II

The nature of the underlying myth in *The Cantos* begins
to become really clear about half way through, in the two
long sections where the anecdotes, of which the poem is
largely composed, are no longer broken off in the middle to
be taken up, in a different setting, several Cantos further on.
Of these two large monolithic chunks, intruding so strangely
into a kaleidoscopic poem, one is about John Adams, the
second President of the United States ; it consists largely of
extracts from letters by him or about him, of documentation.
For most readers, just as poetry, it is one of the least successful sections ; it presupposes, for the English reader at
least, a grounding in the early history of the United States
which few English readers are likely to have. The other
section is a condensed version of the history of China ; and
on the whole most readers, I imagine, will find this one of the
most wonderful sections of the poem—it is, perhaps more than
any other part, properly epical. But, failures or successes,
these two sections give the key to the myth.

It is the myth of the noble leader and the stable community, of the good society which has been, and can be
again, and which wicked men seek to destroy. The good
society, for Pound, is stable rather than changing ; the only
natural kind of change is deterioration, and therefore to
preserve the stability of society a constant, daily effort of
renewal is required. Certain sacred exemplars of stability
must be kept in mind, figures like Confucius and Adams,
documents like the Confucian writings and the American Constitution. The noble leader, like Adams, and the stable
society, like China, have qualities in common. Their stability
is preserved by the exercise of an acute but severely practical
intelligence. They both respect tradition, but by that they
mean the cultural inheritance of skills and insights and wisdom ; not merely anything at all that has come down from

177

the past. There are times when a break must be made,[1] but
when the break has been made, it has something of finality
about it—just as for Burke, for instance, the "Glorious
Revolution" of 1688 was, among other things, a kind of
sacred barrier against any subsequent revolutions whatever.
Stability has two enemies besides its own natural tendency to
decay. One is the activity of the moneylender, the tax-
gatherer, the banker, the great financial combine ; the other
is the other-worldliness—like Taoism in China—which treats
life as a vain dream.

Pound thus thinks of certain purposes as valid throughout
history, but as constantly thwarted. He thinks it possible to
separate the wheat of history from the chaff ; and this distinguishes him from historicists in the strict sense like Hegel,
Marx, Croce, or Collingwood, for whom such a distinction
is untenable, for whom everything that happens in history is
necessary, and reasonable, and therefore right. To separate
the wheat from the chaff, Pound must feel sure that he has
a stance *outside* history ; or access to certain permanent values.

What set ? Partly those of the artist who keeps his eyes
open. " By their fruits ye shall know them." There must be
something right about the society that produces Chartres and
something wrong about the society that produces, say, London
south of the river. Men like Adams and Jefferson respect the
arts, but they are not in Mauberley's sense " æsthetes ", and
indeed throughout *The Cantos* Pound seems to be moving
away from Mauberley's still faintly ninetyish attitude towards
one more like Ruskin's in *Unto This Last* ; it must be good
men, in a good society, who build a good cathedral.

The odd thing is that in religion Pound is a kind of eighteenth-
century deist (one of his literary heroes, and an oddly assorted
set they are, is Voltaire), and there must be a sense in which
the cathedral, and the whole outer fabric of mediæval life that
he loves so passionately, is nothing for him but an adorable
mockery or a beautiful empty shell. Critics have noted, and

1. But those making the break—Confucius, the Whigs of 1688, the American
Founding Fathers, Pound himself as a poetic innovator—will claim always to be
going back to an earlier and sounder tradition.

very rightly, the new and very moving note of religious humility in the "Pull down thy vanity" passage in *The Pisan Cantos*; but none of them have noted that the divinity not exactly invoked but hinted at there—the deity that sheathes a blade of grass more elegantly than a Parisian dressmaker sheathes a beautiful woman—is just the divinity of the Deists: "Nature", or "Nature's God", it hardly matters which one calls it, for it is just enough of a God to keep Nature running smoothly. The *feeling* of the passage is anything but Voltairean, but the *notion* is quite Voltaire's: the God envisaged is wholly immanent. There is a good deal of disquiet and horror at odd moments in *The Cantos*, but so far as I can see there is no sense of the transcendental, no awareness of the great gulf that separates finite existence from the mystery of nothing ɔr the mystery of being. These ultimate questions are for Pound, as for Confucius or William James, vain distractions from the immediate business of living. There is work to be done, danger to be met; do not let us, Pound seems to be saying, vainly sit and brood, in solitary uselessness.

The anguish that Pound feels most acutely is not about eternity, but about time. "Time is evil. Evil." That couple of tiny sentences comes in a passage where Pound is describing how Ignez da Castro, who has been murdered because the old King of Portugal did not want her to be the wife of the young Crown Prince, was dug up from her grave when the Prince ascended the throne, how she sat crowned with "the King still young beside her", and how "a day, and a day, all the Lords of Lisboa" filed past her to kiss her hand. Time is evil that has corrupted her beauty in the grave, that has left of the young King's love only pride and bitterness and a dry ache for revenge. Such are among the most moving moments in *The Cantos* and they break through the sturdy and enclosed optimism which is (surprisingly, when one considers the violence and cruelty of so many of the incidents related) the prevailing mood of the myth. The *myth* of *The Cantos* is that of the stable society, the good society, which has been and which, if only men will let themselves be guided by the sacred exemplars, can be again. The *truth* of *The Cantos* which comes out very often, for instance, in *The Pisan Cantos*, is that of a total waste, bitterness, and loss, which it is not really within human power to compensate or repair. It is something other than man himself that gives him strength to recognise, and to outface, the worst. " It was not man Made courage, or made order, or made grace." Who was it then? This question, in *The Cantos* that are still to come, seems to demand a more positive answer. There is something in the whole pattern of the poem that demands an encounter with the transcendental at a culminating point.

The Cantos started off with a Homeric sea voyage (significantly enough from Circe's island, where Mauberley perhaps, like poor Elpenor, might have been glad enough to linger), and with a visit to hell-mouth, the sacrifice of a sheep, and a raising of the spirits of the mighty dead ; while another sort of hell, the hell, as some critic has acutely said, of *others*—of newspaper proprietors, war profiteers, puritan bishops, and those who think of sex in terms of rubber goods, but certainly not of " ole Ez " himself—plays a prominent, if jarring part in the earlier *Cantos*. There are glimpses, too, of a kind of earthly paradise, sea and sun dazzle, nymphs, Bacchus transforming pirates into furry animals, masts into trees, of troubadours, of Renaissance soldiers, of American businessmen, of the Cid—a great froth and flurry of everything that is lively in Pound's memory or imagination ; a great invocation, with sidelong snarling glances at the present, of everything that seems splendid in the real or legendary past. The effect is wonderful, but would be bewildering if the pattern—of interweaving stories started, dropped, taken up again at random—were continued indefinitely. The first thirty or so Cantos state a " matter " one might say, in the mediæval sense, the " matter of Europe ". The American episodes there come in with a strange, disquieting gritty effect, more " realistic " but less " poetic "; the Chinese allusions with an effect of remote, grave, and not immediately relevant wisdom.

Then come, soberly, the great exemplars; the poem touches, if sometimes a little leadenly, the ground of China and America. We know where we are, we have a clearer sense of direction. After all, against brilliant and unstable Europe—and the European ghosts have all been called up from Hell, after all—some more stolid but safer concept of society is to be justified. Then, with *The Pisan Cantos*, there is a change again ; we have left hell, and the heavenly phantasmagorias that a classic hell affords, the

> hero's iron shade
> Glittering through the gloomy glade,

and we have ascended from the broad plains of earth, of America and China, to the mountain of purgatory.

The poet moves for the first time mainly through his *own* past, recalling dead or distant or estranged friends—Yeats, Hueffer, Jepson, Newbolt, Nancy Cunard—with a new tenderness ; expressing his personal feelings more frankly and on the whole with less toughness than in the past—there are no just wars in spring or autumn (ancient Chinese wisdom, but he feels it personally, the sacredness of sowing and harvest), and, however unpractical and sentimental such a view is, he has learned, from his own sad experience, that he does not like the idea of either animals or men being in cages. Things have not worked out either as he had hoped or as he had calculated. His poem itself, which was to be an impersonal epic, is taking an unexpected direction. He must cast down his vanity. . . .

There are, I believe, about eighteen Cantos still to come. It would be rash to make any predictions about them, but we have had a long sea journey and we must have a return to Ithaca ; we have had a raising of many ghosts, and they must be ceremoniously laid ; we have had the gods of Greece, and the sacred human wisdom of Confucius and Adams, and the *Deus sive Natura* of Spinoza or Voltaire ; it is time, as I have already suggested, for us to confront the Transcendent. We have had hell, and earth, and the earthly paradise, and a personal purgatory ; of a truly supernatural paradise (not necessarily or very probably a Christian one) we must also have a glimpse.

But these are abstract formal demands, and about abstract form in this sense, a preconceived form into which whatever matter immediately available must be moulded, Pound has never cared much. All these prophecies may be wrong. What does seem certain is that, in *The Pisan Cantos*, he has been forced for the first time to come to grips in poetry with *himself* ; to recognise to what great extent the whole pattern of his long poem is, as it were, not objectively read off from history, but projected from his own inner being. If one takes them as an objective statement about history, *The Cantos* are, one must recognise, a failure ; a great deal of evidence is presented but in the nature of the case it is not, and cannot be, exhaustive ; and even if one accepts it as tendentiously selected, it is not certain that it will prove what Pound wants it to prove. Even as a special pleader, he does not quite make out his case.

He will be forced, I think, in the Cantos that are to come, to recognise that *The Cantos* are an objective failure (that flattened and smoothed into prose, so to say, they would not make a convincing thesis about history), but at another level, which one cannot call a merely subjective level, this recognition might set the seal on the poem's success. Pound might recognise that, like Langland, he has written a *vision*. And it is a much more personal vision than Langland's. Pound is free, certainly, of the shadows of Freud and Proust, but we are none of us free of the shadow of Rousseau. The structure of *The Cantos* has in fact no exact analogy in previous literature, but if it is in some sense epical, it is also in some sense confessional. Pound is quite without *introspective* interest in himself, yet perhaps the clearest concrete impression *The Cantos* leave with us, after we have rejected their myth, and accepted their truth, is one of Pound the man. It is perhaps

Pound the man at the centre of *The Cantos* that prevents them falling apart into mere fragmentary chaos.

III

Yet about the man himself, apart from his poetry, it is perhaps not critically proper to say very much. I shall merely say one word about what I think is the main error in his thinking ; an error responsible for flaws in his work and also, of course, for his personal misfortunes. It is a very common error, especially among loyal, active, passionate, and courageous men. It has to do with his ideal of stability. I am not writing as an irresponsible advocate of change for its own sake. We are creatures of habit and, though some changes are always necessary, change in itself is always disagreeable to us. Like Ezra Pound, I too think we should aim at stability in society. But I do not really think that we shall get it, ever, in any permanent sense. We are aiming at something ideal : we have no models of a really stable society in history (certainly neither China nor mediæval Christendom is such a model, if one looks into its history in any detail, since the one society stagnated and rendered itself vulnerable to outer pressure and inner upheaval, and the other, a society of perpetual war and debate, was shaken to pieces by its own inner strife). We have only models of more or less striking and ambitious failures to achieve stability.

We seek society's stability, by a kind of instinct, as we seek our own health ; though we know that in the long run we shall fall ill and die. It is this instinct, or this impulse, to stabilise that seems permanent in history. There are probably also permanent *elements* of human behaviour ; but there are no permanent stable social forms. Every social form is at the best showily, and imperfectly, stable ; it will be broken down in time, and a new form (still imperfect, but more suited to new times and circumstances) will take its place. Politics is a heroic activity just because, almost by definition, it is bound to fail.

It is Pound's error, it seems to me, not to recognise this ;

to believe in stable forms that have been destroyed by malice, and to believe in the possibility of reinstating them, and of curbing the malice that would destroy them. Malice, certainly I would agree, is something that works permanently for the destruction of stability. But whose malice? That, for instance, as Pound sometimes suggests, of those who sell armaments? What about the malice of those who buy? We are *all*, in fact, malicious, and must curb our malice (or seek divine or scientific help to curb it) as well as we can. The human race cannot be divided into the many simple, innocent good and the few cunning wicked. That way lie persecution and death-camps. It is Pound's weakness, as a man and a poet, to be able to spot evil in his enemies and not in himself and his friends. The problem of evil, or of innate human self-centredness and aggressiveness, is the one problem with which his life, his poetry, and his politics, have never come to grips. He has been right to stand up, indeed, for human dignity in an age in which there has been an almost hysterical cult of guilt.[1] But there is a sense, and perhaps he has failed to recognise this, in which human dignity is itself a *persona*, a mask, a rôle. I would rather read Pound any day than Kafka; but there is a sense, after all, in which Kafka goes more deep.

We should think not of this error and these misfortunes but of the man himself, as his works and his friends present him to us, the most generous and impulsive and unworldly of men; devoting two or three hours every day to his poetry and the rest to helping and encouraging younger friends. The evocation of comradeship in *The Pisan Cantos* has a peculiarly touching and genuine quality, and my own feeling, for what it is worth, is that there is more natural goodness in Pound than in half a dozen of his distinguished contemporaries who have had enough common sense—Pound has no common sense at all, I would say, he is a kind of eternal schoolboy, or magnificent *naïf*—never to put a foot wrong. Where he

---

1. By talking loudly about *universal* guilt one intends, generally to assuage an uneasy sense of *individual* guilt. "You are, at least potentially, as bad as me." True: but not *actually* so bad, and this is resented.

yields himself to blind and stupid hate, or to harsh, uncharitable, destructive anger, I shudder ; but whether or not we can hold him fully responsible for such outbursts (and it seems clear that he is the victim of certain compulsive obsessions), it is clear also that they are not *central* to what he has to say. In the perspective of history, his errors will seem incidental ; his epic, his vision, his confession, his discovery of himself through his exploration of history, of humility through the assertion of pride, of truth through persistence in error, these will seem typically and broadly human, and in their pathos noble and profound.

TOWARDS AN A.B.C. OF HISTORY

by Henry Swabey [*1949*]

Ezra Pound looked at the rows of a million books in the British Museum and decided against reading them all. (*Guide to Kulchur*, 1938, p. 53-4.) Instead, he has concentrated attention on a progressively wider selection. He has treated History in the same selective method, by which persons or periods illuminate decent living. " The study of history should instruct," he wrote in a review of a history book, and in *Kulchur* (pp. 259 and 260) gives the canon, " History that omits economics is mere bunk, it is shadow show," and the warning that " there is no use in trying to ' understand ' history as a mere haphazard list of events arranged chronologically." The many historic characters who make their vivid appearance in the Cantos and elsewhere are the instructors of the present. The Cantos are not exclusively a study in success, and the weeding process is applied—we hear little of Egypt or Meso-potamia—but the periods given detailed study are those in which the right idea goes into action.

Gesell (died 1931) is not of such importance only because he entered the Lindhauer government, " which lasted rather less than five days," or even because

> the state need not borrow
> as was shown by the Mayor of Wörgl.[1]   (Canto 74.)

Gesell restates Mencius in our idiom; Lancelot Andrewes did the same for his age when he commended tithes, " because priest and people share the vagaries of nature." The mayor, incidentally, used *stamp scrip* to lift a derelict town out of its depression and was successful until the central bank stopped the experiment. The tithe is one of the threads which runs from Mencius to modern days.

Pound's treatment of history, in fact, follows that of the philosopher historians of China. Introducing the *Great Digest*, he writes : " Confucius's . . . analysis of why the earlier great emperors had been able to govern greatly, was so sound that

1. Austrian Tyrol —*Editor.*

every durable dynasty since his time has risen on a Confucian design, and been initiated by a group of Confucians. China was tranquil when her rulers understood these few pages. When the principles here defined were neglected, dynasties waned and chaos ensued. The proponents of a world order will neglect at their peril the only process that has repeatedly proved its efficiency as social co-ordinate."

Mencius gives details of how the empire was divided into homesteads and tithed, and the following quotations from Legge's translation give the pith of the system (3.1.3.6) : " *The sovereign of the Hea dynasty enacted the* 50 *mow allotment and the payment of a tax;* (Should not this be " tithe " ? Each family had 50 mow, and the produce of five was paid to the government.) *The founder of the Yin dynasty enacted the* 70 *mow allotment and the system of mutual aid;* (630 mow were divided into 9 ; eight families had an allotment of 70 mow each and united to cultivate the central reserve for the government.) *The founder of the Chou dynasty enacted the* 100 *mow allotment and the share system;* (100 mow to each family, which cultivated the 100 mow in common, divided the produce, and paid 1/10th to the government.) *In reality, what was paid in all these was a tithe. The share system means mutual division. The aid system means mutual dependence.* . . . (7) ' *Lung said : " For regulating the lands, there is no better system than that of mutual aid, and none which is not better than that of taxing."* '

So, " YAO, CHUN, YU, controller of waters . . .
kept down the taxes ". (Canto 56.)

This was some time before 2,000 B.C. The same YU *"let his men pay tithes in kind"* (53). The cantos dealing with China give examples of Confucian principle understood, and the contrast is between those who extorted a fixed tax and those who used a tithe of what is actually produced ; Gesell's tithe (or 12%) on circulating medium itself is a modern application of what has so beneficially worked. Mencius also adapted the

principle : "*In the more central parts* . . . *make the people pay
for themselves a tenth part of their produce*" (3.1.3.15). This,
of course, is not the only thread. Tching Tang (1766 B.C.)
was the next restorer, and

wrote MAKE IT NEW
on his bath tub.

Wen Wang in 1231 B.C. practised another principle :

" Kids 8 to 15 in the schools, then higher training."

Tcheou Kong (1122) advised :

' A good governor is as wind over grass
A good ruler keeps down the taxes '.

In 1079 Tching Ouang kept lynx eye on bureaucrats
lynx eye on the currency

Chao Kong (1078) introduces another thread of modern
application :

On the table of the throne of the West
laid out the charters

constitutions of antient kings and two sorts of stone . . .
' Left in my father's orders, By the table of jewels
To administer as in the law left us
Keep peace in the Empire. . . .'

I should like to know more about these charters, constitutions
and laws. There are some further details about the laws in the
same *Canto,* matchless for its historical content and beauty of
language, which includes a notice of Kung's death in 479 B.C.
and ends with

" Sou-tsin, armament racket, war propaganda."

Landor complained that Dante left his characters in skeleton form, but Pound is able to clothe them with a phrase.

> KAO brought calm and abundance
> No taxes for a whole year . . .
> And he told Siano-ho to edit the law codes . . .
> And this was written all in red character,
> > countersigned by the assembly   (202 B.C.)

Under HAN SIEUN (died 49 B.C.) :
> The text of books re-established.

TAI TSONG (639-662 A.D.) ordered :
> Let judges fast for three days before passing capital
> sentence . . . (Canto 54.)

And TAI in his law code cut 92 reasons for death sentence.

In Canto 55 there is something like a complete dynasty of Confucian emperors : HIEN, who *"reduced the superfluous mandarins"*; SIUEN *"stood for just price and sound paper"*; TAI-TSOU (A.D. 953) said : *"KUNG is the master of emperors."* The principles, in fact, were what did not change. Ngan, in 1042, began *"by making to circulate the whole realm's abundance"*. Nor are mulberry trees forgotten. YONG TCHING, who decreed *"No death sentence save a man were thrice tried"*, remitted taxes, used something similar to the Italian tithe system known as AMMASSI, opened undeveloped land, was effective in relief work, and, I regret to say, found himself under the necessity of putting out Christianity because *" Chinese found it so immoral "*. He died in 1735, which was the year of John Adam's birth.

When the system was violated, hunger and revolution followed, and Sir Thomas Moore unconsciously repeated Mencius' words when he complained of *" greedy sheep devouring men"* through enclosures. Mencius recorded : *"Oppressive sovereigns pulled down houses to make ponds and lakes . . . and threw fields out of cultivation to form gardens and parks . . . in their stables there are fat horses, but the people have the look of hunger. This is leading on beasts to devour men"* (3.2.10.6). The English struggled to limit afforestation by charter for centuries after William the Conqueror.

The contemporaneous value of Mencius may be judged from the following extracts : *"The people brought baskets of rice and vessels of congee to meet your Majesty's host . . . they hoped to escape out of fire and water. If you make the water more deep and the fire more fierce, they will just in like manner make another revolution."* (Mencius.) *" I think Great Britain missed an historical chance in 1943 and after, when so many Italians were genuinely waiting for the arrival of her troops as 'liberators'. It was then a question of letting byegones be byegones and starting a far-sighted policy which would 'integrate' Italy in a new Eurafrican system of which England would have been the natural and undisputed leader . . . they were utterly unconscious of the excellent 'trumps' they were wasting."* (C. Pellizzi, author of *The Defective Revolution.* Rome. 1948.)

King, in his *Forty Centuries of Farming*, described how the allotment system persisted in China. Elsewhere it has been destroyed by enclosures and by usury. Pound is often called a crank for attacking usury, as he does directly in Cantos 15, 45, 51, and in its modern phase in Canto 12 : Baldy Bacon extorted from the public a

> Percentage when they wanted centavos,
> Public centavos

The Directors are *"the quintessential essence of usurers"*. But the effects of usury were stigmatised by Amos and Isaiah, by Plato and Mommsen, the historian of Rome, and were the common theme of Anglican church leaders until 1640.

Aristotle likewise examined how men had actually lived in community, but his system was based on slavery. (*" Those who*

190

cultivate the soil . . . should be slaves." Politics, **7, 9, 9.**) His
dislike of trade (*"it is not in accordance with nature"*) was
doubtless derived from Hesiod (*"What do you want with
ships?*), who is quoted by Pound ; his condemnation of usury
(a way of getting wealth *"of all forms the most contrary to
nature"* 1.3.23), and his requirement of self-sufficiency, show
why Pound has commended the book. But in the Greek period
the action of the State, when

> . . . the fleet that went out to Salamis
> was built by state loans to the builders
> hence the attack on classical studies   (Canto 74)

is most significant to Pound, together with the social responsibility that appears in the Tragedies in advance on the
Odyssey. The heroes of Pound's epic are those who have
accepted and discharged responsibility, in contrast with those
who have shirked or have used irresponsible power. *' " The
most powerful men are not public men,"* said the baron. *"A
public man is responsible and a responsible man is a slave. It is
private life that governs the world ",'* wrote Disraeli in Endymion.
Lt.-Col. A. C. Murray, in *At Close Quarters,* describes a more
recent instance of irresponsible power : *"It gradually became
the habit of Gray, as Foreign Secretary, and later of Arthur
Balfour, to exchange messages of an intimate and confidential
character with President Wilson* through *Colonel House . . .
Wiseman was gradually drawn into the political net. . . ."*
At least two code clerks have broken down in the last decade
owing to their horror of what was happening behind the
scenes. One was an American, the other a Russian.

In Roman times, burgess farmers combined to form a pros-
perous state, still with the assistance of slaves, but Mommsen
described in the first and second volumes of his *History of Rome*
how they were ruined by usury, latifundia and the import of
cheap grain. Rome was great as long as she kept to the pattern
of small estates, which Cæsar tried to revive. But as she
deserted the canon, she became more and more like today's

commercialist barbarism. Corinth was destroyed because she was a commercial rival, and family and individual were precipitated into landless *plebs*. "*We recognise as the most prominent feature in the private economy of this epoch the* financial oligarchy *of Roman capitalists standing alongside of, and on a par with, the political oligarchy.*" (Mommsen, 3,385.) Execution of prisoners and of political opponents was as extensively practised as it is today. Ovid's exile in Tomi is a close parallel with that of his admirer in Washington.

From the time that St. Ambrose said "*Maledictus captans annonam*" to that of the economic refinements of St. Antonino, the Catholic Church kept society near the canon with its tenacious hold on the just price, its prohibition of usury, its teaching on partnership, and fulfilled religion's duty of binding back life to reality. These were "*the thousand and more years of Europe, during which the intellectual hard work of the West occurred INSIDE the Church Catholic*". (Kulchur, p. 26.) "*The fibre holds strong from St. Ambrose* (340-397) *to St. Antonino da Firenze* (1389-1459)." (p. 30.) Internal decay came to a head in 1527, while usury rotted the fabric, found an advocate in Calvin, and rendered the Christian message of "*verbum caro factum*" ineffective. Clean laws, clearly defined, are essential to bring the idea into action. ("*When the prince has no principles . . . and his ministers have no laws . . . in court obedience is not paid to principle and in the office obedience is not paid to the rules.*" Mencius 4.1.1.8.)

Nevertheless, Mr. Pound writes : "*The real revolution continua, it goes on.*" (*Kulchur*, p. 249.) "*Siena was flat on her back, without money, after the Florentine conquest. Cosimo, first duke of Tuscany, had all the Medici banking experience behind him. He guaranteed the capital of the monte,*[1] *taking as security the one living property of Siena and a certain amount of somewhat unhandy collateral. . . . Siena had grazing lands . . . worth* 10,000 *ducats a year. Cosimo underwrote a capital of* 200,000 *ducats to pay* 5% *a year to be lent at* $5\frac{1}{2}$% *a year.*" (Social Credit : An

---

1. The *Monte dei Paschi* or communal bank of Siena, which today is still one of the leading banks of Tuscany. It regularly pays out dividends for the benefit of the sick and the poor in Siena.—*Editor*

Impact, p. 11.) Details of the Medici may be found in Raymond de Roover's *The Medici Bank*, where the same kind of contrast is made between members of the *Arte del Cambio* (the bankers' guild) and *"manifest usurers"*, as Pound makes between the Monte dei Paschi of Siena and the Banca S. Georgio, *" the pitiless company of Genovese creditors."* (Social Credit, p. 12.) Readers of Cantos 40 and following will be familiar with the foundation of the Siena Bank :

> Ob pecuniæ scarcitatem
> because there was shortage of coin, in November,
> because of taxes, exchanges, tax layings and usuries
> legitimate consumption impeded.   (Canto 43.)

In Canto 52, the moral is drawn :

> And I have told you how things were under Duke
>   Leopold in Siena
> And of the true basis of credit, that is the abundance
>   of nature
> with the whole folk behind it.

This was around 1624. *" The real history went on. 1760 to 1790 in Tuscany with the work of Pietro Leopoldo and Ferdinand III of Hapsburg-Lorraine, wiped out by the Napoleonic flurry."* (Guide to Kulchur, p. 263.) Pietro Leopoldo

> that wished state debt brought to an end:
>   . . . that ended gaolings for debt ; . . .   (Canto 44)
> . . . that abolished death as a penalty and all tortures
>   in prisons . . .
> that split common property among tillers. . . .
> His son the third Ferdinando cut taxes by half, . . .

'The foundation, Siena, has been to keep bridle on usury.' *"THAT ain't wot you are told about Habsburgs, i.e. it's wot you AIN'T told,"* he remarks elsewhere. *"Ideas of the American*

revolution were tried out, excesses corrected by light discipline,
ALL snowed under and forgotten in frog-volution." This would
lead to a study of Mirabeau, which I am not at the
moment able to pursue.

Some of the materials for a note on Pound's treatment of
American history are not yet available, but Cantos 62-71, and
Jefferson and/or Mussolini penetrate deep into American
history, and are most absorbing to read.

In Canto 80 he refers to

> the old charter
> forgotten, oh quite forgotten,
> but confirming John's first one

This is the fourth and final (1225) version of the Great
Charter, and has been translated by an American only fifty
years ago. The charters were wrung from the Norman kings
by the people, and bound them to the common law of England
which Alfred, Edgar and Edward the Confessor had codified.
No copies of the codes have survived, but Blackstone (Com-
mentaries, 1765, Vol. I, p. 234) traces the restriction on
monarchy still further back. *"The principal duty of the king is*
to govern his people according to law. Nec regibus infinita aut
libera potestas (And kings have no boundless or unrestricted power)
was the constitution of our German ancestors on the continent
(Tacitus, Germania, 7). *And . . . has always been esteemed an*
express part of the common law of England, even when prerogative
was at its highest." We need not follow Blackstone through
Bracton and Fortescue, but note that William II had to sign
a charter, now lost ; and that charters of Henry I, Stephen
(two) and Henry II are preserved ; and that the ninth charter
which Pound mentions was either the beginning of statute law
in England, or was put on the statute book by Edward I,
according as we follow Blackstone and Maitland, or
MacKechnie. It was frequently re-enacted.

Magna Carta (1215) was immediately occasioned by a
50% increase in *scutage*, which was money paid to compound

for military service, and clause after clause curbs unjust taxation, and binds the king to govern constitutionally, which is the opposite of absolute government. In 1225, a separate Forest Charter was granted to prevent afforestation. The yeomen consisted mainly of those fortunate enough to hold by *"socage"*, which required agricultural and not military service, while the villeins were probably depressed Saxon *ceorls* (free peasants). But they gradually won their status of copyholders, and the pattern worked in England for 300 years after *"the old charter"*. It is not irrelevant that Grossteste, St. Hugh of Lincoln, and St. Richard of Chichester were among charter signatories, and the Primate's part is well known. During this happy period for husbandry, when—somewhat to Blackstone's disgust—the Church frowned on trade and lawyers, local bishops' mints supplemented the King's currency. When he lost his land through encosure and usury, the copyholder sank into the worse villeinage of *"parochial settlement"*, and has now disappeared as an independent family unit into the mobile labour pool. Recent proposals suggest mobility through Europe, which would be the final reverse of Edward I's policy of England for the English. *"Whig historians have not emphasised feudal distributism,"* remarks Pound ; *"Feudal dues have been stressed and feudal duties (noblesse oblige) overshadowed." "The praise of largesse in the troubadours is a fact in history." "Madox Ford used to talk very vehemently, but not very coherently, of the damage done by commutation of duty of overlords to their people into mere money payments."* (K.261.)

Loyalty to the American Constitution is a fundamental, perhaps the fundamental, American loyalty. Dr. Beard, in his *Economic Background to Jeffersonian Democracy*, holds that it was framed in the interests of *"security holders and manufacturers"*, and it is certainly more favourable to creditors than, for instance, the 1215 Great Charter. But the Constitution, so conspicuously violated in Pound's case (it prohibits *"unusual and cruel punishments"*), was an attempt to improve on the English model, so admired by John Adams. Adams had read in Blackstone (1-155) : *"And herein . . . consists the true excel-*

lence of the English government, that all the parts of it form a mutual check upon each other. . . . Thus every branch of our civil polity supports and is supported, regulates and is regulated, by the rest. . . . Like three distinct powers in mechanics, they jointly impel the machine of government in a direction different from what either, acting by itself, would have done; but at the same time in a direction which constitutes the true line of the liberty and happiness of the community." The British lost the residential qualification for representatives, which had been essential to knights of the shire and burgesses, and this was replaced in the American document. Another attempt at improvement, which is still a debating point, was the substitution of a wholly elective machine for one in which the elected are, in theory, checked and balanced by the hereditary principle. *"Elections of every kind are too frequently brought about by influence, partiality and artifice"* (Blackstone, 1-193). And (p. 53) *"the constitutional government of this island is so admirably tempered and compounded that nothing can endanger or hurt it, but destroying the equilibrium of power between one branch of the legislature and the rest".*

Almost while Blackstone was writing, "Lord North, purblind to the rights of a continent, eye on a few London merchants" (Canto 52) was violating the principle of taxation by consent which had been granted in the Great Charter. Madison, says Beard, *"turned very early against Hamilton and his policies; he fought for a discrimination between original holders of securities and the speculative purchasers; and he soon became an avowed partizan of Jefferson"*, the agrarian leader. John Taylor, in 1793, demanded that the Senate no longer sit behind closed doors, but *"subject their legislative discussions to free and common audience of every citizen"*. Pound's opinion of Hamilton is quite consistent with support of the Constitution, and his suggestion that parliamentary debates should be broadcast—as is done in New Zealand and Bonn alone— would implement Taylor's idea. Jackson of Georgia realised that Hamilton's proposition of a large national debt *"simply implied purchase of prosperity at the expense of the taxpayer and of future generations"*. This was an unconscious quotation from Blackstone, and he quoted him with an acknowledgment when he mentioned that the debt was established to create a monied interest.[1]

The establishment of the Bank of England (1694) at the dissolution of the feudal system of rights and duties was a precedent understood no less by its opponents at the First Congress than by Brooks Adams and Ezra Pound. For Pound is in the direct tradition of John Taylor, who complained of usurpation, when *"a faction of speculators seized upon its legislative functions"*, with Hamilton their *"apt instrument"* to ensure *" high taxes and their rigid collection"*; warned against *"a dangerous inequality of rank"* which laid *"foundation for the subversion of the government by undermining its true principles"*; and pleaded, *" Let us return to the Constitution"*. Taylor foresaw the capital-labour conflict which the imposition of *"usurious and compound interest"* would cause, and the federalists replied that small holdings but no slavery were to be found in New England. The Republicans saw what we have forgotten, that there was the gravest danger to their constitutional government from *"Dutch finance"*—Disraeli's phrase—and Excise, of Dutch-Cromwellian descent and reprobated as such by Blackstone, even if there was no powerful Dutch press, as Macaulay describes, to promote the system, or Dutch troops to enforce it.

Before one sees Pound's " Introductory Text Book ", it may seem inconsistent for him as a follower of Jefferson to write ten Cantos in praise of John Adams, Federalist President in 1796 and Jefferson's adversary in 1800. But Adams's economic and political outlook was not that of Hamilton, and Pound considers that he *"formed own view of Hamilton's game"* (Canto 62). Pound calls Hamilton " the Prime snot in ALL American history".

" Property equalled land in J.A.'s disposition " (Canto 63). Adams pointed out:

---

1. Blackstone did not quite say this, but rather that the new monied interest supported, naturally, the new arrangements.

late attack flagrant and formal
on the constitution itself
and the immunities of our charters
    this 41st. section repeals MAGNA
CHARTA the 29th chapter . . .
common law of England BIRTHRIGHT
of every man here. . . .   (Canto 66.)

On the constitutional issue, Pound writes :

in Tacitus, in Homer, 3 orders, in Greece as in Germany
and mankind dare not yet think upon
    CONSTITUTIONS . . .   (Canto 68).

In Canto 70, Adams says :

eternal neutrality in all wars in Europe . . .
I am for balance.

In Canto 71, views of his on banks are given that would
shock the moderns quite as severely as Pound has done. There
is little wonder that Cobbett saw much to approve in America.
Cobbett was using identical language in England to that of
Bryan, an agrarian pamphleteer, on *"stock jobbers"* and
"muck worms".

Jefferson opposed Hamilton's system of financial oligarchy,
and aimed to resolve the conflict between rich and poor
which Adams described by extending the middle class of
small farmers. But the sage of Monticello was a practical man
—Beard tells of Hamilton's support for him against Burr,
the "Catiline of America"—and for this reason Pound wrote
Jefferson and/or Mussolini. *"We have an immensity of land
courting the industrious husbandman"*, Jefferson wrote, and
held that the proportion which the aggregate of other classes
of citizen bears in any state to that of its husbandmen was
*"a good enough barometer whereby to measure its degree of
corruption"*. Beard concludes that the U.S. Constitution was
"the product of the conflict between capitalistic and agrarian

interests", and that it took ten years to swamp the corrupt minority which had dominated the country, *"while Jeffersonian Democracy simply meant the possession of the federal government by the agrarian masses led by an aristocracy of slave-owning planters, and the theoretical repudiation of the right to use the government for the benefit of any capitalistic groups, fiscal, banking or manufacturing"*.

Ezra Pound's book on Jefferson is unfortunately out of print. *"Jefferson"* (p. 14) *"governed our forefathers for twenty-four years, and you might almost say he governed for forty-eight . . . with a limited suffrage, and by means of conversation with his most intelligent friends."* Jefferson's principles are summarised on pages 115-116, and the best use I can make of space available is to repeat them in their shortest intelligible form : (1) *No hereditary privilege.* (2) *No unpayable national debts.* (3) *State control only where necessary.* (4) *Newspapers should be factual.* (5) *Peace.* (6) *The Constitution* (with the Amendments or " Bill of Rights "). (7) *" Ideals."* (8) *The advantage of the "ubiquity" of money.* (9) *The practicability of "national bills".* (10) *"National control of the national finances ceased when the administration changed WITHOUT there being a corresponding change in the control of the bank . . . the fights against the First and Second U.S. Banks were fights to keep the control of the nation's finances out of control by a clique, and to attain the use of the national resources for the benefit of the whole nation."* (11) *The nation should own its own paper money.* (12) *"No one has a natural right to the trade of a money lender but he who has money to lend."* (13) and (14) concern *debt.* (15) *The value of internal commerce.* (16) *Napoleon's ignorance.*

"A second bank was rigged up after another war. It took all Jackson's military popular prestige and Van Buren's brains and persistence to get the nation out of its talons. Van Buren wrote out the story in 1860. . . . The people did vote out the bank . . . the Treasury was made free, and remained so until the slithering Wilson erected a Board" (121, 124). *"All American and republican principles were lost during the damnable reign of the infamous Woodrow, but even Woodrow did not favour the XVIIIth*

Amendment." (A.B.C. of Economics.) The *Board* was instituted in 1913, under the guidance of Mr. Warburg. In a word, *" We were diddled out of the heritage Jackson and Van Buren left us "* (J/M, 97).

> Hic est hyperusura. Mr. Jefferson met it :
> . . . Van Buren met it.   (Canto 46.)

Elsewhere he blames on the Civil War the forgetfulness of these historic events. *(A.B.C. of Economics,* pp. 25 and 26.)

Time, and probably quite a short time, will be needed before Dr. Pound's more recent pronouncements are considered dispassionately. His views have been grossly misrepresented. Signora Olivia Rossetti Agresti, the great-niece of D. G. Rossetti, wrote : *" When Fascism fired the Italian imagination it was by seeking a solution for a world-felt need, that of harmonising the interests of capital, management and labour in the Guild or Corporative State. . . . The Guild State may yet save the world from the servile state. . . . When Fascism rejected parochialism (the individual) and internationalism (mankind) for nationalism, it ceased to be Italian and it died before the 'liberators' arrived. But a day will come when the contribution Fascist Italy made to the solution of both local and universal problems will be studied and perhaps understood."* It is not easy, even now, to take seriously the proposition that Eza Pound was an advocate of despotism. His ideal, and a practical one, was balance between the nations and within them.

> . . . despotism
> or absolute power, . . . unlimited sovereignty,
> is the same in a majority of a popular assembly,
> an aristocratical council, an oligarchical junto,
> and a single emperor, equally arbitrary, bloody,
> and in every respect diabolical. Wherever it has resided
> has never failed to destroy all records, memorials,
> all histories which it did not like, and to corrupt
> those that it was cunning enough to preserve.
>   (Canto 33.)

Mencius found the same historical gaps in his time. Pound is not the solitary crotchet that the mesmeric press would have us believe, and was certainly not alone among Americans in deploring Roosevelt's policies. The late Dr. Beard wrote two detailed books, one on the change in foreign policy to an aggressive open door policy in 1933, the other giving some distasteful facts about Pearl Harbour. There have been many others with exciting titles. ("The Roosevelt Myth"; "Government by Treason", etc.) In his economic and historic writings, Ezra Pound has tried to carry on the realistic tradition of John Adams and Jefferson, of Jackson, of Taylor and Brooks Adams. The Americans appear to forget their past even quicker than the English do. I am attempting a clarification rather than an apologia, for good work can stand on its own feet : but misrepresentation on the "racial" issue needs clearing away. Pound, throughout, is far less consciously "racial" in outlook than were, for instance, Disraeli or Lord Byron. He admired David Lubin, or any other individual of any other race who had personal merit and integrity.

There is, of course, another view of history which is taught in the schools. F. J. C. Hearnshaw complains in his "British Prime Ministers of the 18th Century" : "Blackstone . . . seemed to know nothing of the prime minister or the Cabinet or the party system or parliamentary sovereignty. . . . It would be difficult to conceive a picture more remote from reality." Pound is well aware of this current view, and has some scorching sayings on the swindle of the "party system", as well as (in 1933 !) on the welfare state. Hearnshaw, incidentally, confuses "parliament" with the House of Commons, which is doubtless what a good many political adventurers would approve of. Any healthy system guards against the bloated buzzard and the swarm of locusts which are no less predatory. John Adams, in Pound's view, is the corrective to Jefferson : "'*You fear the one, I the few', said the second to the third President.*"

the Foundation of Regius Professors
was made to spread lies and teach Whiggery. (Canto 46.)

Readers of C. Hollis's *The Two Nations* will doubtless recall the author's conclusion that it has taken but two generations of compulsory text-book education to make the poor as ignorant as the rich.

I have had to omit grain and loot dividends, and other interesting facts with which the Cantos abound, and it is to Pound's work that I would commend the reader. *"No one can understand history without understanding economics. . . . The best facts of history are not in the school books."* (*Social Credit*, pp. 5-6.) Pound is a genial, if exacting, guide and, although vilification of him and his work is the latest " racket" in America, one who has studied his work cannot quit the subject without a word of gratitude.

EZRA POUND AND HIS CHINESE CHARACTER:
A RADICAL EXAMINATION

by Hugh Gordon Porteus [*1950*]

" Wang Wei in his landscapes couldn't care less about
details appropriate to the Four Seasons. Thus,
in the matter of flowers, he would slip into the same
picture blossoming sprigs of peach, apricot, hibis-
cus, together with lotus. I happen to possess a
sketch of his which actually shows a fruiting banana
plantain loaded with snow ! Just a flash of vision,
suddenly seized and fixed by the hand of a master
—an inspiration of sheer genius ! Ah, but what a
tedious thing it can be, to find oneself embroiled in
controversy over such phenomena—especially with
the unwashed."
—Shen Kua (Sung Dynasty Art Critic, circa 1066 A.D.)

" For that matter explain to me how the pages of *Cathay*
Came out of the time-bound Ezra

into the light of common day !"
(*One-Way Song*).

Throughout the works of Ezra Pound one comes across
references to Chinese literature, and to quotations from the
Chinese classics—sometimes in English paraphrase, sometimes in Chinese character. Increasingly, since the first world
war, Pound has busied himself with things Chinese. Constantly he has advocated the inclusion of Chinese language,
poetry, and (Confucian) doctrine in the English educational
system. " A sane university curriculum," he holds, " would
put Chinese where Greek was." Confucius is recommended
to redress the state of affairs brought about ever since " Aristotle's parrots left *techne* out of the kinds of intelligence ".
The nine so-called " Confucian " classics comprise the five
Ching (canons) and the four *Shu* (books). The latter include,
besides the sayings of Confucius himself (Analects) and the
works of Mencius (Mengtze), two books which deserve more

attention than they have hitherto received in the West. The
first is the *Ta Hsüeh*, or the Great Learning. The second is the
Chung Yung, or the Doctrine of the Just Mean. Originally
these two books formed part of the *Li Ki*, or Book of Rites.
Of the first, the opening section alone is ascribed to Confucius, whose grandson is credited with the compilation of
the second. And of the first, Pound has made two English versions. More recently he has made translations of the *Chung
Yung* and of the *Analects*. One might wonder why Pound
should choose, out of the vast corpus of Chinese literature,
these three hackneyed works, known by rote in childhood to
every scholar in China, and long available in European
versions. One might also dwell upon the peculiarly Chinese
paradox involved in Pound's advocacy of strict orthodoxy
and orthology. But Pound's avowed ignorance of Chinese
literature in general and of the Chinese language in particular
makes only the more spectacular his singular achievements
in these two fields. It must meanwhile be conceded that Pound
is not only the latest, but the most exhilaratingly unorthodox,
and the most intelligent, of a very long line of Confucian
editors and commentators.

One of Pound's most certain claims to immortality rests
upon his paraphrases and pastiches of Chinese poetry. While
China barely subsists, Pound has put Cathay back on the
map, and made it live again in all its glory. In this he has
done only what the great poets of China have done in various
times for their own mythical Golden Ages. Pound's *Cathay*
comprises a set of paraphrases made from the notes of one
American and two Japanese professors. It represents a
Japanese selection of Chinese poems, the better half of which
are attributed to the T'ang poet Li T'ai Po (in sino-Japanese:
Ri-ha-ku). Some of these have been known in the West from
numerous translations made ever since the publication of
the French versions of the Marquis d'Hervey-Saint-Denys in
the 'eighties. That Pound's versions are incomparable, no
poet will deny. "As for *Cathay*," Mr. Eliot wrote, in
1928, "it must be pointed out that Pound is the inventor of

Chinese poetry for our time." As early as 1914, **Mr.** Waley was publishing admirable translations of Po Chü-I in *The Little Review,* to which Pound was then a regular contributor. Yet between them it seems there has been no commerce. Mr. Waley is the most widely read and respected of translators from Chinese. That he has received no mention in this context is no matter for surprise. Pound is first and last a poet. Waley is first and last a sinologue. In sinological circles, no doubt, Pound's excursions into Chinese raise no more than a wry smirk. For he has always treated Chinese as though it were an extinct, well-nigh indecipherable script, akin to the hieroglyphics of Harappa and Mohenjodaro, Easter Island, or of the Hittites. On the other hand, those responsive to the subtle niceties of Pound's verse cannot be expected to take seriously, on the same level, the hit-and-miss poetic technique of Mr. Waley: although all contemporary poets must be in his debt. What is remarkable about Pound's Chinese translations is that so often they do contrive to capture the spirit of their originals, even when, as quite often happens, they funk or fumble the letter. Pound's knowledge of Chinese, at least up to the time of his second version of the *Ta Hsüeh,* was so inadequate that he had been incompetent even to use a Chinese dictionary properly. This has, however, by no means impaired the value of his achievements. In his edition of Fenollosa's essay, " The Chinese Character as a Medium for Poetry ", Pound provides an illuminating commentary on his own practice in the form of " some notes by a Very Ignorant Man ". And one might go so far as to argue that it is rather because of that frankly acknowledged ignorance than in spite of it that his Chinese "inventions" (to follow up Eliot's hint) are so valuable.

For Pound, the Chinese character is a mysterious and magical unknown quantity, which sets all his faculties vibrating at the highest pitch of excitement. His pseudo-sinology releases his latent clairvoyance, just as the pseudo-sciences of the ancients sometimes gave them a supernormal insight. A Chinese text serves Pound as a receipt for the elixir served a Chinese alchemist, as a hand serves a palmist, as a horoscope serves an astrologer. The result is a phenomenon of psychometry abetted by æsthetics.

"Things have their roots," as it is written in the *Ta Hsüeh*, "as well as their branches." In the ensuing pages I wish to prod the roots from which Pound has reared his great tree, laden with the fairest flowers of the orient. The branches may take care of themselves.

In connection with the Chinese epigraph at the head of this essay, it may be interesting to quote from the notes of Wang Wei himself. Wang Wei was one of the finest painters, poets and calligraphers of the Sung heyday. He observed : "Art is not the mere exercise of manual skills. It must reveal its relations with the phenomena of the cosmos. Those who engage in discussion upon the arts commonly confine their attention to formal considerations. The old masters were not however motivated merely by a wish to record sites, boundaries or waterways. The forms in the arts must be infused by spirit, after which the mind effects further transformations. Without this spirit, form itself is powerless to move us." These two quotations together suggest an analogy which may be useful in establishing a point or two about translation. No amount of information is enough to put us in possession of all that matters about a poem, or a place, beyond our reach. Suppose you wish to know about, say, Venice. You may collect all sorts of factual and graphic information from books and tourist agency brochures. You may gather statistics, photographs, plans, topographical drawings, and a thousand kinds of data. And this may add up to nothing. And a rough sketch by Turner, or Canaletto, may give you the whole place at a glance. The sketch may be rough and factually inaccurate or outmoded in detail. But it may give you the precise feel, smell and *stimmung*. Campanili are shuffled about with reckless indifference to topography. None of the detail will stand scrutiny. Yet it gets across something that your data leave out. Something similar is true of translations. The problem of translating from one language to another is a complicated one. The problems involved in translating Chinese are many and peculiar. The problem of translating verse is especially tricky. There is room for many kinds of valid and valuable approach. But in judging translation one should not give priority or an exclusive monopoly of truth to the equivalent of a piece of cartography or a list of the number of hotels open to non-residents. These details are not useless. Archæology has its value. But sinologues who attempt to translate poetry tend to be inhibited by their own specialised knowledge, and it is only the fools who rush in where this angel host fears to tread who succeed in carrying off a Chinese poem intact into English. Notoriously the most readable translations from the Chinese have been made by European writers with practically no knowledge of Chinese. Sinologues, who are a jealous crew, famous for their fighting footnotes, should learn to suffer these fools more gladly. For we need the expert's data as well as the amateur's rough sketch. Pound, of course, it not an amateur poet, but a professional who, like Waley, stands at the very top of his own profession. It is in the nature of things impossible to reproduce in a foreign medium all that gives value to an original poem. We can do with innumerable versions : indeed, the more the merrier. Each translation can do no more than open a lens on certain selected facets of the original. Bearing in mind that in translating a poem the most valuable end product is another poem, that shall soar and sing by its own right, all other data have their place. Pound produces living poems, and not stuffed museum specimens that are true to everything else except life. The following pages focus attention on one or two simple facets of the problem of translating Chinese, as Pound had to face it. The reader is invited to join a short excursion into semantics.

Pound has the vices of his virtues. Sometimes imagination leads him to see too much. At other times a headlong enthusiasm propels him so impatiently that he misses the obvious. In his attempts at dissecting the Chinese character, his tendency towards over-literalism would matter less if his procedure were not radically wrong. In his *Cathay* translations, Pound was able, fortunately, to check up from both ends, rationalising Fenollosa's notes with the aid of Morrison's dictionary. No praise is too high, in any case, for the results, however arrived at, and it is good to see this acknowledged by Chinese scholars of evident authority. But from some of Pound's subsequent, presumably unaided, work on Chinese, it is plain that in several particulars he misunderstood, and so misinterpreted and misapplied, the method of Fenollosa. Not only has he entirely ignored the function of the phonetic in the structure of compound characters (owing doubtless to the complications introduced by using Sino-Japanese texts), but the formula he uses is incorrect. A few illustrations will show how he adds up the components of his characters, instead of multiplying, and so gets the sum wrong instead of the right product.

(1)   (2)   (3)   (4)   (5)

I pick at random, from the poem on Plate I of Pound's notes to Fenollosa's essay, the symbol for flower (1). Pound correctly sorts out its three components, noting that the top bit is an abbreviated form of plants (2), the left-hand bit an abbreviation for man (3), and the remaining pieces the usual symbol for spoon (4). Now plants plus man plus spoon hardly add up to a very convincing definition of flower. (Pound tries to explain : " Flowers at height of man's head.") The dictionaries, on the other hand, simply give "plants" as radical plus the phonetic group *hua*, implying that it is no more than a sort of plant pronounced *hua*. The dictionary gives the right procedure ; Pound has the right idea. The character must first be divided into radical and remainder, and the latter resolved separately. The phonetic group *hua* represents a person wielding a ladle, and means "to melt", hence to transform, to change (5). Therefore, a plant that changes its hue with the seasons—a flowering plant, a flower. (That the whole character is only a comparatively recent simplification of an ancient picture of a bush covered with blossoms does not invalidate the truth and "poetry" of this analysis.)

Sometimes Pound just can't read straight. On Plate V of the same book are two characters (6), (7) of which the radicals are on the left in each case :

(6)   (7)   (8)

Even for one who has to refer to a table to find common radicals, there seems little excuse for confusing the abbreviated 3-stroke radical 64 (hand) with the 4-stroke radical 93 (ox). For one who deems all professors moles or bats, it was surely unwise to go on to mistake both radicals for still a third (8). Pound's interpretation in each case being "a measure" (radical 68). The two characters together actually mean "to sow things" or "to publish matters abroad". Pound's deliciously fantastic translation runs "and knoweth measure in dividing and in bringing together"

The confusions into which Pound can be led when he combines misreading with bad method are less remarkable than the manner in which, by a combination of intuition and ingenuity, he is able to extricate himself again—with a squint at his crib. The following character, from the poem already cited, is a relatively complex one—indeed, it is a good deal more complicated even than it looks—and one which any amateur might be forgiven for botching (9):

(9)

This is the character which Pound translates "admire" in his line : "We can admire the bright turning disc." If we analyse it according to the correct formula :

$$R.61 \; \frac{R.119}{R.136}$$

where $R =$ the generic radical (and R the other components with their numbers as found in the dictionary under the 214 radicals), we get the generic *heart*, showing us at once that the character has something to do with the emotions, and the phonetic group *lin*. That is as far as the dictionary takes us in analysis. If we care to resolve the phonetic *lin*, we find that its meaning as a separate word is "will-o'-the-wisp", and that it apparently represents the character for "uncooked rice", over the character for "perverse".

$$\text{heart X} \; \frac{\text{uncooked rice}}{\text{perverse}}$$

This is what Pound would have got, had he not misread all except the first component. How he would have cooked up the meaning "admire" out of this I cannot imagine. But in fact Pound transcribes (p. 41, *op. cit.*) thus :

> "ADMIRE
> (be in love with)
>   heart +
>   Fire
>   girl +
>   descending
>   through two "

His "heart" is in the right place. "Fire" is evidently his misreading for "uncooked rice": and yet here, in his curious prophetic way, Pound is right, if not for the right

reason. For an earlier form of the character, still current as
a precious alternative, does in fact show the "fire" picture
repeated (10) above the "perverse" symbol. The latter,
mistaken by Pound for two separate characters, is in its
ancient form a representation of two persons sleeping back
to back (11).

(10)   (11)   (13a)   (13b)   (12)

In its modern form, it does resemble the two characters
respectively meaning "evening" (13a) (veiled moon) and
"ox" (13b). Mr. Pound, not recognising the indivisible 6-
stroke hundred and thirty-sixth radical (12), mistakes the
left half for the thirty-eighth radical ("girl") ; while his
"descending through two" is presumably a very desperate
guess at the rest, which he can't find in Morrison.

Now in the case of this character, it will be noted that had
the lexicographer's intention been merely phonetic, so that
he desired simply to add to the "heart" or "feelings"
radical the sound *lin,* he might just as well have used the
commoner character *lin* (a wood) already mentioned ; and
this, indeed, might have been poetically suitable too ("wood-
land feelings"). It happens that such a character does, in
fact, exist ; with the sound *lin,* and the meaning "chilly".
But he required something more exotic and elusive, and
found it in the rarer phonetic group *lin,* comprising fire
repeated over perversity, hence *ignis fatuus.* Thus the whole
character signifies "will-o'-the-wispish feelings", something
nostalgic and pathetic, commiseration, sympathy, pity with
a dash of envy in it : in the context, I should say, *envy* :

     able   envy   gold   disc   turning

Pound explains his choice of "admire" in a note as follows :

"Fenollosa had translated admire, then changed to love ; I have taken back to admire, for the sake of the Latin ad-miror, and to absorb some of Morrison's 'implement used to reflect' (i.e. disc), though I do not imagine this will reach many readers."

From this cursory examination of a single character, certain conclusions may be drawn. Plainly Pound, handicapped as he necessarily is, sees something—or at any rate looks for something—that sinologues in general are blind to. Plainly, too, we must dig down deeper than the 214 radicals of the dictionaries before we can get at the true roots of Chinese. We must go back to the fountain head, the pictogram, if we wish to trace the source from which may well the various submerged "meanings" of a character.

(14)   (14a)   (15)   (16)   (17)

"There is a character," says Karlgren (*Sound and Symbol in Chinese*, p. 64) "for the word 'spring, well', which in a primeval form (14), and even in the 'small seal' (14a) was an unmistakable picture of a well or spring : a basin from which water flows. The corresponding normal character (15), however, looks as if it were composed of 'white, pure' (16) and 'water' (17) ; and as this is a good definition of the notion 'spring', it is evident that some *speculative scribe* in transforming the 'small seal' into a normal character has introduced an element of *popular etymology*." And again (p. 62) Karlgren observes that Li Si, the scribe responsible for the " small seal " stylisation of bronze and bone pictograms, " had often *misunderstood* the old symbols, and had sometimes deliberately substituted new characters for them. There was, for example, an old character for a word meaning ' extend, pull out, notify '. *Not understanding this,* he put in its place a somewhat similar character—perhaps a variant

invented by *some careless scribe*—two hands stretching something long ". I have italicised, in these two passages, the
expressions which seem to me characteristic of the insensitive
solemnity of the professional philologist. I submit that there
is not a shred of evidence to show that Li Si was the blind
fool implied above, and masses of evidence to show that he
was a poet of great resource and imagination. The changes
from pictograph to seal, and from seal to Sung style, all bear
witness to the sophistication of the scribe. Faced with the
task of transposing a picture into simple and more formal
terms, in his anxiety to guard against losing the image, and
so bogging the language in abstraction, the scribe sensitively
and good-humouredly rehabilitated the decayed character
with fresh imagery ; thus preserving the concrete and poetic
essence of Chinese, and saving it from the fate that overtook
cuneiform when it got stumped in the clay of Babylon. These
changes were made by the *literati*, it must be remembered,
and they were in the nature of donnish *jeux-de-mots*, the
products not of accident or vulgarian fancy, but of art and
wit. " Popular etymology " does, it is true, sometimes produce something in English that succeeds and survives by its
sheer effectiveness, but more often still something absurd and
grotesque (e.g., " Goat and Compasses " for " God Encom-
passeth ", or, on the orthographic plane, the " ye olde " Y
for the " thorn " rune). Nevertheless, even popular etymology
is not to be despised in a consideration of the growth of roots,
and English affords at least one excellent example, as we
shall see in a moment, of a type of analogic-semantic change
parallel to that which the professors so scorn when they spot
it in Chinese.

Was it not Aristotle who announced that a man's
genius was commensurate with his power to make good metaphors ? Certainly one of the non-transferable endowments of
genius appears to be the gift for analogical as against logical
thinking. (T. E. Hulme understood this, but never lived to
develop his theory in detail.)

In this respect Pound exhibits all the signs of the greatest genius. His particular gift is for linking up the seemingly disparate in order to generate something new. In the field of words and images, this is the creative gift of the artist. In the field of ideas the same faculty may operate. And in both fields it is a gift which, when its possessor is thwarted, may get him locked up. The second sight which enables the seer to detect secret liaisons between matters which to the normal observation have no apparent commerce can easily take some form of paranoia. I leave it to experts in these matters to decide how far Pound's present distress is due to persecution mania : no doubt he *was* persecuted. And I note in passing that paranoia in some form is clearly an occupational disease among sinologists. What I wish to point out is that a person like Pound with a gift for metaphor and image-making and punning (with the seven or seven hundred and seventy-seven types of ambiguity), is quite likely to let his gift run away with him. Pound's epistolary style is well known: it sparkles very like the incandescent foam of *Finnegan's Wake*. An early and I think uncollected epigram *On a Cake of Soap* well exemplifies his mastery of the multiple ambiguity:

> Lo, how it gleams and glistens in the sun :
> Like the cheek of a Chesterton.

The same faculty has led Pound sometimes into the nightmare no man's land of name swopping and etymological fantasy. Thus in one place in *The Pisan Cantos* he actually equates "Wanjina" (an African rain god out of a Frobenius legend) with "Ouan Jin" (French transliteration of Chinese for "literary gent"—in Wade transcription : *Wên jen*). When, in the same *Cantos*, he runs into Provençal with "cette mauvaiseh vengg", one almost expects to see stamped in the margin the Chinese character for wind, *fêng* (cf. German fohn). But do we know enough to say that these are all mere winds of chance ? Typhoon, it may be observed in passing, is not exclusively Greek. *Tai-fêng* ("great wind") is a familiar phenomenon to those who sail the China seas. All this may seem by the way, but (further to illustrate my point) these matters are not unconnected. Pound is much attached to the word "ideogramic". Just as the arts reach their peaks of greatest significance where there are suitable racial or cultural "crosses", so do the faculties of individuals of genius, and so do words when they are coined or used to satisfy as many "cognate" meanings as possible. We speak also of the genius of a language. Highly inflected tongues like Latin, or German, with their interminable tables, suit the logical thinker very well, and serve admirably for scientific card indexing work. Languages like English and Chinese, which make syntax and suggestion do as much as possible of the work of grammar, have other properties. In English we have a tongue adapted to every variety of subtle quasi-onomatopæic expression, as readers of the neglected works of Sir Richard Paget will know (e.g., his discovery of the gestural implications of groups of words of the order of *string, stretch, strain, stroke, strand, stream, street, strake, stride,* etc.). The great virtue of the Chinese language inheres in its written characters, which so often contrive to suggest by their graphic gestures (as English does by its phonetic gestures) the very essence of what is to be conveyed.

The reader may be left to judge how far the traditional middle way of the Chinese is exemplified in the various styles of the character for "man" (3).

(18)   (19)   (20)

The earliest known form (18) derives, according to the latest researches of Mr. L. C. Hopkins, from a profile. The "small seal" (19) suggests, perhaps, man's peneal attribute. The modern form (20) evokes an immediate picture of man as biped, or, the "bifurcation", as Karlgren notes, of Shakespeare's "forked radish".

Here an English parallel suggests itself. The Concise Oxford Dictionary simply gives the derivation *radix,* which would
also be the bright schoolboy's guess. This ignores the fact
that the radish flourished, under a similar name, long before
the Roman invasion. The O.E.D. admits earlier spellings,
adding that the word was "re-adapted" later. The poetic
point is missed. *Radix* is abstract, generic, any old root.
Reddish, the early native name, is concrete, particular, gives
the colour that distinguishes it from the turnip and the
parsnip. The fusion of the two words gave the vivid ideogram
radish.

It would seem that the survival values, in English words
as in Chinese characters, depend on properties of evocation
which only the poet consciously apprehends. Professor Forest
(*The Chinese Language,* pp. 41-2) concedes the principle that
even where the function of the phonetic element in a compound
character is primarily phonetic, the associations of the
character so used are generally weighed. Mr. Payne (*The
White Pony*) holds that no Chinese seeing the character for
"autumn" thinks of its components, "fire" and "corn":
though other writers on Chinese have seen in it an evocative
picture. Mr. Forest cites the character for "sadness", which
happens to be compounded of the "autumn" symbol over
the "heart" radical (=autumnal emotions, the heart bleed-
ing for the decay of the year). But he goes on to note that it
is hard to find a case where the graphic etymology has actually
influenced semantic development as clearly as in the case of
the phonetic similarity of "sorrow" and "sorry" in English
—"which most English speakers apprehend as related".
He then says that "for those educated in the written
language, writing rapidly becomes so far an automatic gesture
that the written word is hardly analysed. It is probable that
few, however steeped in the classics, have even the faintest
suggestion of astrology in their minds when they read or write
such a word as 'disaster', or even dream of white raiment
in connection with a candidature". The answer here, and it
should settle a crucial point, is that it is precisely those *few*

216

who matter, at any rate in connection with poetry. Mr. Eliot's dictum about the importance for poets of knowing everything possible about *words* will be recalled. A poet insensitive to the origin, shape, tone and colour of such words would be, as a poet, simply a candidate for disaster.

All the urgent problems of our time are, after all, in some sense, communication problems. In all fields there are gaps to be bridged. It is easy to see the immediate importance of the more obvious kind of bridge-builder: the structural engineer, for example (a man apt to be too handy with sticks of dynamite). It is never so easy to vindicate the bridge-building functions of the artist, whose parallel activities take place on a higher level. At no time in history have the gaps been so wide between specialised departments of knowledge, between the arts and the sciences, between east and west. The significance of China for the future of the world cannot be over-estimated. It is especially necessary that the breach between the Chinese and English-speaking peoples should not be widened. That is something more important ultimately than, say, the dollar-gap. The value of Ezra Pound's lonely pioneer work in the higher orders of gap-bridging will one day receive the honours due to him now.

About other aspects of Pound's great work I have written elsewhere, in appreciation and appraisement, I suppose as voluminously as anybody during the past twenty years—and consistently, too. Naturally, one expects no change from Pound himself. But I hope that these extremely rough and elementary notes may serve to even enlighten some who have been very ready to find fault with his translations from languages more familiar than Chinese.

SOME CONSIDERATIONS ARISING FROM
EZRA POUND'S CONCEPTION OF THE BANK

by Max Wykes-Joyce [1949]

In a life-long advocation of clarity, Pound has rarely troubled
to annotate his own work, reasoning, with justice, that its
meaning was evidence without the need of gloze. His chief
exception was the careful consideration given to Canto 45
in a broadcast from Rome : which should lead us to one of two
conclusions. Either Canto 45 is in Pound's view obscure, and
the reader not in possession of the full facts of the case that
Pound sets forth in it, which the reader can prove untrue for
himself on a cursory examination : or, and this I believe is the
true explanation, the Canto is of such importance in his system
of thought that he will not take the risk of being misunderstood.

Now this Canto has usury as its subject, detailing its evil
effects ; and it is a fact that our banking systems are based on
usury, no matter by what sweeter name we call it to salve our
troubled consciences, or to shrive ourselves of some atavistic
condemnation. Hence Pound's first modification of the commonly held view of the function of banks. The levying of
interest whether at two per cent. or twenty per cent. is
usurious, and usury stands condemned as strongly in this
American's view as it did in the teaching of the mediæval
Fathers.

In all his economic writings, he makes the basic distinction
between banks founded for the good of their shareholders and
regardless of the wellbeing of any and everyone else, which
means almost all banks as we now know them ; and banks
founded primarily for the good of the whole people. As
examples of this difference in attitude and aim, Pound posits
two Italian banks, the Banco S. Giorgio, usually known as
the Bank of Genoa, and, together with the Bank of Amster-
dam, lauded in every English text-book as the ideal banking
organisation ; and the Monte dei Paschi of Siena. The Banco
S. Giorgio, well-styled by the bank historian Thorold Rogers
"a republic within a republic", was founded in 1407. Loans

made to certain citizens became the bank's capital. Later eight
directors were elected by the stockholders. The State made
over to this board of directors certain cities and territories,
including Caffa and Corsica, the latter of which was sold to
France at the convenience of the bank. Over a period of many
years the board acquired the right to levy all taxes, including
those on the Church. After the revolution at the end of the
eighteenth century, the absolute right of civil and criminal
jurisdiction in the Republic was taken from the bank directors
in whom it had been vested (which meant that the bank, even
in cases against itself was both prosecutor and judge) as being
incompatible with the Republic's unity and the sovereignty
of the people. The Monte dei Paschi, founded for the good of
the whole people by Cosimo I of Tuscany, and based not on
gold, nor on mere juggling with the accounts to produce paper
credits, was an experiment following the Florentine conquest.
Cosimo guaranteed the bank's capital of 200,000 ducats,
accepting as security the grazing lands belonging to the city.
The shareholders were to be paid five per cent., money to be
loaned to the public at five and a half per cent. All overheads
and salaries were to be kept at a minimum, and all profits were
to be expended on hospitals and public works within the city.
" The lesson," writes Pound, " is the very basis of modern
banking. The CREDIT rests, *in ultimate*, on the ABUN-
DANCE OF NATURE, on the growing grass that can nourish
the living sheep."

With these two examples in mind, we find throughout
Pound's work references to many world famous banks, most
of which on analysis prove to be fashioned after the Genoan
rather than the Sienese prototype. It is unnecessary for our
present purpose to consider the references in detail, but one
or two specific points demand attention. The foundation of the
Bank of England was, in itself, immoral, based upon a fraud,
in Pound's opinion. Paterson, in his public circular soliciting
investments, had written: "The Bank hath benefit of the
interest in all the moneys it creates out of nothing." The
process by which banks created and create money *ex nihil* is

too large a subject in which to engage here : the interested
reader is referred to R. McNair Wilson's *Promise to Pay*
for a complete exposition. In his *Carta da Visita* Pound
specifically dates the modern phrase of the war against usury
from 1694, the year in which the Bank was founded. Lest it
be thought that Pound's objection to the creation of credit for
private profit is merely the aberration of an inept visionary,
let it be recorded that two years after the Bank's foundation,
a pamphlet opposing it contained the following epitaph:
" Here lies the body of the Bank of England, who was born
in the year 1694, died May 5th, 1696, in the third year of its
age. They had issue legitimate by their Common Seal,
1,200,000 called Bank Bills, and by their cashier two million
sons of ——— called Speed's notes."

Pound objects to the American banks for quite another
reason; he is intensely patriotic (indictment for treason not-
withstanding), and it is his opinion that the American revolution and the aims of the American republic were betrayed to
the usurers by the American banks. He speaks with bitterness
of the "great betrayal", and the ensuing decadence, against
which only Martin van Buren and Jackson warred in the
public sphere, and Adams in private. One of the few passages
specially emphasised in the Cantos (No. 71) is a quotation
from John Adams:

Every bank of discount is downright corruption
taxing the public for private individuals' gain
and if I say this is my will
the American people would pronounce I died crazy.

It is a tragic thought that on the repetition of this and similar
statements the American people bases its belief that Pound is
crazy.

Somewhere Pound distinguishes between the "Monte dei
Paschi and the devils"; of this latter group one more remains
to be detailed, for the connection between armaments and
usury. It is acknowledged that the usurer's chief interest is

his own profit; it is also acknowledged that the manufacture of armaments is one of the most lucrative of occupations. It is reasonable to assume, therefore, a close connection, indeed an interdependence, between international usury and the international arms trade. The best example is to be found in the Mitsui bank of Japan, where European and American banks have bought

> a lot of shares in Mitsui
> who arm 50 divisions, who keep up the Japanese army
> and they are destined to have a large future.

The motive of these three immoral actions: in the case of the Bank of England the creation of money, in the case of the Banks of America the betrayal of the State, in the case of the Mitsui Bank the financing by foreigners of an army likely to be used against their own compatriots—is private gain at the expense of public good. Since so much banking activity is of this nature, one wonders why Pound does not advocate the complete rejection of the banking system as we know it, since its very operation is almost certain to be anti-social. But there *are* a few banks like the Monte dei Paschi; and it is upon such slender foundations that he hopes to create a new and valuable banking system, with a new aim. He introduces his idea of necessary reform early in the Cantos, by approving the Mantuan banking legislation of 1401, which virtually set up a credit bank in Mantua. The relevant passage is from Canto 35.

> That there be made a fontego (a chamber)
> to lend money on cloth, so that they cease not to
> labour for lack of money. . . .

This advocacy of the credit bank necessitates a short explanation of the credit theories to which Pound adheres.

The economic problem of this century is not one of production; we have enough machinery to fulfil adequately all our

needs; the problem is now one of distribution. In the 'Thirties
the catchphrase about poverty in the midst of plenty became
familiar; and to some of us it appeared then as it now appears,
that the spectacle of Brazilian coffee and Canadian wheat
being destroyed while a large part of Europe existed in semi-
starvation, was a result of our inability to grasp a few simple
economic facts and to act upon them. Fact one. Distribution
depends upon the amount of money in existence in a country
being equivalent to the amount of goods for sale in that
country. Which means that if some organisation produces
goods which are going to sell to the consumer for a million
pounds, and directly or indirectly only half a million pounds
are payed out for the production of the goods, then there will
be half a million pounds' worth left at the factory or in the
shops solely because of a lack of vouchers with which to
transfer them from shop to table, or wherever they would be
most useful.

Fact two. At present any creation of such credit (the
vouchers for the second half million pounds' worth) is haphazard, arranged by bankers, understandably but lamentably,
for their own gain, and with *no* reference to the public weal.
Again the reader is referred to McNair Wilson's *Promise to Pay*.

Fact three. Any government to be effective, must have
control of the state's finance (this, be it noted, without prejudice to the adjunctive political organisation, for, as Pound
writes: "Economics is concerned with what should be done,
not with how you are going to get a controlling group of men
to carry out an idea"), and, broadly speaking, will take the
same economic measures for the health of the state whether it
be an individual dictatorship, a monarchy, a soviet, a democracy, or an oligarchy. One of its chief functions will be to
create and distribute credit.

At any suggestion of printing more money, tickets, vouchers,
without more work, there is raised the inevitable cry of inflation, as though of necessity inflation must be evil, and without
any consideration as to whether such controlled production of
credit is inflationary at all. The correction of such a miscon-

ceived notion was ably voiced by A. R. Orage, quoted by Pound in his *A.B.C. of Economics*. "Would you call it inflation to issue tickets for every seat in a hall, despite the fact that the hall had never before been filled, or more than a fourth of the seats sold, because of there not being enough tickets available? Inflation would consist in issuing more tickets than there are seats."

It should be obvious that any pieces of paper will serve as money, so long as they are honoured by those who use them. Private money has been produced many times in history— Pound instances the issue of paper bills under the T'ang dynasty, between the years 841 and 847; the production, by his grandfather, of private paper money, backed by lumber, in pioneer America; and the Wörgl experiment, in which this small Tyrolese town issued its own credit with complete success, thus at one stroke of the pen freeing itself of the necessity of borrowing from the bankers:—

> all the slobs in Europe were terrified. . . .
> . . . 'no one,' said the Frau Burgomeister
> ' in this village who could read a newspaper article.
> Knew it was money but pretended it was not
> in order to be on the safe side of the law.'

In each of these three cases, and there is documentary evidence for many more, the credit was based, in the last analysis, upon one factor, which Pound emphasises over and over again in his Cantos, in the as yet untranslated Italian sociological pamphlets, in his purely economic treatises:

> I have told you . . .
> . . . of the true basis of credit, that is
>   the abundance of nature
> with the whole folk behind it. . . .

As example of this realisation in good rulers, Tai Tsong is cited, who released three hundred men from jail for the spring sowing, and all of whom returned in October.

223

Given the true basis of credit, which is the same for individual or state, the actual distribution of credit can be left in private or public hands; but Pound, in agreement with Silvio Gesell, suggests that credit could best be organised and distributed by a national central bank, controlled by the government. This, he asserts, was originally proposed in Mazzini's *Doveri Dell' Uomo*. The chief function of the bank in Pound's economics is to distribute credit.

It is important in any study of national and international economics to remember that political power, dissociated from economic, is valueless. The majority of nations still leave their financial affairs to the care of their Central Banks, some examination of which will not be out of place here. My example in this paragraph will be taken from English banking, but with minor variations the system is similar throughout the whole world with the exception of Soviet Russia and some of the Eastern European countries. The Central Bank (the Bank of England in our example) acts as banker to the local banks, just as the local bank acts as banker to individuals. The assets of a local bank are approximately fifty-five per cent. notes and coin, and forty-five per cent. bankers' deposits with the Central Bank; this last is a fact which should be carefully noted. If a large loan is required of a local bank, it is forced to ask a loan of the Central Bank; its ability to loan to an individual or group will depend on the willingness of the Central Bank to make a loan to it. Moreover, it should be obvious that the Central Bank can control the amount of credit available to the public by simply altering the total of bank deposits, or by varying the bank-rate. A further element has yet to be considered; the Central Bank also acts as the State's banker; and thus has power to finance or to decline to finance any government project at will. " But," the alert reader will enquire, "in such case is not the Bank the real governor of the State, and not the nominal government?" True, and if the government declines to be governed, the Central Bank, by manipulating the bankers' deposits, can vary the whole economic pattern of the State in any way that it desires. Hence the commotion made by just men who object to the rule of Wall Street or the Exchange. Is there no way then that the government can circumvent the international banking system (for each Central Bank is connected to the rest in an international group, basing its transactions upon gold, a medium acceptable to all, at a price)? There is. It is so simple that most governments stand aside amazed at the prospect, and allow the financiers to continue their infamous rule. The solution is for the government to issue its own credit, through the already existent banks for convenience, based on the wealth and potentialities of the whole people, and not on gold, which can be used by any unscrupulous profiteer to his own advantage.

Pound affirms the independence of a government from the banks in a memorable fashion. "*Dire che lo Stato non può fare e creare perchè, ' manca danaro' è ridicolo quanto dire ' non può fare strade perchè mancano i kilometri'.*"[1] There is nothing save economic ignorance to prevent the State from issuing credit, without paying interest to the bankers. " Statal money based upon wealth must replace *gold* manipulated by the international usurers." And in Canto 49, the obverse of the medallion :

> State by creating riches should thereby get into debt?
> This is infamy ; this is Geryon.

Pound's view of the function of banks, and the economic importance of Statal credit independent of them, illuminates some previously puzzling contradictions in his character. His pleasure at a ruler who ruled, accepted responsibility for his rule, and attempted economic reform of the sort advocated by Pound, accounts for his praise of Mussolini, and for his Fascism. His is economic Fascism. Had some absolute monarch attempted similar economic discipline in his kingdom, I do not doubt that Pound, living in the kingdom, would have

---

1. To say that the State cannot make or create because it " lacks money " is as ridiculous as saying that they cannot make roads because " they have no kilometres ".

become an absolute monarchist. Fascism carried the implication of something positive; it was a revolution *for* certain standards, unlike the Bolshevik, which was directed against certain evils, and in itself negative. It was based on the progressive prosperity of the whole people; it typified for the many honest Fascists what Pound calls "the increment of association", that economic element possible only in a group of people working towards a common end: thus "the increment of association . . . is affirmed in every fascio, clamped on to a public building; in every bundle of rods set up as a symbol." It is this vision of economic co-operation, unhindered by usury, which prompts him to write : "*Mille candele insieme fanno splendore. La luce di nessuna candella danneggia la luce di un' altra. Così la libertà dell' individuo nello stato ideale è fascista.*"

His detestation of universal usury accounts for his antisemitism. His is economic antisemitism. That he is not racially anti-Jewish can be abundantly proved. One instance is in his choice of performers for the Rapallo concerts which he organised there over a period of about ten years, which included Lonny Mayer, a Jewish singer, and, *after* the inception of the race-laws in Italy, the Jewish pianist Franchetti. Among the usurers, however, there are so many Jews; and against that sort of Jew Pound is justly merciless. I hasten to add that he would be equally ruthless with its Gentile counterpart. His most important book in prose is dedicated to the Jewish poet, Louis Zukofsky, who has testified to the absolute lack of racial feeling in Pound.[1]

It is to be deprecated that no-one, except Montgomery Butchart to a limited extent in the field of money, has ever troubled to collect the economic observations of literary men. There is an immense body of economic material as yet untapped; research into it would provide us with some marked surprises. Pound is *not* the first poet to introduce economics into his poetry, as practically all literary critics would have us believe. It is in Dante, where Geryon (*vide supra*) is con-

[1]. Charles Norman: *The Case of Ezra Pound.*

226

demned to the deepest Hell. It is in Shakespeare, in Bacon, in Hume. It is in Skelton's

> Counterfeit maidenhood may well be born,
> But counterfeit coins is laughing to scorn.

In Ben Johnson's *Epigramme on Banck the Usurer*

> Banck feeles no lamenesse of his knottie gout,
> His monyes travaile for him, in and out:
> And though the soundest legs goe every day
> He toyles to be at hell, as soone as they.

In Gascoigne's

> Not that they hoard the grain when it is cheap,
> Not that they kill the calf to have the milk.

In all these poets is an instinctive feeling for the just. "The study of monetary economics is worthy because it leads to the contemplation of justice." To the contemplation of justice, then, Pound's study of banking and economics has lead him. And not of justice alone; but of æsthetics and ethics and morals.

When economic corruption—and the banking system is corrupt, almost beyond belief—is permitted to flourish, all other decadence flourishes with it. When the Church ceased to care about usury, or rather, permitted it, the influence and importance of the Church declined. When Statal responsibility decreases, the beauty of coinage decreases. When one part of society collapses, the whole culture of necessity follows.

> and if theft be the main principle in government
> (every bank of discount J. Adams remarked)
> there will be larceny on a minor pattern
> a few camions, a stray packet of sugar.

Once more I would emphasise the importance of economic study. It leads to justice in government and in personal conduct. A study of personal behaviour leads almost inevitably to Confucious, that most human, and therefore perhaps most humane, of all philosophers, whose thought has so much influenced Pound. It is the humanity of his philosophy which has most attracted Pound. Accused, in 1934, of writing Fascist propaganda, he cries, "I am writing for humanity in a world eaten by usury."

Almost alone among contemporary poets Pound has fought to preserve economic truth. And let there be no illusions; every day that we permit what he calls usurocratic rule to continue, we are making the ultimate overthrow of usury more difficult. Why should this concern a poet? Why can he not leave the whole settlement to the "professional" economists? His reply is in that section of *Carta da Visita* entitled *Gli Iconoclasti*. "*La forza del putridume vuol distruggere ogni bellezza intrinseca. Che questa forza sia portata di alcuni o da altri è da determinare. Viene portata come i bacilli del tifo e della peste bubbonica, che vengono portati dai topi incoscienti. Diffidate di chi distrugge un' immagine, e di chi vuol cancellare la storia. Il latino è sacro, il grano è sacro. Chi ha distrutto il mistero della fecondità, portandovi un culto della sterilità?*" Or more plainly in these remarkable lines from Canto 51 :

Usury rusts the man and his chisel
It destroys the craftsman ; destroying craft
Azure is caught with cancer. Emerald comes to no Memling
Usury kills the child in the womb
And breaks short the young man's courting
Usury brings age into youth ;
                it lies between the bride and the bridegroom
Usury is against Nature's increase.

EZRA POUND:

SOME NOTES ON HIS PHILOSOPHY

by Brian Soper [*1948*]

It is a tragic, but highly typical symptom of our time that Ezra Pound should have been persecuted and imprisoned. His condemnation by all except a very few indicates the rigidity of the categories instrumental to the judgment passed upon him. I shall not attempt to discuss Pound at the simple level of political morality ; the matter goes essentially deeper : it is rather the case that Pound's nature as a critical and philosophic force makes that aspect of his problem necessarily irrelevant. It is the purpose of these notes to try and explain why.

We must first of all understand in what sense Ezra Pound may be termed a " philosopher ". To most of the people who are familiar with his work he would probably not seem to be a " philosopher " at all. Yet it is precisely in the light of a most valid sense of the word " philosophy " that his critical and poetic achievement must be appraised : this is the root meaning—love of wisdom. As a philosopher, Pound is not concerned with systematisation of thought, the classification of ideas into academic categories, which philosophy has come to mean for us. He *is* concerned with the achieving of wisdom, and by wisdom he means specifically the right relation of knowledge to action, on the one hand, and on the other, of knowledge to contemplation. To this end, he has developed a particular, individual poetic as his philosophical method. This method is not exegetical, in that it neither propounds criteria of thought or action in the accepted sense, nor does it, either directly or indirectly, re-establish " schools " of ideas. What it does is to unify history, not categorically, but through an apotheosis of the individual contemplative mind and the seeing eye ; Pound re-establishes " goût " rather than specific norms of judgment. That is to say, he enters into the minds of his readers preceptually and by example, rather than canonically and through dogma.

For Pound, poetry is criticism of itself as well as of life, and his poetic work acquires its bulk and complexity by virtue of the great scope which this implies : the various forms of poetic expression, epic, lyric, elegiac, tragic, dramatic, satirical, didactic, must correspond verbally to their factual counterparts in human history ; moreover, by "human history" Pound does not merely mean a temporal sequence of events, but also significant moments in the lives of individuals. This complex of events and moments must be reinforced by purpose and informed with imagination, and Pound selects his moments in imaginative order. The imagination involved—and this is the fundamental point —is not merely his own, but also the imagination of persons within history. These distinct imaginations are fused together by Pound's particular poetic technique : he himself re-creates and re-lives the events and moments he selects, so that their interpretation is not contingent but necessary, and the selective re-creation is in every case implicit with its own explanatory comment. Thus Pound's poetry does not need to be "written about" in the sense that it requires the usual kind of textual explication : it requires rather that the reader, if not already sufficiently informed, should have lessons in literary and political history. At a first glance this requirement may seem to be unreasonable, and indeed a very common basis for attacks upon Pound has been the feeling that his literary eclecticism is unnecessary, a form of gross intellectual snobbery. The answer to this charge is simply that the artist is not subject to the limitations of his audience. If he were, there would be cause indeed to despair of art.

Such is the principle behind Pound's poetic method. We must now inquire into its validity and raison d'être as far as generalised philosophical implications are concerned, and I am now using the word "philosophical" in the sense in which we would normally understand it.

In order to justify the special rôle to which he has assigned himself, Pound must believe in the validity of certain premises. He must, for example, believe that history is capable

of *being* understood, and that the internality of the historical
"standard" in no way alters this. That Pound does in fact
hold this belief is plain from the sense of purpose that one
feels on reading him, even though the precise nature of this
purpose is not visible at a glance in all its detailed extent.
Now the question of whether history is comprehensible is
philosophically debatable, and it devolves upon the individual to make his own judgment. Pound at all events has
come to the conclusion that his aim at a certain balance between knowledge, action and vision can only acquire significance teleologically. He is compelled by the very method he
adopts to identify his own purpose with an historical one, or,
to put it another way, the purpose he finds in himself must
also be the purpose he discovers in history. To be consistent,
therefore, Pound must regard himself as a microcosm in
which selected moments of time and thought re-appear in
imaginative order and gain significant pattern (not form :
their intrinsic formal values are subordinated to intrinsic
structural values in the historical *pattern* that Pound is trying
to build). Yet it is precisely because of their *formal* values
that these moments have been selected ! The concept would
seem to anticipate the fact. Nevertheless, the argument is not
quite a closed circuit, for Pound believes that a pattern of
significance must not be defined by reference to an idea of
what a pattern of significance ought to be like. That is, significance must not be inferred from sequence. Pound believes
that this sort of pattern is something essentially creative, that
the knowing and the known combine imaginatively to create
a significance which should be valid. History is revealed by
the organisation of the spiritual and imaginative faculties :
the past is understood by the actions of the present. In sum,
history separates itself out into groups, each of which has its
own original formal value, e.g., the Hermes of Praxiteles has
a unique formal value deriving from the period of its creation.
This formal value can become a pattern-value in two ways :
(a) within the "fix" of an artistic canon ; (b) as an integral
and vital part of a creative activity. Art dies without art ;

and for Pound the great moment in literature is precisely equivalent to the great moment in history.

All Pound's early poetic output and much of his prose criticism lead up to the work of his maturity, the Cantos, and the critico-philosophical precepts which we find summarily expressed in the prose-work are activated and exemplified in the Cantos themselves. Very often, we may infer something of Pound's philosophical position from his formal critical remarks, which we also find embodied in his poetry. For example :

(a) Criticism is not a circumscription or a set of prohibitions. It offers *fixed points of departure* . . . that little of it which is good is to be found mostly in stray phrases.

(b) An " image " is that which presents an intellectual and emotional complex in an instant of time. . . . It is the presentation of such a ' complex ' instantaneously which gives *that sense of sudden liberation, that freedom from time and space limits : that sense of sudden growth, which we experience in the presence of a great work of art.*

(c) . . . consider the three propositions (demanding direct treatment, economy of words and the sequence of the musical phrase) *not as a dogma . . . but as the result of long contemplation.*

(d) Pay no attention to the criticisms of men who have never themselves written a notable work.

These four quotations (from *A Stray Document*) are good illustrations in differing ways of the philosophical attitude underlying Pound's criticism. The path to right judgment is through creation ; creation is criticism and a function of the *poeta*, the " doer ". But the creative act of the artist must arise not from " a malpractice of heart or illegitimate process ", but through contemplation ; and for Pound contemplation is the interaction of cognition with vision.

Pound's technique, which began comparatively humbly as " imagism ", is therefore the practical result of a true love of wisdom, of a belief that the precept or moment of interpreted "onsight"—Anschauung—is the true key to reality, whose *cor*rectness varies in proportion to its *direct*ness. It is certainly true to say, I think, that the Cantos do in fact consist of such moments, and that their obscurity, where it exists, neither conceals an intellectual ellipsis—which would make the "thought" "difficult"—nor indeed arises, as some enemies of Pound have suggested, from private musings of no importance ; but that it represents rather a difference in focus and visual scope. To accuse Pound of obscurity is like accusing an Alpine guide of lying when he reports the presence of a crevasse, although one's own untrained eyes can only see an expanse of snow.

The charge of obscurity is often coupled with that of obscurantism. How far is it possible to justify Pound's choice of "moment" ? The answer is that it is not each "choice" which *has* to be justified, but their total effect. Pound's method of individual creative interpretation makes this inevitable. It is of course true that many—and among them those whose opinions must be taken into account—find they do not have the patience to let this "total effect" accumulate. It is not to be denied that in his extreme personalism Pound eschews ontology and cosmogony inasmuch as the Cantos reflect no rational system, theocratic or androcratic, which sets forth an external standard or scale of historical values, such as we find more or less explicit in most epic poetry. Yet while we may find lacking a vertebrate *a priori* background such as informs the Divine Comedy, for example, we can none the less observe the empirical search for a philosophy, conducted not with an irresponsible dilettantism but with an assiduous regard to an honest interpretation of history and the need to establish the poetic terms of historical relationships. We are losing the mental habits necessary to sustain interest in and concentration upon epic poetry—our society lacks the requisite spaciousness and sense of leisure—but this ought not to disguise the fact that Pound's poem is an epic truly consonant with our time, and interprets our own dismays and bitternesses, whose roots stretch deep into the past. Furthermore, although we may look in vain for an authoritative evaluation of reality in terms of those major branches of philosophy which I have mentioned, we have an account of ontological and epistemological thought made explicit pragmatically by "ideas in action", and also some formal statements in philosophy of value, in which Pound makes his own important contribution to the theory of æsthetics. Here his fundamental proposition is, briefly, that art belongs to the realm of ends :

Ut doceat, ut moveat, ut delectet.

Notice the order : teaching or discipline, inspiration, pleasure. Art is not esoteric or mystic, nor is it "classical" or "romantic". Art teaches, stirs, delights, and does so not mediately but directly.

So much we may state in general terms. We have now to consider Pound's philosophic method in its particular applications, which are always closely related to literature. Time and time again Pound emphasises the importance of certain writers, because of their contribution in terms of literary art to the philosophy of living. Constantly he draws our attention to the neglected truth that Nature copies Art, and that it is only by perpetually injecting into his bloodstream the antitoxin of genuine art that man is empowered to resist the infections of barbarism. Pound's rejection, sometimes abhorrent and vituperative, of works long-established in the favour of the more conventional academicians and scholars is not mere idiosyncrasy, but a considered judgement based on knowledge and insight. Conversely, this acumen re - assesses and restores the value of many neglected authors, particularly from the point of view of the practising poet. I think it is important for us to examine in more detail the cause and effect of this admitted re-alignment of literary criticism.

Ezra Pound directs us away from many "accepted" authors because their import, in the last analysis, is impersonal. They are thrown up by the tendencies of the age and reflect its spirit. But they are not of primary importance to Pound in his selective re-interpretation of history, because they are not, for him, the formers and initiators of styles, but either (a) exponents—it may well be the greatest—of styles already historically inevitable, or (b) writers who accept implicitly the current theory of society, and whose genius consists rather in exploiting or expressing it, rather than in submitting it to tests. In neither category do these writers stand out, according to Pound, from the *materia* of their intellectual and social environment. Since this is so, they fail, despite their other excellencies, to fulfil the essential condition Pound submits for his "interpreted reality", which is that the structure of the visible world of scene and event is most meaningfully analysed, not in terms of mechanics or biology, but in terms of art, and is most significantly and satisfyingly expressible in those terms. Moreover, I think Pound would say that such an analysis was *intentionally inherent* in reality. We cannot be surprised, therefore, to find that Pound's philosophy, that is, as we have seen, his concern for wisdom, is closely related to the right use of language, for language is the only means we may use to communicate *in any detail* our discoveries of what is wise. The logical positivists and their post-empiricist successors—the new empiricists—who are, so to say, philosophers too, also concern themselves, *bien entendu*, with the right use of language. The difference is, however, that whereas the latter are concerned with what language can *say*, Pound is concerned with what language can *do*. This is a most important distinction, and clearly illustrates the difference between Pound's idea of philosophy and the more scientific and methodological idea of it. It is doubly important because it is significant at a more general level. The logical positivists tend to conclude that, on account of certain logical inaccuracies and semantic illusions, allegedly ineradicable, human speech, spoken or written, is inadequate as an instrument by means of which to measure the extent, scope and texture of reality ; and that propositions in metaphysics have no meaning valid outside their own verbal composition. This concern with pure epistemology emphasises too dogmatically—and it may well be quite wrongly—the point of view that language, at any rate language based on speech, is " extra-essential ". In contrast, Pound affirms the " philosophically " pragmatic use of language as a factor in *determining* rather than in *defining* the real. The pragmatic effect operates at two levels : at the creative level of the world of poetic imagination which constructs patterns out of the unfigmented possibilities of worlds ; and at the critical level, by reducing terms and categories to their artistic essence and refining them to their artistic limit. In this way all superfluous and irrelevant material is removed, while at the same time concentration is raised to its highest power. A parenthesis may be added here : Mr. T. S. Eliot has defined poetry as " an exploration into the possibilities of language ". The logical positivist methodology might also be so described. The difference in outlook, however, is not difficult to see.

Pound's pragmatism is not a thing isolated, but stretches far back into literary history. We must attempt to trace the " tradition ", keeping in mind our particular philosophical reference. Any assiduous student of Pound will not be long in coming across a line from Propertius :

> Ingenium nobis ipsa puella facit.

Pound quotes the line in a wide variety of contexts, and obviously attaches great importance to it. We must examine the relevant passage in Propertius' Elegies 2, i. :

> Quæritis, unde mihi totiens scribantur amores
> unde meus veniat mollis in ore liber
> *Non haec Calliope, non haec mihi cantat Apollo,*
> *ingenium nobis ipsa puella facit.*

The second distich is the important one. It is the realisation,

probably for the first time in Latin literature, of the directness
of poetic inspiration. The creation of artistic monuments,
Propertius saw, might not depend upon the mediation of the
" Muse ". The content of poetry might not perhaps be fixed
for all time by the classic canons—generalisations about what
beauty ought to be like. Love, despised as a passion, might
yet have a salutary effect if its function were properly recognised. It is unfortunate that Propertius has not more to say on
this subject. Elsewhere in the same Elegy is another passage
which Pound does not quote, although no doubt he has
regarded it as significant :

> Laus in amore mori : laus altera, si datur uno
> posse frui : fruar o solus amore meo !
> ....
> una meos quoniam prædata est femina sensus,
> ex hac ducentur funera nostra domo.
> omnes humanos sanat medicina dolores :
> solus amor morbi non amat artificem.
>
> (II, i., 47/8 & 55/8.)

Here the emphasis is rather different. The last four lines hold
a notion which, to us, is at least familiar : love is a disease,
and, what is more, a most peculiar disease in that it "loves
no physician of its ill". LL.47/8 are a defence of constancy,
and, more surprisingly, of the worthiness of death for the
sake of love. None of these sentiments commended itself
highly to the ancient world. In a different way, they are as
strange-sounding as the first passage. What is the connection?
I think it is, as Pound has realised, that "ingenium nobis
. . . " is an "idea in action", immediately explicit in two
distinct types of personal attitude. We can, in fact, observe
the beginning of the post-classical rationale of love, which
separated itself out at some time during the middle ages into
two opposing traditions, the realist tradition of the mediæval

singers, the Provençal lyrists, the early Italian poets and
Villon, and the mystical tradition of " Tristan and Iseult ",
which by-passes the Pléïade and the later Renaissance to
emerge once more during the so-called Romantic Revival.
As may be seen, the original dichotomy is implicit in Propertius. (We might remark in passing that the sentiment of line
58 is found again in Ovid, and it is indeed through him that
the conception of " romantic " love notably descends to the
Middle Ages.)

If this all seems at first sight somewhat remote from a
discussion of Ezra Pound's philosophy, we must remember
that he can only look at the world " philosophically " through
the eyes of those whom he considers best practised in the
art of expression. He seeks to unite the categories of " known "
and " felt ", so that " æsthetics " assumes its Kantian sense
of " transcendental " perception. But, let me repeat, this
is achieved dynamically, through and with the aid of those
who have stripped language and emotion of its superfluous
trappings, the unnecessary adornments which contribute
nothing to the quality of idea or image. Chief among them
are : Sappho, Homer, the Provençaux, Cavalcanti, Villon,
Rimbaud, Laforgue, Corbière. These poets have common
qualities—an astringent clarity, precise freshness, the plan-
gency of finely-tempered metal or of a perfectly-strung
instrument, an irony never inhuman or merely sardonic,
and, above all, the quality of light ; they are suffused, bathed,
impregnated with light ; their words glow, not with the fire
of rhetoric, but the lucent penetration of æsthesis, the
interaction of seeing and knowing. Pound himself in a famous
passage has well described this alchemical process : " We
appear to have lost the radiant world where one thought cuts
another with clean edge, a world of moving energies, ' mezzo
oscuro rade ', ' risplende in sè perpetuale effecto ', magnetisms
that take form, that are seen, or that border the visible, the
matter of Dante's paradiso, the glass under the water, the
form that seems a form seen in a mirror, these realities perceptible to the sense, interacting, ' a lui si tiri ' untouched

by the two maladies, the Hebrew disease, the Hindoo disease, fanaticisms and excess . . . the envy of dullards, who, not having ' intelletto ', blame the lack of it on innocent muscles. For after ascetism, that is, anti-flesh, we get the asceticism that is anti-intelligence . . . the cult of naïveté. To many the term ' mediæval ' connotes only two diseases. We must avoid these idea-clots. Between those diseases existed the Mediterranean sanity . . . this ' harmony in the sentience ' or harmony *of* the sentient, where the thought has its demarcation, the substance its virtù, where stupid men have not reduced all ' energy ' to unbounded, undistinguished abstraction. . . .'' '' For the modern scientist, energy has no borders,'' adds Pound, '' perhaps algebra has queered our geometry.'' Elsewhere in the same article he is even more explicit :

'' The mediæval Italian poets brought into poetry something which had . . . not been in any so marked or developed a degree in the poetry of the troubadors . . . this quality, *or this assertion of value* (my italics) has not been in poetry since . . . the Greek æsthetic would seem to consist wholly in plastic, or in plastic moving to coitus, and limited by incest which is the sole Greek taboo. . . . Erotic sentimentality we can find in Greek and Roman poetry, and one may observe that the main trend of Provençal and Tuscan poets is not toward erotic sentimentality. . . . What is the difference between Provence and Hellas? There is, let us grant, a line in Propertius about *ingenium nobis facit*. But the subject is not greatly developed. I mean that Propertius remains *mostly* (my italics) inside the classic world and the classic æsthetic, plastic to coitus. Plastic plus immediate satisfaction.

'' The whole break of Provence with this world . . . is the dogma that *there is some proportion* between the fine thing held in the mind and the inferior thing ready for instant consumption. . . . The Tuscan demands harmony in something more than the plastic . . . there is the residue of perception, perception of something which requires a human

being to produce it. Which may even require a certain individual to produce it. This really complicates the æsthetic.
You deal with an interactive force : the *virtù*, in short. . . .
It is more than the simple athleticism of the ' mens sana in
corpore sano '. The conception of the body as perfected
instrument of the increasing intelligence pervades. The lack
of this concept invalidates the whole of monastic thought. . . .

" Whether it is necessary to modernise . . . our terminology
and call this ' the æsthetic or interactive vaso-motor
mechanism in relation to the consciousness ', I leave to the
reader's own taste and sense of proportion. I am inclined to
think . . . such terminology somewhat takes the bloom off
the peach. . . . I am not considering the merits of the
matter, much less those merits as seen by a modern æsthetic
purist. I am using historic method. The god is inside the
stone . . . the *force* is arrested, but . . . *essential* . . . the *shape*
occurs." (My italics.)

I have quoted at length from this essay (on Cavalcanti)
because it seems to me to illuminate the essential core of
Ezra Pound's philosophy. The zeal, the sense of conviction,
the clarity of these phrases disclose Pound's notion of the
relationship between life and art, expressed as a philosophical
concept : reality attains to its peaks of self-consciousness
and " value " in the active, creating minds of certain individuals ; the nature of reality is at the same time noumenal
and phenomenal, and the known and the felt are constantly inter-related. There is no question, however, of
noumenal forms being imposed upon an amorphous chaos.
The pattern is *there* ; the god is indeed inside the stone. The
reality which we usually call ' external ' has already within
it the force creative of its patterns, in other words, its λόγος,
either implicitly (and *a priori*) or explicitly, in the works of
man. The cosmic harmony is not something given which we
learn to " appreciate " as if it were some tangible object to
be picked up and examined under a glass ; rather is it a quality
responsive to principles of order in human consciousness,

both controlling it and being controlled by it in turn. Pound puts this succinctly in *The Pisan Cantos* :
" The stone knowing the form which the carver imparts it."
Specifically, for both Cavalcanti and Pound, the term is " virtù ". " The light of light is the virtù "—a quality common to both man and nature, which unifies, correlates, and mediates the purposeful will of the former with the grace of the latter. Gérard de Nerval wrote :

A la matière même un Verbe est attaché :
Ne la fais pas servir à quelque usage impie.

Certainly Pound is in accord with these lines. He protests against the idea that the grace of nature can somehow survive the loss of conscious art and the fact of voluntary subversion of art. Interpretation, indeed, creative evaluation of experience—that which is real for us and the manner in which we become conscious of it or give it consciousness—depends on the use of methods of communication. But communication affects both originator and recipient mutually and simultaneously. If we build ugly cities, we will have ugly art ; if we put up with bad art—jejune painting, insipid poetry— it will be natural for us to build ugly cities and live lives devoid of style. The god is in the stone. What conceals him is a mode of expression—whether it be language or music, sculpture or painting—lacking in virtù. In Cavalcanti and Villon, to take two examples which are typical, virtù is inherent in the language : each word rings with the fine trueness of a newly-minted gold coin, and has a transparency through which one can look direct to the meaning. Pound would not, nevertheless, say that this precluded the harmonics of meaning, which have become so important in a richly allusive language like English ; but he would say that the tendency of words, like cities, to become " tentacular " is not without its dangers. The " impious use " is more or less prevalent as the way of life of the user is more or less *contra naturam,* and the loss and obsolescence of terms does not help.

It may perhaps be of greater value at this point to recapitulate a little. So far, I have attempted to define the philosophy of Ezra Pound in terms of a relation between language, art and history. I have also tried to define it in terms of value ("art belongs to the realm of ends"). I have spoken of Pound's æsthetic, Pound's view of historical significance, Pound's conception of reality—his "metaphysic"—and in a particular sense, his theory of knowledge. Nevertheless, all of this does not yet amount to a comprehending of his philosophy. A philosophy must be consistent, for wisdom is homogeneous in nature if not in effect. It must also be an "outlook" and a mode of action. In appreciation, we must pass from thought to action, from the analytic to the synthetic.

I have been careful to emphasise that Pound is not a phliosopher in the exegetical or the dialectic sense. Yet he is not an "ideologist" : his philosophy is "thought out", even though pragmatic. We must ask the question : What *ratio vivendi* can account for both Pound the poet and Pound the man ? We can perhaps best introduce our answer to this question by saying that it is a rationalisation of everything which is antithetical to what Pound understands by USURA —the corruptive influence on art and society of money considered as a thing of intrinsic value. Pound does not see "usury" necessarily as the symbol of capitalism, as one of the Church's deadly sins, or as one of the more unpleasant characteristics of Jewry, but as any or all of these things (and others) according to the ebb and flow of forces exercised by characters in history. Pound sees USURA introducing mean, niggling, irrelevant considerations to obscure a world of colour, light, pride and self-assertion which never perhaps existed as a continuity, but which Pound has stitched together into poetry from the strands pre-eminently visible to him at certain recognisable foci of interest. As a poet writing in epic form, his claim is that this rhapsody is viable. The main problem for the inquiring reader must be (since the epic form in Pound is not universally recognised by critics) :

is this true? A recurrent charge against Pound arises out of comparisons with other epic poets, particularly Milton and Dante : history is not held up against, and illuminated by, spiritual forms which transcend it. There is no vision of the Absolute. It must be admitted that there is a great deal in this charge. The conception of USURA, itself, is something negative and local. It cannot be used, even inversely, to suggest, *a priori*, answers to the question of universal destiny ; and whatever *purpose* in history the Cantos, for example, may detail, it is hard to see that they uncover a vaster, cosmic purpose, in the Miltonic sense. In the strictest sense, indeed, Ezra Pound eschews ontology and cosmogony : there is no religious sense, no intense feeling of "numen" or "pietas". Nevertheless, in the Cantos, "the birth of worlds, gods and systems" does have a place. But we must bear in mind that Pound does not look through a partisan or avenging eye. He is anxious to create, poetically, conditions appropriate to the most finely patterned world. His universe may well be emergent. Marx has said that force is the midwife of progress. For Pound, insofar as the consideration is relevant, poetry is the midwife of cosmogony. The true teleology of history is for him the study of literary eugenics. The world of the Cantos, the enormous ant-hill of Europe, is the chaos out of which the new gods shall step.

This, at any rate, is a possible interpretation if we take the established standards of the epic. But not only do we not need to take these standards ; we find it almost impossible to do so any longer, because the societies, the dynastic and hierarchical evolution which made them valid, has come finally to an end. A remnant only survives, and a remnant only can be saved. The heroic situation, as Pound has shown, is reversed. Words no longer spring from actions, but action from words. A new basis for action must be worked out. The creative word of the poet must cause the creative act of the man.

Pound's philosophy emerges, therefore, as first and foremost a philosophy of language. His word tries to re-articulate a world powerless to move on account of its many compound

fractures. Sometimes, many times, there are too many
breaks, and the effort is too much for him. But the significant
common factor, the opposition of light, of chiarità, to the
excremental, vertiginous obscurity, the turgidness of USURA,
is everywhere present, and is ᴗeen by Pound to be moving
forward, in the form given it by literary expression, towards
something simple and self-contained. And to look forward
to this, paradoxically, Pound has to look back—to the poetry
and philosophy of classical Chinese. Here all Pound's philosophical and critical ideas unite. His critique of language
becomes embodied in the ideogram. His a-religious pragmatism is not dissonant from the Confucian and Taoist ethos.
His humane eclecticism is well matched by the temperate
warmth of the scholar-poets. His joy in the spirit of light
responds to the clarity which illuminates Chinese art. His
arrogance is welcomed yet tempered by its aloofness. The
ideogram, let it be added, is both instrument and symbol
of the growth of the analytic and the decline of the synthetic
in language. Its meaning and the beauty of its effect are not
merely in its abstract nature, but in the formalism of the
calligraphy. Here indeed is the apotheosis of the interaction between cognition and vision. Confucius once said
to a disciple: " In all I have written, you will find that the
most important things is SHU—the principle of reciprocity."

The foregoing pages have attempted to define the general
terms of Ezra Pound's position as artist and thinker. The
remainder of this essay must enter the rôle of the con-
tentious, although I shall repeat that my aim is to remove
misconceptions rather than effect an apologia. What is now
known to certain sections of the world public as "the Pound
controversy" or "the Pound question" is based on the
following argument: Pound is supposed to be a great modern
poet in the "European" tradition; during the recent war,
Pound sided with the Italian Fascists; therefore either Pound
is a traitor to the European tradition (or, if you like, Western
culture) or he is not in his right mind. Now, a board of
American doctors recently examined Pound and declared

him to be insane—specifically, to be suffering from paranoia. Good, said the great world, our system of values is secure ; Pound was merely out of his mind. But the very next thing that happened was that Pound published *The Pisan Cantos*, and was awarded the Bollingen Prize. The public naturally concluded that either the doctors were wrong or that it is possible to be an important poet and a madman at one and the same time. This is clearly the sort of puzzle which the majority of people, who prefer things cut and dried, do not like at all. However, I believe that the propositions I have just set down do not exclude a middle. I believe that clinically speaking Pound may not be normal. I also believe that it was with clear purpose that he chose to align himself, if not against the Western democracies, then certainly away from them. Furthermore, I believe that his decision was the logical and proper outcome of his whole intellectual development as poet and critic. He believed quite genuinely that the real cause had already been lost, and that the technical victories or defeats which might follow could not make any fundamental difference. The world was the world he had put down in the Cantos. Collective action, mass movements, the old idealism, were delusions and had resulted only in breakdown. Further disintegration was all that could follow. Nothing more would avail to shore up the *anciens parapets* of Europe. In the Cantos and elsewhere, Pound tries hard to salvage valuable articles from the wreck, but it is clear that he sees history in a sense as a vast junk-shop :

> For two gross of broken statues,
> And a few thousand battered books.

This is not a cynic's jibe. The inheritors of the " tradition " had cluttered up their waste lots with these objects. They had sucked their sustenance, like leeches, from so much artistic capital that, in the end, only the outward and visible form remained : the capital paid no more dividends. Pound has been accused of a lack of architectonic power ; it has been said that the Cantos do not *inform* history. Yet their whole object is to contrast the nine-tenths of dross, the coprophagous universe of USURA, with the tenth part of pure metal. This waste-matter cannot be digested, but only thrown up and thrown aside.

For Pound, therefore, the partisan action we might have perhaps expected from a humanist poet was impossible. Taking sides meant nothing to him. Nor was he to be inveigled by the philosophy of " as if "—frequently the intellectual's compromise with the demands of *force majeure*. The linear movement of history is a foreign conception to Pound. He is concerned, not with the transient attachments of strict temporality, but with projects, tending always towards logo grammatical expression, for the re-vision of history in terms of permanently valid patterns, lucid, economical, self-coherent, existing within a temporal matrix, but not subject, except within the limits imposed by the immediate context of situation, to the " normal " conditions of historical time. For Pound, " European values " are discontinuous, and all he has dared to say is that within the total complex of events certain moments of thought or action give the promise of possible optimum validities of experience and language.

I have possibly said sufficient to prepare the ground for my answers to more commonplace questions. However, I must repeat that I attempt to answer these questions not in any polemical or apologetic spirit, but simply as they appear to me in the light of the philosophy which I discern in Pound's works.

First, did Pound become a Fascist and betray America? If so, is this action consistent with his philosophy? Certainly, it is difficult for most of us to accept that the Fascist régime in Italy is one of the " significant moments " of history in the " good " Poundian sense. It may be that we are too close to the event to be dogmatic, but the evidence seems to suggest that Pound never actually *allied himself*, or threw in his lot with the Italian Fascists, in the positive sense of political *engagement*. He never condoned acts of barbarism, except, it may be, in a spirit of contemptuous irony. His broadcasts, his pamphlets with their Fascist superscriptions, were never acts of deliberate political opinion in the sense that his defamers would wish. Pound still claims to this day that he remains a loyal American, admittedly according to his own estimation of what a loyal American ought to be. He had remained a voluntary expatriate partly as a protest, because he felt that the latter development of the American state was a betrayal of a truer conception of America, an America without USURA, the Jeffersonian ideal. It is no doubt probable that there was sufficient of value in the Italian Fascist state, especially with regard to theories of autarchy, which suggested to Pound a genuine revolution from usurious society (as he understands it), and which was able to convince him that a significant moment might be in process of eventuation. This seems the more likely because the formal apologiæ for Fascist economics and statecraft do not relate to any explicit "Fascist philosophy", for the simple reason that the latter does not exist.

Pound's attacks on the Jews present a more difficult problem. But his objections to Hebraism, despite their violence, are not racial. For him, "Jewish" is a term of opprobrium comparable with "baroque", and defensible on similar grounds. He objects primarily to the Jewish conception of culture, the exaggeration of its sentiment, its "ventral" interpretation of life. His attacks are confined to cultural values. He believes that Jewish life and art tend to be vitiated by a false romanticism, expressed in *weltschmerz*, or in a characteristically nostalgic millenarianism. Pound's holoscoptic poetic vision arrives naturally at this kind of conclusion, and he tends to exclude from his favour elements he considers alien to a proper *Kulturgeschaft*.

On the subject of Pound's alleged paranoia I am prepared to say little. It is true that his work suffers from hyperbole and a sense of being persecuted, but, taken as a whole, it is impossible to describe it as paranoiac. In no sense is his work a *symptom*, or a reject-product, of our maladjusted and disintegrating society.

Naturally, it must not be imagined that Pound's outlook upon knowledge is consistently whole. There are errors of taste and judgment, indeed entire misconceptions. For example, Pound's introduction to Rémy de Gourmont's *Physique De l'Amour* is, from the point of view of natural philosophy, arrant nonsense and nothing less. It may well be that certain preferences and points of view of his have an obsessional flavour about them. But *quantus homo tantus error*. These are small things in comparison with his positive and manifest achievement.

Comprehensive criticism of the work of Ezra Pound is still to be done. The time for it has not quite arrived, partly because the passions and prejudices of war are still hot, but chiefly because at the present moment there is no apparatus criticus of the Cantos, which in any case have yet to be finally achieved. All we can expect to do until proper conditions occur is to make a few positive statements and to attempt to clear away a few misconceptions. Many will find it strange and hurtful that this "traitor" and "mountebank" is not only taken seriously, but taken at his own value. The fact remains that the work is great enough to testify to the man, and the aggressiveness and hyperbole which have alienated many would-be sympathisers must not obscure the final purpose of Pound's writings, which, so far from being pusillanimous and contingent, bids fair to measure up to these lines from *The Pisan Cantos* :

> . . . seized the extremities and the opposites
> holding true course between them
> shielding men from their errors
> cleaving to the good they had found.

THE LAST HUMANIST

by John Heath-Stubbs [*1950*]

It may possibly be not quite irrelevant to our understanding of Ezra Pound, if we remind ourselves that he is represented— if only by a charming but very light-weight lyric—in the *Oxford Book of Victorian Verse*. Pound, born in 1885, was one of those whose formative years were spent in the period of calm and prosperity which preceded the 1914-18 war—a period in which, however, the portents of the coming storms could not be wholly undiscernible. But, as an American, he was, in some respects, several decades behind his time—as he himself, in *Mauberley*, has ironically suggested. Mr. Eliot has pointed out, in his introduction to Pound's *Selected Poems*, that there is a 'ninety-ish, Celtic twilight, or even pre-Raphaelite background to much of his early poetry. But it is possible also to regard him as the last exponent of a characteristic tendency in certain late or mid-Victorian writers. This tendency we discern in Arnold, Browning, Swinburne and Pater. All of these, in their different ways—the first and the last most specifically—are philosophers of culture. The culture which they uphold is a particular European tradition which can be traced back, through the Renaissance in France and Italy, to the Greeks. This tradition they oppose to the false values of contemporary philistinism, which they hope, by this means, to ameliorate. They love to think themselves back into their chosen periods of the past, and to treat of their own problems—emotional, intellectual, or spiritual—in such terms as, by analogy, they might have confronted real or imaginary characters in these periods. Thus, Arnold expresses his own very personal sense of tragedy in terms of the quasi-Homeric epic of *Sohrab and Rustum*. Browning, confronted by problems raised by the Higher Criticism of the New Testament, expresses himself through the mouth of an imaginary Greek poet of the first century A.D. He makes Fra Lippo Lippi or Andrea del Sarto discourse on the nature of the artist, and the relation of his personal life to his art. Pater presents the Victorian æsthete's wistful approach to Christianity by writing the imaginary biography of a young man of the time of Marcus Aurelius, while Swinburne places the frustrated passion engendered by his own abnormal temperament into the mouth of Sappho.

All these writers, furthermore, are dominated by a special and marked enthusiasm for particular periods of the flowering of culture, and for particular figures—comparatively few in number. These form, as it were, a series of key-points, round which the whole of their work is deployed, and the standards by which their measurement of cultural values are made. This characteristic is very well-marked in Swinburne, the whole of whose work, extending as it does over a period of several decades, is dominated by a series of unwavering allegiances—to Sappho, Catullus, Villon, the border ballads, the Elizabethan dramatists, Landor and Hugo, in the tradition of literature, and to Mary Queen of Scots and Mazzini among historic figures. Much the same sort of thing, formulated more critically and intellectually, finds expression in Matthew Arnold's doctrine of " touchstones "—single lines of verse held to embody those virtues of style which he most approved, against which, in all too schoolmasterly a fashion, other poetry is measured.

Now, Ezra Pound also has his touchstones. They are certain writers—the "inventors" and the "masters"—who originated or brought to perfection certain technical devices, forms, or qualities of style, and who likewise furnish the standards by which poetry as a whole, particularly contemporary poetry, is to be judged. By reference, paraphrase, imitation, recommendation, or direct translation, these writers dominate alike the critical and the poetic work of Pound. They are in reality comparatively few in number, and the reader who has followed Pound's advice, and has taken the trouble to furnish himself with some knowledge and understanding of them, will soon find that they provide the key to Pound's own work. In the light of such knowledge, the *Cantos,* for instance, will not— as hostile critics seem to imagine—appear as a chaos, demanding from their readers a mass of eccentric and irrelevant erudition, but as a region easily charted by reference to its few major roads. To these "masters" and "inventors" Pound's own critical writings furnish, in many ways, the best means of approach. In particular, in *The ABC of Reading* and in the essay *How to Read* (included in *Polite Essays*) he has furnished his readers with a brief list of those writers a knowledge of whom he deems necessary to the discerning and intellectually mature student of literature, together with the reasons for their inclusion. It is by these writers that Pound's critical and imaginative universe is dominated, though not, it is perhaps necessary to add, bounded.

A consideration of them, their collective characteristics, and their historical relations both to one another and to the cultures which they represent, may give us a clue to Pound's own approach to art and to life, both in its strength and its limitations.

If we consider those writers whose names are most frequently on Pound's lips we find that they typically belong to what Professor Toynbee terms the " growth-stage " of the civilisations which produced them (or which they produced). Thus, Homer and Sappho represent the growth-stage of the Hellenic civilisation, the authors of the songs of the *Shih King* that of the ancient Chinese civilisation. These poets are preeminently concrete in style, giving us direct narrative or direct lyric. Their language serves to express objects, actions and emotions as immediately as possible, without metaphysical or rhetorical elaboration. Their world is that of man's mundane existence, but seen, as it were, in the clear light of early morning—transfigured only by a kind of primal innocence. The 'Tang poets, such as Li Po (Rihaku to the Japanese) belong to the growth-stage of a second Chinese culture (Toynbee's "Far Eastern" as distinguished from his "Sinic" civilisation). This second civilisation had grown up on the ruins of the old one, its ethos being a Confucian-Buddhist-Taoist synthesis, with "other-worldly" elements. The Mediæval civilisation of Western Europe, was, historically, in an analagous relationship to the ancient Græco-Roman civilisation—Christianity taking the place of Buddhism as the non-indigenous "other-worldly" religion which interpenetrated the old classical culture. Its growth-stage is represented in Pound's scheme by the line of Romance lyric poets which begins with the Provençal troubadours, and runs through the early Italians to Dante and Cavalcanti—(of this line Chaucer and Villon are later off-shoots). The Troubadours, and (I suspect) the Chinese 'Tang poets, are much more introspective than Homer and Sappho, or the poets of the *Shih King*; and Dante and the Italians of the *dolce stile nuovo* are, of course, deeply concerned with metaphysics. But they write while their civilisation is relatively un-subject to those stresses which lead men to ask unanswerable questions, and to be torn apart by indissoluble conflicts of spirit.

Those writers who most elicit Pound's admiration, and who represent later, more disintegrated phases of civilisation ("Civilisation" in Spengler's definition, as opposed to "Culture") form a much less coherent assemblage. Some of them, such as Catullus and the Alexandrian Bion, one might perhaps regard as having preserved, in their times, because of special reasons, a purity of style belonging to an earlier age. Catullus modelled himself closely on Sappho, and Bion, like the other pastoralists, was not un-influenced by the traditional Doric folk-poetry of Sicily. Propertius and Ovid, on the other hand, might be regarded as looking forward, from their historical position in the early Roman Empire, to the Romance poetry of the Middle Ages. Pound lays great stress on Propertius's line: *Ingenium nobis ipsa puella facit*, which contains, in germ, the troubadour ethos of Courtly Love ; and Ovid was, to the Middle Ages, the great " doctor " of love, as well as a romantic story-teller. It is the Mediæval Ovid which finds expression in Golding's translation, another of Pound's touchstones.

In general, when dealing with these writers of a disintegrated culture, Pound's preference is for those who face up to the complexities of their situation with the intellectual weapon of irony, rather than by withdrawing themselves behind a screen of rhetoric, and by making their language hieratically remote from common speech. This quality of verbal irony—a form of "logopeia"—Pound detects in Propertius; it is found also in the seventeenth century Metaphysicals, and in Laforgue and Corbière, and others of the French Symbolists. These—Metaphysicals and Symbolists— largely through their influence on Pound's pupil, T. S. Eliot, have become the progenitors of much modern English poetry. For in the twentieth century, the intellectual countering of a disintegration has become one of the main tasks forced upon the poet.

Lastly, we must consider three nineteenth century English poets whom Pound has praised, and from whom many elements in his own style obviously derive. These are Swinburne, Browning, and Landor. Pound's praise, at any rate of the first two of these, has had its reservations. It could hardly be otherwise, for their faults are obvious, and of a kind particularly irritating to the twentieth century reader. Their superiority to their contemporaries is not so obvious; in the opinion of the present writer, Browning may with justice be set beside, but not above, Tennyson; Swinburne by Rosetti; and Landor by Wordsworth. It is therefore instructive to enquire for what particular virtues Pound has picked them out of the general nineteenth-century Romantic rag-bag.

At their best, all three of them exhibit a certain cleanness of line, and a sharpness of physical impact—visual in the case of Landor and Browning, aural in that of Swinburne. They are, all three, *extoverted* writers, and are oriented towards the southern, Mediterranean culture which Pound himself admires. All three were no mean classical scholars. But they showed, in addition, an active political sympathy with the cause of Italian unity and freedom as it then presented itself. Fundamentally, I think, they belonged to a liberal tradition which was older than the nineteenth century. This was not so much Romantic Liberalism, with its belief in progress (represented by Tennyson—in his more liberal moods), but a classical, humanistic, aristocratic Republicanism. This aristocratic

Republicanism was the creed of the Girondins in the French Revolution, and of the poet André Chênier, who met his death on the guillotine. In the eighteenth century, it saw the world, not in terms of modern political necessity, but of Plutarch's idealised Greek and Roman heroes. It could not foresee the mob-violence of the Terror, still less the rise of Napoleon. Much of its idealism went into the framing of the American Constitution. This idealism was to be falsified by the development of Northern Big Business after the Civil War.[1] This aristocratic Liberalism, limited by its too purely humanistic conception of Man, always makes insufficient allowance for the dæmonic, destructive forces which human history may release. Of this tradition Pound is, perhaps, the last and most tragic representative.

Pound, an American, and therefore native to the periphery of Western Civilisation, has striven to affiliate himself to the " Mediterranean sanity ". And beyond this, in his world-picture, is the profounder, though less passionate, Chinese sanity. Both these cultural traditions are founded, in their different ways, on a doctrine of the Mean, and are concerned, mainly, with the outward appearances of things. But the philosopher of culture, in the twentieth century—it is Pound himself, among others, who has taught us this—must be a philosopher of world culture. In spite of the diversity of Pound's interests, one cannot help noting his lack of response, in any of his published writings, to either the Indian or the Hebraic traditions.[2] He has spoken, indeed, of "the Indian disease, asceticism, and the Hebrew disease, fanaticism". But if these are diseases, they are the diseases of civilisations for whom Man is not the measure of all things, because they possess the consciousness of realities which transcend the human. The Indian tradition, profoundly unhistorical, empha-

---

1. This is well borne out by Mr. Pound's views on American history, economic and social, as exemplified in *The Economics of the United States* (Venice, 1944), his broadcast talks from Rome Radio and a number of other pamphlets published in Italy between 1939 and 1945.—*Editor.*
2. The Indian tradition includes, of course, the Buddhist element in Far Eastern civilisation, just as the Christian element in Western and Eastern European civilisation is, at bottom, a product of Hebraism. Islam may be regarded, for our purposes, either as an extreme, anti-Hellenic Christian heresy, or as a militant, de-nationalised Judaism.

sises the immanence of the Absolute in all things. In the Hebraic tradition, the idea of Divine transcendence is related to an eschatolgical view of history.

In the second place, one notes Pound's lack of interest in the Drama, and, in particular, in Tragedy. In *The ABC of Reading* he justifies the omission of the Attic dramatists from the list of books recommended to his ideal student on the grounds that "the words are only a part of the medium and the gaps between them, or deficiencies in their meaning, can be made up by 'action'."[1] But this argument, though convincing, can hardly be the whole of the truth. Elsewhere, Shakespeare's Histories are recommended, but on the grounds that they constitute "the true English epos". This is clearly an attempt to see Shakespeare in terms of Homer, from whom the Attic dramatists are also said to "decline".[2] Now, the tragic consciousness, whether it finds expression in Drama or not, is the product of certain tensions which arise at a later, more complex, stage of civilisation, than that which finds its natural expression in heroic Epic. Man is called upon to face the destructive forces he finds within his own nature, and to ask what is his ultimate place in the Universe. Tragedy includes the problem of freedom, which may be freedom to self-destruction.

Aeschylus, Sophocles, and Euripides are each, after his own fashion, concerned with the problem of justifying God's ways to Man. And there is a line which leads from Sophocles to Virgil, and thence to Milton—where the tragedy of Good and Evil is played out on its ultimate, cosmic stage. Virgil is a tragis, as well as an epic poet ; Aeneas, it has been wisely said, is not so much a feeble imitation of Achilles and Odysseus, as a forerunner of Hamlet. He is torn between his Roman destiny and Dido's passion ; initiated by the Sybil, he has seen both Tartarus and Elysium.

1. EDITOR'S NOTE.—Mr. Pound seems to have changed his mind on this matter. See *Nine*, Vol. I, No. 1.
2. Pound's early volume of essays, *The Spirit of Romance* (1910), in which we may see many of his leading ideas in a still formative stage, includes, besides essays on the Troubadours, Dante, Villon, etc., a treatment of Lope de Vega's plays. Here we have a drama, mainly comic, with a maximum of rapid action, and a minimum of psychological interest. The same volume also includes an essay on Camoens—the most Homeric of the Renaissance writers of literary Epic.

Hence it is that the rhetoric of Virgil and Milton is not merely a formal evasion of the exigencies of plain narrative and common speech. Its inversions and sonorities are full of overtones, suggesting a complexity of human experience, and a sense of depth, which could not be otherwise realised.

It is this sense of depth, I think, which is ultimately wanting, both in Pound's critical writings and his poetry. It is to be found in his friend and pupil, T. S. Eliot, the range of whose mind and technical accomplishment are, perhaps, much narrower. The figures of Virgil and Aeschylus form part of the background of Mr. Eliot's imaginative world, and he has embraced, moreover, the tragic and meta-humanistic experience of Christianity. It is not my purpose here to suggest a comparison, either of the work or the personalities of these two men. Those of us who have come after them must be profoundly grateful to both for what they have taught us. Pound, on the one hand, has recalled us to a sanity and a humanism which are central to civilisation. Because of Eliot's words, on the other hand, we may be better skilled to face those tragic realities before which that sanity and humanism, and civilisation itself, may be found wanting.

EZRA POUND

by Wyndham Lewis [1948]

In the array of articles, among which this is to take its place, each having Ezra Pound for its subject, verse will be the major theme. The professional poets will expound the astonishing technical feats—the emotional flexibility, the innovatory restlessness. In any case, I feel that Pound, the prosodic magician, will be taken care of—be praised to the skies as he should be, and in the right way. Pound, the great poet, it is to be hoped, will not be lost sight of beneath the magic mountain of the virtuoso's bric-à-brac.

Ezra Pound, I feel, is probably a poet of a higher and rarer order than it is easy at all times to realise, because of much irrelevant dust kicked up by his personality as it rushes, strides, or charges across the temporal scene. *The Cantos*, for example, appear to me to be clogged with deposits of this often quite dense matter, like volcanic dust. I would venture the opinion—though it is with the professional poets that the final judgment rests—that he has written verse of greater beauty than that of any contemporary poet in our language. As to his native talent, that is obviously terrific. He has displayed a demonic power over words.

Since nearly all these articles, however, will have for subject his verse, and since none of those contributing (excepting, if they are there, Mr. Carlos Williams and Mr. T. S. Eliot) have known Pound, I expect, so well as I have, let Ezra Pound himself be my subject. I will assign to myself the less glamorous task of writing of that Personality, to which I have already had occasion to allude.

When first we met, Ezra Pound was an uncomfortably tensed, nervously straining, jerky, reddish-brown young American. He came straight, I think, into the place in London when I saw him out of the English Faculty in Hamilton College, N.Y., where he had done a short spell of " instructing ". Anyway it was the first days of his début over here. The impression he made, socially, was not a good one. He was a drop of oil in a glass of water. The trouble was, I

257

believe, that he had no wish to *mix* : he just wanted to *impress*. The British in question were not of the impressionable kind—hated above all things being impressed and people who wished to impress them. I may add that they also disapproved of Americans.

Pound approached these strangers as one might a panther, or any other dangerous quadruped—tense and wary, without speaking or smiling : showing one is not afraid of it, inwardly awaiting hostile action. But when it comes to his desire to *impress*, the panther-image will no longer serve. For he did not desire to prove to the people he had come amongst that he was superior in physical strength, but that he was superior to all other intellectuals in intellect, and all poets in prosodic prowess. *They* were to be the spectators merely—they were of very little account. The feelings of dislike were mutual and immediate, as I could observe, and he never sought to hide the fact that he looked upon them as of very little consequence.

At the beginning in England Pound socially was a little too much like the "singing cowboy". His gaucherie was quite unnecessary. I have met young men from Idaho—or just as bad—with no money, who had the manners of a juvenile Henry Adams. However. *He* had rushed with all the raw solemnity of the classic Middle West into a sophisticated post-Nineties society dreaming of the eighteenth century, discussing the quality of the respective cellars of the Oxford Colleges, calling their relatives' county palaces "places", still *droppin'* their g's from time to time, for whom the spectacle of American "strenuousness"—the Bull Moose tradition—was something that hardly any longer deserved a smile. They looked at it with a stony stare of infinite boredom.

Above all, these people were unready to be lectured to : to have their shortcomings, as to literary taste, dissected, to have their chronic amateurism exposed.

The particular group in whose company I met him were apt to be learned too. Those were the days when a man going on a long train journey would be apt to slip in his pocket a copy of *The Iliad* in the Greek text : and there was after all Lionel Johnson's definition of a gentleman—a man who knows Greek and Latin. Ezra Pound seemed forgetful at times of these details. His lecture would, at that period, have introduced a much-needed discipline into English literary culture—which has in fact been demonstrated by his great ultimate influence, by Mr. Eliot's and that of others. As to the learning, those possessing it usually did nothing with it, and he showed them its uses (however faulty his own may have been). But Pound arrived as an unassimilable and aggressive stranger : with his Imagism he became æsthetically a troublesome rebel.

It was not the fault of England nor was it his, but I hope I shall not seem sensational if I say that looking back I cannot see him stopping here very long without some such go-between as Ford Madox Hueffer. A short while ago a request from an American editor set me hunting for old Ezra-letters. So far I have succeeded in turning up only a few. None are of interest, or good specimens, except perhaps one but it is marred, from the editorial point of view, by a nationalistic outburst. This refers to a young English biblio-phile I had sent him in '38 to Rapallo. What happened I never knew : his letter contained the savage axiom : "There's only one thing to do with an Englishman—kick him in the teeth."

His patience must have been sorely tried, he would not have written in that way otherwise. Yet a great incompati-bility existed, first and last, between Pound and The English-man. It is regrettable. But it is an indispensable clue to his character. Further, this relationship colours one of his prin-cipal biographical compartments, just as his unfortunately more cordial relationship with the modern Italian over-colours the last-but-one biographical compartment.

He writes of England, in *Pavannes and Divisions* (1918):

In a country in love with amateurs, in a country where the incompetent have such beautiful manners and per-

sonalities so fragile and charming, that one cannot bear
to injure their feelings by the introduction of competent
criticism, it is well that one man should have a vision
of perfection and that he should be sick to the death and
disconsolate because he can not attain it.

Although my feelings with regard to the Englishman are
as different as possible from those of Pound, nevertheless I
would endorse everything he says above as to their cultural
delinquencies.

Professionalism even as long ago as Congreve (and that in
spite of recent laughable attempts of whitewashing) was
looked upon in England as something to shun and to disown.
With the passage of time people have not grown *less* snob-
bish. Indeed, every decade seems to mark an advance upon
the last in that respect.

The word *perfection* (the key word in the above quotation)
has obvious professional associations. Perfection implies the
highly finished product, result of competent craftmanship,
and consequently it is tabu in a society where a well-to-do
class desire the fruits of craftmanship without its toils, or in
one where time is denied the workman, and what is done
can only be fragmentary, superficial, hasty, in-the-rough.
"It is impossible," wrote Pound (*Pavannes*), "to talk
about perfection without getting yourself much disliked. It
is even more difficult in a capital where everybody's Aunt
Lucy or Uncle George has written something or other." He
recognised, as you see, that *nowhere* does it make things more
comfortable to talk about perfection.

A huge middle class rentier army of the intellectual or the
artistic emerged, like a cloud of locusts, from the Victorian
Age, and it covered the entire landscape, to the dismay of
the authentic artist. They drifted dreamily out, paint-brush
in hand, or with the novelist's notebook tucked away in their
overcoat pocket, choking professional talent—drawing all the
applause to themselves, as Pound indicates, because they were
such awfully nice people (and the critics were not looking

for artistic *perfection*, needless to say, but for social *niceness*). This lifeless host of niceness eyed Pound, very naturally, askance. A *professional* ! Hum ! But that, of course, was what was the matter with the Americans ! They take their sports too seriously.

Pound did not remain the raw post-graduate figure of the first days. By the time of *Pavannes* (1918) he had married, acquired a beard, grown into a sort of prickly, aloof, rebel mandarin—as it would be viewed by the world. He now knew his England very well, without ever really having come to terms with it. After the first world war he suddenly departed, never to return. This seems the logical thing for him to have done.

Ezra Pound has now come home. But Paris was his next stopping place then, in the long exile, after he had found that he was after all too American, or something, to dwell with people " still dominated by an xviiith century verbalism "—exponents of " the opalescent word, the rhetorical tradition." And other things. Retrospectively I am only astonished at his Kensington life enduring as it did, at the foot of what he describes as " Rotting Hill."

First sight of him in his Paris studio for me was a great change from the dark Kensington quarters. Having found his abode, I rang the bell. A good deal of noise was to be heard but no one answered : therefore I pushed the door, which opened practically into the studio. A splendidly built young man, stript to the waist, and with a torso of dazzling white, was standing not far from me. He was tall, handsome, and serene, and was repelling with his boxing gloves—I thought without undue exertion—a hectic assault of Ezra's. After a final swing at the dazzling solar plexus (parried effortlessly by the trousered statue) Pound fell back upon his settee. The young man was Hemingway. Pound got on like a house on fire with this particular statue. There is a logic in that too. He was much more in his element in Paris. I actually believe he cooked better in Paris than he did in London—and like Sickert he is an excellent cook.

My remarks so far have not so much been aimed at estimating the value of Pound's stay in England—to himself or
to the Englanders—as to bringing out something about him
of primary significance where his personality is concerned.
It is this : Pound is—was always, is, must always remain,
violently American. Tom Sawyer is somewhere in his gait,
the *Leaves of Grass* survive as a manly candour in his
broad and bearded face : the "tough guy" that has made
Hemingway internationally famous, and the "strenuousness"
of he of the Big Stick, are modes of the American ethos with
which Pound is perfectly in tune. The good, bad, and indifferent in Americanism all goes in, to make the perfect
specimen—where *that* is concerned it would be impossible
to be more unselective. He exercises a sort of tribal attraction
for his fellow-countrymen, over and above the effect of the
glamour of his poetic genius. In his present great misfortune
the sympathy has been markedly spontaneous. I suggest that
the spectacle of a great American in eclipse in this way has
an effect beyond the question of the welfare of American
Letters.

Pound's nearest American analogue in the past is not
Whitman, however, or Mark Twain, but a painter, James
McNeil Whistler—the "gentle master of all that is flippant
and fine in art." Whistler signed his pictures with a butterfly.
Indeed, their delicacy would not admit of the intrusion of
the customary extrovert clodhopping calligraphy in the
lower right-hand corner, where the authorship of the work
is proclaimed. Only by the unobtrusive presence of this
winged insect was the artist's identity revealed. Like Pound
in the literary art, it was in the extreme-orient that Whistler
had discovered the fundamental adjustments of his preference.
But what I would say here is how strangely in contradiction
American "toughness" and so much that is American is to
the Butterfly—taking that as a symbol.

Two of the most famous pictures of the last century, the
Portrait of Thomas Carlyle and the *Mother*, were of course
Whistler's. That Pound was conscious of affinity is suggested

by the frontispiece to *Pavannes and Divisions,* in which he is posed in raking silhouette, his overcoat trailing in reminiscence of the Carlyle (though with swagger and rhetoric). But being an interloping American—like " Jimmie" before him—aggressing among the sleepy islanders, ramming novelties down their expostulating throats—and so on—it would be the " gentle master" at the easel (a " Bowery tough" according to his disciple, Sickert, in conversation with me—a tough in defence of his own most gentle and defenceless art) rather than the sitter of whom Pound would be thinking : the author of *The Gentle Art of Making Enemies,* not the old sage responsible for " Latter Day Pamphlets".

We heard Pound just now allude to *perfection,* where he was speaking of the cult of the incompetent, which he encountered in England. And among artists of the modern age —since the time of the " old masters", that is—there have been very few indeed who attempted perfection as did Whistler, or, I may add, attained it. Whether Pound himself, in his department of the arts, has compassed perfection in the same massive proportions will be decided I suppose in the end, one way or the other, by *The Cantos.* But certainly he has been bitten by the same inexorable bug, strained fanatically towards the same limits of human expression.

As to his present predicament, as a martyr of " credit" economics, at least one knows (irrespective of one's personal opinion regarding those economics, and although it is small consolation for one of his oldest friends) that Pound is sincere. Once, in a moment of impatience, I used the word " simpleton": and—in addition to everything else—I am again impatient. Of course he is not that. But he demands *perfection* in action, as well as in art. He even appears to expect perfection, or what he understands as such, in the world of politics.

Economist Pound certainly is immeasurably more sophisticated than William Jennings Bryan, we know that : nor has any such electrifying cry come from him as—" Thou shallt not crucify mankind upon a Cross of Gold !" But with him Gold is a great bugbear too. Half a century has elapsed, the

Problem has changed : with the contemporary prophet
"gold" would not be the magic word so much as "debt"
—and with debt, *Usury*. The universal slavery of Debt, rather
than mankind's crucifixion by means of Gold, is the burden
of the modern economist's jeremiad. Usury (usuria—usura)
sometimes in one tongue, sometimes another, dominates
Ezra's incantation.

> with usura
> ... ...
> no picture is made to endure nor to live with
> but it is made to sell and sell quickly
> with usura, sin against nature,
> is thy bread ever more of stale rags
> is thy bread dry as paper,
> with no mountain wheat, no strong flour
> with usura the line grows thick
> with usura is no clear demarcation
> and no man can find site for his dwelling.
> Stone cutter is kept from his stone
> weaver is kept from his loom
> WITH USURA
> wool comes not to market
> sheep bringeth no gain with usura
> Usura is a murrain, usura
> blunteth the needle in the maid's hand
> and stoppeth the spinner's cunning.

That is from Canto XLV. Usury is everywhere, as a per-
vasive rot, such is the teaching. If that is the sinister picture
arrived at by this analytical intelligence—even though you
regard it as mistaken or perverse—any actions engaged in
by him must be of an extremely different order from those
undertaken by politicians. It is as a moralist only that he can
be judged.

.It is the magnificence of Ezra Pound's poetry—his own
work—that causes very different kinds of people who have

contributed articles to respond, however busy they might be, to an editorial summons. But in his attitude towards other people's work Pound has been superlatively generous. It is unlikely that a quite accurate account of Joyce's fortunes from Trieste onwards will be written. All the facts I am not in possession of, but I was seeing Pound a good deal in those years. Though my own interests lay in other directions, MSS. always were lying around in his Kensington apartment, sent by divers strangers, who subsequently might appear in the flesh. Some, like Eliot, became habitués. Many facts, therefore, in the nature of things, I am acquainted with which enable me to say that without Pound the author of *The Portrait of the Artist* might never have emerged from his central European exile, nor *Ulysses* and *Finnegan's Wake* been written.

It is to take nothing away from that admirable and self-denying Quaker lady to point out that it was not Miss Weaver, after all, who came across Joyce's novel, *The Portrait of the Artist,* and recognised its value : as a result of which recognition and warm support it was serialised in her review, *The Egoist.* (Nor was Eliot's verse, nor my novel, *Tarr*—which she likewise serialised—material dependent on her editorial initiative, but work brought to her notice by Pound.) In a word, Ezra Pound " sold " the idea of Joyce to Miss Harriet Weaver. Subsequently that lady set aside a capital sum, variously computed but enough to change him overnight from a penniless Berlitz teacher into a modest rentier; sufficiently for him to live comfortably in Paris, write *Ulysses*, have his eyes regularly treated and so forth. These *rentes* were his— I know nothing beyond that—until he had become a very famous person : and the magician in this Arabian Nights Tale was undoubtedly Ezra.

That is the most spectacular instance of the dynamic rôle of his critical sympathy : in very fact a *creative* sympathy. It extends far and wide. He does not in the least mind being of service to somebody (as do other people it is usually found) if they have great talent. No envy of the individual attached to the work. I have never known a person less troubled with personal feelings. This probably it is that has helped to make of Pound that odd figure—the great poet and great impresario at one and the same time. Also, he is a born teacher; and by his influence, direct and indirect, he has brought about profound changes in our literary techniques and criticisms: changes, in both cases, for the better.

SELECT BIBLIOGRAPHY OF EZRA POUND

* Indicates that an English edition is appearing shortly.

1908 *A Lume Spento.*

1909 *Personæ.*

1909 *Exultations.*

1910 *The Spirit of Romance.*

1911 *Canzoni.*

1912 *Ripostes.*

1912 *Sonnets and Ballate of Guido Cavalcanti.*

1914 *Des Imagistes.*

1915 *The Poetical Works of Lionel Johnson,* edited with an introduction by Ezra Pound.

1915 *Cathay.*

1915 *Catholic Anthology.*

1916 *Certain Noble Plays of Japan,* with an introduction by by W. B. Yeats.

1916 *Noh,* or *Accomplishment.*

1916 *Gaudier Brzeska : A Memoir.*

1916 *Lustra.*

1917 *Passages from the Letters of J. B. Yeats to his son, W. B. Yeats.*

1918 *Pavannes and Divisions.*

1919 *Quia Pauper Amavi.*

1920 *Hugh Selwyn Mauberley.*

1920 *Umbra.*

1920 *Instigations,* together with an Essay on the *Chinese Written Character* by Ernest Fenollosa.

1923 *Indiscretions.*

1924 *Antheil,* and the *Treatise on Harmony.*

1925 *A Draft of XVI Cantos.*

1926 *Personæ* (Collected Poems of Ezra Pound).

1927 *The Exile* (Periodical, edited by Ezra Pound).

1927 *A Draft of Cantos XVII—XXVII.*

1928 *Selected Poems,* with an Introduction by T. S. Eliot.

1928 *Ta Hio,* or *The Great Learning of Confucius.*

1930 *A Draft of Thirty Cantos.*

1930 *Imaginary Letters.*

1931 *How to Read.*

1931   *Guido Cavalcanti, Rime.* Critical text with notes, etc., by Ezra Pound.

1932   *Profile.*

1933   *Active Anthology.*

1933   *A.B.C. of Economics.*

1934   *A Draft of Cantos XXXI—XLI.*

1934   *A.B.C. of Reading.*

1934   *Make It New.*

1934   *Homage to Sextus Propertius* (printed originally in *Quia Pauper Amavi*).

1935   *Jefferson and/or Mussolini.*

1935   *Social Credit: An Impact.*

1937   *The Fifth Decad of Cantos.*

1937   *Polite Essays.*

1938   *Guide to Kulchur.*

1939   *What Is Money For?*

1940   *Cantos LII—LXXI.*

1940   *A Selection of Poems* (Sesame Books).

1942   *Confucio : Studio Integrale.*

1942   *Carta da Visita.*

1944   *Introduzione alla Natura Economica degli Stati Uniti.**

1944   *L'America, Roosevelt e le Cause della Guerra Presente.**

1944   *Oro e Lavoro.*

1947   *The Unwobbling Pivot* and *The Great Digest*, translated by Ezra Pound.

1948   *The Pisan Cantos.*

1948   *The Cantos* (The whole poem to date.)

1948   *If This Be Treason.*